HEALTHFUL
FOODS

from
Back to Eden

HEALTHFUL
FOODS

from
Back to Eden

Jethro Kloss

THUNDER BAY
P·R·E·S·S

San Diego, California

Thunder Bay Press
An imprint of the Advantage Publishers Group
10350 Barnes Canyon Road, San Diego, CA 92121
www.thunderbaybooks.com

This book was conceived, designed, and produced by Ixos, an imprint of
Ivy Press
The Old Candlemakers
West Street, Lewes,
East Sussex BN7 2NZ, U.K.
www.ivy-group.co.uk

Creative Director Peter Bridgewater
Publisher David Alexander
Editorial Director Caroline Earle
Art Director Clare Harris
Design Michael Morey
Picture Research Joanna Clinch, Katie Greenwood, Sarah Skeate

DISCLAIMER

This book contains the opinions and ideas of its authors. It is intended to provide
helpful and informative material on the subjects addressed in this book. It is sold with
the understanding that the author and publisher are not engaged in rendering medical,
health, or any other kind of personal professional services in the book. The reader should
consult his or her medical, health, or other competent professional before adopting any
of the suggestions in this book or drawing inferences from it. The authors and publisher
disclaim all responsibility for any liability, loss, or risk, personal or otherwise, which is
incurred as a consequence, directly or indirectly, of the use and application of any of the
contents of this book.

ISBN-13: 978-1-59223-869-9
ISBN-10: 1-59223-869-6

Library of Congress Cataloging-in-Publication data available.

Printed and bound in Thailand.

1 2 3 4 5 12 11 10 09 08

Contents

Jethro Kloss

Jethro Kloss:
A Pioneering Nutritionist

In 1939, Jethro Kloss published *Back to Eden*—a book that was to become one of America's all-time bestsellers. In it, Kloss distilled a lifetime's experience as a herbalist and nutritionist, a career in which he blazed a trail as one of the United States' earliest and most persuasive advocates of a careful diet to prevent disease and promote lifelong good health.

By the time *Back to Eden* hit the bookstores, Kloss was already a well-known manufacturer of health foods. Indeed, farming and food production were in his blood. Born in 1863, he was brought up in near self-sufficiency on a pioneer homestead in Wisconsin, and as a young man he worked on Florida's fruit farms. In 1911 Kloss bought his own farm in Tennessee, and he was soon also managing a health food factory at nearby Amqui. He later established his own manufacturing operation and retail market at Brooke, Virginia.

Some of the mainstays of the Kloss business were soybean products, and Kloss pioneered the use of soy milk and soy protein as part of a diet which cut down on red meats. He originated and produced about twenty recipes, including meat substitutes and soybean bread, butter, cheese, and ice cream. Few Kloss meals did not use soybeans somewhere or another. The menu from a demonstration vegetarian dinner given at Washington D.C. in 1933 contained sprouted soybeans as a side dish.

Accessible healthy eating
Another core group of health foods produced by Kloss were zwieback breads and crackers, which he believed are "very wholesome and very easy to digest. A good way to make zwieback is to slice the bread about one-half inch thick and let it dry out in the sun, or in a slow oven until it is entirely dry."

Zwieback means literally, in German, "twice baked," and the cracker recipes which Kloss developed came out of his childhood experiences as the son of German settler parents. In an age before refrigerators and freezers, when storing food safely was a huge problem, Kloss's advocacy of cracker breads was an important element in his work to make good, healthy eating accessible even to the poorest Americans. As he pointed out, zwieback was not liable to mold like ordinary bread: "I have kept zwieback an entire year in fine shape in a common barrel lined with heavy brown paper. During this time there was a long period of wet weather, and it seemed as if the zwieback had gathered a little moisture, but there was not a trace of mold; I put it outdoors on paper in the sun and let it dry out thoroughly again, and after it had been heated in the oven, it was just as good as when it was freshly made."

When *Back to Eden* was first published, many Americans were woefully unaware of the need for a balanced diet, or how they might achieve it. Today we take this understanding for granted—children in grade school learn about vitamins, proteins, and how much of each type of food is good for us. Yet the recipes and advice of Jethro Kloss still have much to teach us—his common-sense, homespun beliefs in the need to eat well and stay healthy were rooted in his own zest for life, and he was motivated by a religious conviction of his duty to better the lot of his fellow humanity. Through his writings, Kloss's own energy and passion for promoting wholesome lifestyles live on, over sixty years after his death.

TASTY TREATS

Jethro Kloss was motivated by the desire to produce healthy foods but, like all good nutritionists, he knew that healthy food can—and should—taste delicious. Kloss's granddaughter recalled: "Often Grandpa would prepare soybean ice cream to serve at the close of his lectures. One of my favorite treats was to lick the paddle for the ice cream freezer before we left home to go to the lecture." Kloss's son, Eden, often wrote of the way his father would prepare special treats for his family even when working long hours at the food manufacturing plant: "One way Papa expressed his loving care for his family was to include in the Friday baking a large pan of good old German coffee cake . . . Also, often a steaming kettle of rice, sprinkled with raisins, would be brought out of the fireless cooker for our breakfast."

Your Body and Its Needs

The Importance of Good Nutrition

The true science of eating should be thoroughly understood by all—what elements the system requires in order to build and repair, how best to supply then, and how to prepare them in the most appetizing manner without destroying their life-giving properties.

The human body is a finely constructed machine and transforms the food supplied to it into energy. As the automobile burns gasoline, the human body burns food. All the parts on every machine are constantly wearing and require renewal; just so, the body must have proper food to build new tissues and to repair worn-out ones.

The best way to obtain the nutrients that are needed by your body is from natural foods the way nature prepared them, and not from pills. Nearly 40 percent of Americans over the age of 16 regularly take some form of dietary supplement.

Several recent surveys that included thousands of American families revealed several potential or real areas of nutritional deficiency. The vitamins that tended to be low were vitamin A, B_6 (pyridoxine), and C. The minerals that were often deficient were iron, calcium, and magnesium.

In order to ensure the proper function of the nearly limitless and complicated reactions that are necessary for our body's optimum health, good nutrition is absolutely essential. This means not only supplying the body with a sufficient amount of food, but just as important is eating the right kinds of food and eating them in the proper proportions. Strangely enough, many overweight

Your body needs a large amount of energy just to maintain life even when you are sleeping.

persons, although they look well fed, are not getting the proper kind of nourishment.

In all the food we eat, whether it comes from plants or animals, there are roughly 50 different nutrients—substances necessary for life and growth. These can be arranged into six basic groups, as follows:

Basic nutrients

1 Carbohydrates   4 Minerals
2 Fats   5 Vitamins
3 Proteins   6 Water

The first three of these six—carbohydrates, fats, and proteins—provide energy that is used by the body to perform all the functions of daily living. This energy is measured in small units called calories. Calories are used to measure not only the energy used by the body, but also to tell us the amount of energy present in food.

Even when a person is lying down completely relaxed, awake, and with an empty stomach, a large amount of energy is necessary just to maintain life. This energy is known as the

Grapes are a good source of carbohydrates, vitamins, minerals, and water.

basal metabolic rate (BMR). In the average person the BMR is 1200 to 1800 calories per day. This represents more than half of the daily expenditure of energy. A rough estimate of your BMR can be found by multiplying your body weight in pounds by 10. The brain is responsible for about one-fifth of our total basal metabolic rate. But, unlike most other parts of the body such as the muscles, the amount of energy used by the brain stays about the same throughout the day, even when we are mentally very active.

Energy supply

While carbohydrates, fats, and proteins all supply energy, they are not all equal. As can be seen in Table 1, for any given weight, fat supplies two and a quarter times as much energy (calories) as the same amount of protein or carbohydrate—9 calories per gram compared to 4 calories per gram. Alcohol gives 7 calories of energy per gram; but it is almost totally lacking in any of the other nutrients.

Calorific value of basic nutrients

Calories	Calories per gram	per ounce *
Fat	9	250
Protein	4	110
Carbohydrate	4	110

* approximate weight: 28 grams = 1 ounce

Table 1

Amounts of various foods needed to give 100 calories

High calorie foods	Amount	Low calorie foods	Amount
Chocolate cake with icing	1 ounce	Tomatoes, raw	4 medium
Almonds	16 nuts	Strawberries, fresh	2 cups
Peanut butter	1 tbs.	Pear, fresh	1 average size
Butter or mayonnaise	1 tbs.	Peas, frozen	1 cup
Sugar	1¾ tbs.	Lettuce	2 heads
American cheese	1½ inch cube	Peach, fresh	2 average size

Table 2

Carbohydrates are frequently condemned as being the main culprit responsible for obesity, one of America's most common and serious health problems, when fat actually contains more than twice the number of calories. Today, in the average American diet, 45 percent of our energy supply comes from carbohydrates, 43 percent comes from fat, and 12 percent from protein. This pattern of eating is not the way it used to be in the United States, nor is it the way it is at the present time in less affluent countries, where most of the energy in the diet comes from carbohydrates—in some countries even as much as 80 percent. Although no daily requirement in grams has been suggested for fat or carbohydrates, as there has been for protein, it would certainly be much better for our health if we increased the amount of carbohydrate in our diet so that it provided about 55 or 60 percent of our daily energy needs. At the same time we should lower our fat intake from the present level of 43 percent

Legumes are excellent sources of protein and contain many other minerals and vitamins.

Potatoes are rich in carbohydrates and the skin contains essential vitamins.

down to 30 percent or even less of our energy supply, especially since we know that a high fat diet is strongly associated with coronary artery disease as well as colon, breast, and possibly prostate cancer.

One sure way to know if you are getting too many calories is to watch your weight. Excess calories are mainly stored in the body as adipose tissue, more commonly known as fat. It takes 3,500 calories to make one pound of fat. So, if every day for one week you take in 500 more calories than you burn up as energy, by the end of the week you will have stored those excess 3,500 calories as one pound of fat. The reverse is also true, so that for every 3,500 calories you use in excess of what you take in, there will be a loss of one pound in weight.

What your food contains

Foods that are high in energy value (calories) tend to be those with a low water or high fat content, such as nuts, dried fruit, butter, etcetera. Fruits and vegetables are low in calories, except for avocados and olives. A contrast between the amounts of some high and low calorie foods, showing how much of each it takes to produce the same number of calories, is shown in Table 2.

Foods rich in protein These foods repair and build tissue. Peas, beans, nuts, lentils, milk, eggs, cereals, cow peas (black-eyed peas), soybeans, peanuts, and nut preparations.

Foods rich in fat These foods are used mainly for furnishing fuel and energy. Butter, cream, egg yolk, milk, cheese, cereal, ripe olives, olive oil, vegetable oils, all nuts, and avocados.

Foods rich in carbohydrates These foods also furnish energy and fuel. Malt sugar, malt, honey, ripe fruit, starchy vegetables (such as potatoes), cereals, refined white sugar. (Sugar removes mineral salts as well as vitamin B from the body and should not be eaten.)

Foods rich in protein and carbohydrates Peas, beans, lentils, peanuts, milk, oatmeal, wheat, natural grains.

Although protein is one of the three energy producers, the body is best suited to obtain its energy supply from carbohydrates, with fat as its second choice. Protein is used as a source of energy only when there is more of it present than is necessary for normal growth and the repair of tissues, or when there is not enough carbohydrate and fat to meet the body's energy demand. Protein foods are the most costly way to obtain energy, while carbohydrates are the least expensive.

These three energy-producing constituents of food, plus water, are needed by our bodies in large amounts, and all are present in nearly all the food we eat. Vitamins and minerals, on the other hand, though also essential for the maintenance of good health, are needed in comparatively small amounts.

Carbohydrates

Foods for energy and fuel

Carbohydrates are the cheapest, most efficient, and most readily available source of food energy in the world, since they are the main constituents of the foods that are the easiest to produce and that can be obtained throughout the world, namely, grains, legumes, and potatoes. In many of the less industrialized nations, carbohydrates supply 80 percent or more of the daily calories in the diet, while in the more affluent, highly industrialized countries the calories supplied by carbohydrates

Unrefined grains such as brown rice are more nutritious than refined ones.

in the daily diet are usually much less. For example, in the United States only between 40 and 45 percent of the daily calories are obtained from carbohydrates. Nearly three-fourths of the carbohydrate in the average American diet comes from grains and refined sugar. The rest is divided about equally among potatoes, vegetables, fruit, and dairy products.

As the name implies, all carbohydrates consist of three basic elements—carbon, hydrogen, and oxygen. Carbohydrates vary markedly in their structure, from simple sugars such as glucose, to very complex carbohydrates such as starch, which contains thousands of simple sugars all joined together.

Types of carbohydrate

Carbohydrates can all be divided into three groups: *simple sugars or monosaccharides* such as glucose, fructose, and galactose;

Most of our carbohydrate intake comes from the consumption of grains.

disaccharides, which are made from two simple sugars linked together, such as sucrose, lactose, and maltose; and *complex carbohydrates*, which are made up of hundreds or thousands of simple sugars connected together. Some examples of complex carbohydrates are starch, dextrin, glycogen, and fiber.

The carbohydrates we eat consist mostly of starch, sugar, and fiber. When carbohydrates are eaten either as complex carbohydrates or disaccharides, they must be broken down by the digestive processes in the body to simple sugars before they can be used for energy. Fiber is an exception. Although fiber is a complex carbohydrate, it passes through the body nearly unchanged, since humans have no enzymes that are able to break down fiber to simple glucose.

Fiber is a part of carbohydrate that passes unchanged through the body.

Starch digestion

The digestion of starch begins in the mouth, where it is acted on by amylase, an enzyme in the saliva. It reduces the starch to simpler carbohydrates, preparing it for further digestion in the small intestine. The complete breakdown of starch to simple sugars is accomplished by other enzymes in the small intestine. Some of these enzymes are made in the pancreas and some in the wall of the small intestine itself. After the simple sugars are formed, they are absorbed through the wall of the small intestine into the blood and are carried to the liver. In the liver they are changed to glucose. The glucose re-enters the blood and is readily available to the cells for the production of energy. As the cells use the glucose to make energy, heat is produced as well as water and carbon dioxide. Water is removed from the body by the lungs, kidneys, and skin, and the carbon dioxide is given off by the lungs as we exhale.

Wheat is a source of carbohydrate that is cheap and easy to produce.

A small amount of the glucose is changed by the liver to a form of sugar called glycogen, also known as animal sugar. Some of the glycogen, about 100 grams, is stored in the liver in case of a need for emergency energy by the body. The rest of it, about 200 grams, is stored in the muscles and used when they contract. These stores of glycogen will last only 12 to 24 hours, depending on the amount of physical activity. Any extra carbohydrate that is not used by the body cells or changed to glycogen is stored as fat. Remember that it takes about 3500 excess calories to form one pound of fat, and that each gram of carbohydrate supplies four calories.

In case the body does not receive enough carbohydrate to meet its energy needs, some fat and protein can be changed to carbohydrate, although this is not the ideal situation. Ideally the body should obtain its energy supply directly from carbohydrates.

Types of sugar

Glucose (dextrose, grape sugar, corn sugar) is the only form of sugar that can be used by the body for energy. It is especially vital to the brain and nervous system, which use about 140 grams of carbohydrate a day. Glucose is found in most fruits, some vegetables, honey, and in a nearly pure form in corn syrup.

Sucrose (table sugar) is present in sugar cane, sugar beets, maple syrup, fruit, and some vegetables, especially sweet potatoes. Granulated table sugar is 99.5 percent carbohydrate and, if eaten in large amounts, it will cause fermentation in the intestines. Brown sugar is regular table sugar with a small amount of molasses or burnt sugar added for color. It is about 97 percent sucrose and although it has a slight amount of iron, the amount is negligible. Sucrose consists of a combination of glucose and fructose, the same as honey.

Fructose (levulose, fruit sugar) is found in fruits, some vegetables, honey, and berries. Fructose has 70 percent more sweetening power than sucrose, so it takes fewer calories to produce the same degree of sweetness.

Salad dressing contains refined sugar, which provides calories but little else.

Sweet potatoes are a good source of starchy carbohydrates.

Lactose (milk sugar) is found only in the milk of humans and other mammals. Lactose assists in the absorption of calcium from the intestines. It is composed of glucose and galactose.

Maltose (malt sugar) is present only to a very limited degree in most foods. It is produced during the malting process of grains and is found in beer, malted foods, and sprouted grains.

Starch is the form in which carbohydrates are stored in plants. It is not soluble in water like the other sugars and it does not have a sweet taste. Starch is slowly broken down by the body to many units of the simple sugar glucose before it is absorbed, and because of this it supplies calories to the body at a slower rate than when the simple sugars themselves are eaten. Starch is found in whole grains, legumes, nuts, potatoes and other

tubers, lentils, sesame and sunflower seeds, yams, sweet potatoes, and some other vegetables.

In their natural state, cereals contain starch and fiber as well as various important vitamins and minerals. When cereals are refined, however, most of these important nutrients are lost and it is mainly starch that remains. Some examples of the refining process are seen when sugar beets or sugar cane is refined to table sugar (sucrose) or when whole wheat flour is refined to white flour.

Refined sugar gives only calories and little else in the way of any nutrients, and for this reason the term "empty calories" is used. Refined sugar is present not only in the foods where we expect to find it—candy, ice cream, jam, syrup, pastries, canned fruit, especially those in heavy syrup, etcetera—but also in many other foods such as soup, salad dressing, TV dinners, fruit drinks, breakfast cereal, baby food, peanut butter, tomato catsup, fruit yogurt, granola bars, etcetera.

Honey is a good source of the simple sugars glucose and fructose, used for energy.

Sugar content and cost of various breakfast cereals

Cereal Name	Added Sugar*	Sugar Calories**	Calories Per Serving	Cost Per Serving***	Cost Per Ounces
Shredded Wheat	0	0	90	8.5	10.2
Cheerios	1	4	110	13	13.2
Rice Chex	2	7	110	15	15
Corn Flakes	2	7	110	8	7.7
Fiber One	2	8	60	11.5	11.5
Corn Chex	3	11	110	13	13
Wheaties	3	11	110	12	11.6
Total	3	11	110	16	16
Special K	3	11	110	15	14.8
Product 19	3	11	110	16.5	16.5
Rice Krispies	3	11	110	13	13
Grape Nuts	3	12	100	9	8.7
Team	5	18	110	13	13
Life	6	20	120	12	11.9
Bran Chex	5	22	90	9	9.2
40% Bran Flakes	5	22	90	11	10.8
Raisin Grape Nuts	6	24	100	10	10.3
Frosted Mini Wheats	7	26	110	12	12.1
All Bran	5	27	120	12.5	11.8
Marshmallow Krispies	10	29	140	24	16.5
Fruit and Fiber	7	31	90	13	12
Golden Grahams	9	33	110	15	14.6
Honey Nut Cheerios	10	36	110	13.5	13.5
Nutri-Grain	13	37	140	24	15.8
Frosted Flakes	11	40	110	11	10.9
Honey Comb	11	40	110	16	16.3
Bran Buds	7	40	70	10	9.6
Cocoa Krispies	10	44	110	16	15.9
Pac-Man	12	44	110	17	17.1
Post Raisin Bran	9	45	80	10	10.2
Fruity Pebbles	12	44	110	15	15.3
Apple Jacks	14	51	110	18	18
Honey Smacks	16	58	110	14	13.8

* In grams: 4 grams equals about 1 tsp; ** As percent of total calories; *** In cents per serving

Table 1

The refined sugar in candy contains empty calories and causes tooth decay.

Food labeling

A new law beginning in 1994 requires that most foods in the grocery store must now have a nutrition label and an ingredient list. The new label has the title NUTRITION FACTS. Claims like "low cholesterol" and "fat free" can be used only if a food meets new legal standards. Read the label to help choose foods that make up a healthful diet. Eating a healthful diet can help reduce your risk factors for some diseases. For example, too much saturated fat and cholesterol can raise blood cholesterol (a risk factor for heart disease). Too much sodium may be linked to high blood pressure. High blood pressure is a risk factor for

Not all breakfast cereals are unhealthy—oat clusters with dried fruits and nuts will provide your body with sustained energy.

heart attack and stroke. No one food can make you healthy. In addition to eating healthful foods, stay active, don't smoke, and watch your weight.

As a good example of the use that may be made from nutritional labeling, Table 1 lists the percentage of calories that result from adding refined sugar to the usual serving of various popular ready-to-eat breakfast cereals. Also given is the cost per serving as of 1988 (this will vary in different localities and in different stores). The amount of sugar added to breakfast cereal ranges from 0 to 16 grams per serving. There are approximately 4 grams (16 calories) of sugar in a level teaspoon. This means that the cereal highest in sugar content has had four teaspoons of sugar added to an average serving during the manufacturing process, before any honey, sugar, etcetera, is added at the time it is eaten.

Carbohydrates and the diet

The amount of carbohydrate in the American diet has decreased from 68 percent during the early 1900s to 47 percent at the present time, due mainly to eating less starchy food. Sugar consumption has increased from 30 percent to 53 percent. The average American eats about 380 grams of carbohydrate a day; that is, between 13 and 14 ounces. The consumption of refined sugar and corn syrup in the United States is now nearly 127 pounds per person each year. This figure includes all sugar in the diet, both natural and refined. If food sweeteners containing calories are added, the total comes to about 143 pounds per year. Sugar and sugar substitutes account for more than $8 billion in sales every year. A special note for former President Reagan and others who like jelly beans: one-half cup of jellybeans contains the equivalent of approximately 27 teaspoons of sugar.

Soft drinks

Soft drinks are now the number one national drink, over 30 gallons for each person per year for a total cost of over $9 billion.

In 1984, for the first time in history, people drank more soft drinks than water. During 1986 the average person drank 42.2 gallons of soft drinks—1.4 gallons more than in 1985. The sales of soft drinks increased from $1,857,000,000 in 1960 to $9,426,000,000 in 1975, and the per capita sugar consumption for soft drinks nearly doubled during this same period from 11.3 pounds to 21.5 pounds. A regular 12-ounce can of a cola drink has about 150 calories as well as caffeine, coloring, and other additives, but practically no other nutrients are present. This 150 calories

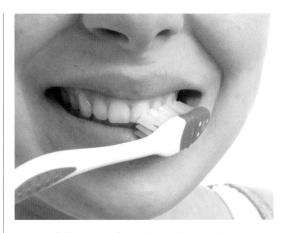

Brush your teeth after meals to cut down on cavities.

represents 9 to 10 teaspoons of sugar, since there are about 4 grams (or 16 calories) of sugar in a level teaspoon. Twenty-one percent of our sugar intake now comes from soft drinks.

In 1930, 64 percent of the table sugar produced in the United States was purchased by the consumer and 30 percent was used in prepared food. These percentages have now been practically reversed so that in 1970 only 24 percent of the total production of 9,000,000 metric tons of sugar was used as table sugar and 65 percent was used by the food industry, about one-third of this being used in beverages.

Grain

As in most of the rest of the world, the largest source of carbohydrate in the United States is grain, with the average American's share being 22,000 pounds. Most of this grain, however, goes to feed animals, and nearly all the nutrients in the grain that are removed during refining are also used as animal feed.

Today people drink more soft drinks than water.

Remember that carbohydrates in themselves are not nutritionally bad or necessarily fattening. In fact, Americans should increase the amount of carbohydrate in their diet and reduce the intake of fat. But the carbohydrate should be of the most nutritious kind, rather than refined sugar and devitalized grains.

Health problems and empty calories

Several health problems have been linked with an excessive intake of "empty calorie" carbohydrates. The most common and best publicized is obesity. Heart disease and diabetes have also been connected with excess sugar in the diet, although this connection has not yet been proven with certainty.

Undoubtedly, tooth decay is largely the result of eating refined sugar. There are several things you can do to cut down on cavities. Don't eat between-meal snacks containing refined sugar. Brush your teeth, or at least rinse your mouth, after eating. Finish your meal with a carrot stick, apple, etcetera, rather than with a dessert filled with refined sugar. Floss your teeth daily. Have regular checkups with your dentist and a thorough twice-a-year cleaning by a dental hygienist.

Most of the nutrients present in grain are removed during the refining process and end up as animal feed.

How to increase carbohydrate intake

In summary, here are some ways to improve the use of carbohydrates in your diet.

- Eat more whole grain bread and cereal. This will also add vitamins, minerals, and fiber to your diet.
- Eat raw fruits as often as possible.
- Cut down on all processed foods. Nearly 70 percent of the sugar we consume is hidden in these foods.
- Eliminate refined sugar and refined cereals as completely as possible.
- Pay attention to food labels. Any word ending in "-ose" is a form of sugar.

Watch out also for corn syrup, corn sugar, molasses, honey, brown sugar, and other forms of sugar.

The closer any sugar is to the beginning of the list of ingredients on a nutritional label, the greater is its percentage in the product.

Whole grain bread adds vitamins, minerals, and fiber as well as carbohydrate to your diet.

Artificial sweeteners

Artificial sweeteners have now been around for nearly 100 years, and at the present time nearly 69 million Americans over age 18 consume products containing these noncaloric sweeteners. Nearly $4 billion is spent yearly on diet soft drinks, and the prediction is that by the year 1990 half the soft drinks sold will be sweetened with artificial sweeteners—a $15 billion market. The cost of the sweeteners for that many soft drinks will be nearly $1 billion.

Saccharin

It was as long ago as 1879 that an intensely sweet compound was accidentally discovered by a chemist working at Johns Hopkins University. This compound had been developed as a preservative and antiseptic. Around 1905 it was offered for sale to the general public as Saccharin, and although it was slow to gain acceptance at first, today 7 million pounds of saccharin worth $3 billion are consumed yearly in the United States.

During the 1960s and 1970s several studies claimed to show an increased incidence of bladder cancer in rats that were fed very high doses of saccharin. Because of these reports, in 1977 the FDA proposed a ban on the sale of saccharin. But because of the public outcry as well as pressure from the manufacturer, Congress imposed a temporary moratorium on the proposed ban. This moratorium has been extended to the present time. Congress also agreed to have a

Fruits are a healthy source of carbohydrate and contain natural sugars such as glucose, sucrose, and fructose.

label placed on all saccharin products warning of the possible risk of cancer.

In 1980 a large research program was started that cost over $1 million and involved the use of 2,500 rats. This study was intended to give a definite answer as to whether saccharin produced an increased incidence of bladder cancer. The final results, published in 1983, were not much different from earlier studies and showed that at very high doses, an amount that would be equal to a person drinking 750 to 1,000 cans of soft drinks a day, saccharin does have a strong connection with bladder cancer.

Cyclamate

Cyclamate was also discovered by accident, at the University of Illinois by a chemist seeking to develop fever-reducing agents. By 1950 it had won FDA approval and was marketed as Sucaryl. It grew rapidly in popularity, since it does not have the bitter aftertaste that saccharin has.

By 1967 cyclamate consumption was 18 million pounds a year. In 1970 this rapid growth in consumption was suddenly brought to a halt when studies showed that cyclamate caused bladder cancer in mice, and the product was banned by the FDA.

Artificial sweeteners have been used for the past 100 years and give drinks a sweet taste without the calories.

Aspartame

While working with some amino acids in 1965, James Schlatter, a chemist at the G.D. Searle Company, happened to lick his fingers and noticed an amazingly sweet taste. This discovery led to the formulation of Aspartame from two amino acids. It was approved for public use in 1973 by the FDA. Aspartame, marketed under the names of Equal and NutraSweet, has no bitter aftertaste. It does have about the same number of calories per gram as sugar, but because Aspartame is 200 times sweeter than sugar, the amount that is used in a 12-ounce can of soft drink adds up to less than 1 calorie. Since it is made from two naturally occurring amino acids, and not from synthetic materials as saccharin is, it can be digested as a protein. Aspartame is more than 20 times as expensive as saccharin, so while it costs over 4 cents to sweeten a 12-ounce can of soft drink with aspartame, eight 12-ounce cans can be sweetened using saccharin for only 1 cent. In 1984 sales of aspartame totaled $585 million.

Aspartame cannot be used in bakery products as it is not stable at high temperatures, nor can it be used by people having the inherited metabolic abnormality called PKU, or phenylketonuria, since its consumption may cause brain damage in such persons.

More artificial sweeteners

Another sweetener, acesulfame K, will likely be on the market soon. FDA approval is expected shortly. It has no calories; is about the same sweetness as aspartame; has some aftertaste; and is not metabolized by the body.

Recently certain plants growing in Africa and Latin America have been discovered that have been used as natural sweeteners by the people living in these countries for hundreds and possibly thousands of years. An African plant called katemfe appears to be the world's sweetest product. On a weight basis it is 3,000 times sweeter than sugar.

In Paraguay the leaves from a small shrub, *Stevia rebaudiana*, contain a substance 300 times sweeter than sugar. The local population uses it to sweeten a popular but bitter drink called *mate*.

Scientists from the University of Illinois, following the description given by a Spanish physician during the conquest of the Aztecs, tracked down a plant known as *Lippia dulcis*. Its sweetening power is 1,000 times that of sucrose and so far no toxic affects have been found.

Licorice, a well-known sweet root, has very few calories and is 50 times sweeter than cane sugar.

None of these sweet substances from plants are carbohydrates, as sugar is, but before any of them can be used on a commercial basis much more testing for safety needs to be done.

Following is a brief review of artificial sweeteners.

- **Saccharin** 300 times sweeter than sucrose. No calories. Inexpensive. Slightly bitter aftertaste. Known to cause cancer of the bladder in animals when very high doses are given. Should not be used by children or pregnant women.
- **Cyclamate** 30 times sweeter than sucrose (table sugar). Has no calories. Is excreted unchanged by the kidneys. Banned by the FDA.
- **Aspartame** 200 times sweeter than sucrose. Same caloric content as sugar but because of its sweetness only a very small amount is needed, which makes the number of calories used very small. Cannot be used in cooking or by those having phenylketonuria. Marketed as Equal and NutraSweet. Approved by the FDA. Is relatively expensive.
- **Acesulfame K** 200 times sweeter than sucrose. Contains no calories. It is not metabolized by the body and does have some aftertaste. Not yet approved by the FDA.

Stevia rebaudiana leaves contain a substance 300 times sweeter than sugar.

Fats

More foods for fuel and energy

Whenever we hear the word "fat," the first picture that comes to mind is often that of an overweight person. Certainly the amount of fat we eat is responsible for much of the extra weight that millions of Americans carry around and that millions of others constantly strive to either keep off or take off. It is estimated that 34 million Americans from 20 to 75 years of age are overweight. Child obesity is also becoming much more prevalent, particularly in those children who spend hours a day watching television. These children tend to get less exercise and to snack more than other children. The weight reduction business in the United States has grown to a billion dollar industry. When all the diet plans, exercise and

Children who watch a lot of television eat more and exercise less than others.

aerobic clubs, books, magazines, reducing products, exercise equipment, etcetera, are taken into account, Americans spend over $10 billion a year in usually unsuccessful efforts to permanently lose weight. At any one time throughout the United States, about 28 million persons are on some sort of a weight reduction program, and more than three-fourths of these will regain the weight they lost within one year of stopping their special weight-reducing diets.

Fat in the diet

In the early part of the twentieth century, the amount of fat in the average American diet accounted for about 30 percent of the total daily calories, whereas now it has increased to between 40 and 45 percent. This increase is largely due to the greater consumption of cooking oils, salad dressing, vegetable shortening, and hydrogenated fats. The average American now eats about 155 grams of fat every day.

This is much more than necessary. Most authorities on nutrition are now advocating a diet in which the calories provided by fat are no more than 30 percent of the total daily calories. For a person on a 2000 calorie per day diet this would be about 67 grams of fat and for a person on a 2800 calorie diet, about 93 grams of fat. In the Orient, the amount of fat in the diet is only one-fourth as much as in the United States and consequently the amount of heart disease and colon cancer is much less.

About one-third of our dietary fat intake consists of foods that are obviously high in their fat content. Such things as butter, cream, cooking oil,

Nuts are a good source of more healthful, unsaturated fatty acids and will keep for up to a year if unshelled.

salad dressing, and fatty meat would fall into this category. But about two-thirds of the fat that we eat is sometimes referred to as "hidden fat," since it is mixed in with our food. Some examples would be whole milk, luncheon meats, avocados, olives, nuts, cheese, and chocolate.

Composition of fats

Fats, like carbohydrates, are composed of carbon, hydrogen, and oxygen, but the amount of oxygen in fat is much less than the hydrogen and carbon. This is what makes fat such a concentrated source of energy, providing more than twice the number of calories per gram than carbohydrates or protein.

Fats are made up of a combination of fatty acids and glycerol. The most common form of fat in our food, and also composing over 90 percent of the fat that is stored in our bodies, is called a triglyceride. This type of fat consists of three fatty acids connected to one molecule of glycerol. The predominant type of fatty acid contained in the fat is what determines its taste and also whether it will be in a solid or liquid form. There are approximately 20 different fatty acids in the food we eat. Each fatty acid contains a long line (chain) of carbon atoms with hydrogen atoms attached to them.

If all the potential spaces in the chain are filled, it is called a saturated fatty acid, since it is completely saturated, or filled, with hydrogen. If there are two empty spaces in the chain that could be filled by hydrogen atoms, the fatty acid is called a monounsaturated fatty acid. If there is room for more than two hydrogen atoms, the name polyunsaturated fatty acid (PUFA) is used. All natural foods contain a mixture of saturated and unsaturated fatty acids. The distribution of fatty acids in the average diet is about 38 percent saturated, 12 percent polyunsaturated, and 40 percent monounsaturated.

Cheese is high in saturated fats but is also a good source of calcium, a mineral needed for the development of healthy bones and teeth.

Saturated fatty acids

Most saturated fatty acids are solid at room temperature. They are found mainly in meat. Other sources are whole milk, cream, butter, cheese, chocolate, and coconut and palm oil. It is important to remember that saturated fatty acids raise the blood cholesterol level and are therefore a contributing cause of atherosclerosis, more commonly called "hardening of the arteries," which leads to coronary artery disease and strokes.

Monounsaturated fatty acids

These fatty acids are found in peanuts, peanut butter and oil, avocados, olives and olive oil, most nuts including cashews, pecans, and Brazil nuts, regular margarine, and vegetable shortening. It was believed until very recently that monounsaturated fatty acids had no affect on the level of cholesterol in the blood. Recent studies, however, suggest that monounsaturated fats, especially olive oil, not only reduce the total cholesterol level by about the same amount as polyunsaturates, but they tend to mainly reduce the level of damaging low-density lipoproteins (LDL) while leaving the protective high-density lipoproteins (HDL) nearly untouched. They do not turn rancid nearly as fast as polyunsaturated fats.

Polyunsaturated fatty acids

Polyunsaturated fatty acids are usually liquid at room temperature. They are abundant in plant oils such as corn, safflower, cotton seed, and sunflower

Margarine is low in saturated fat and high in polyunsaturated fatty acids.

only essential fatty acid; that is to say, it is the only one that must be present in the diet as it cannot be made by the body as can the other fatty acids. Fortunately it is so abundant and widely distributed in our foods that to find a person in the United States with a deficiency of linoleic acid is a rarity. When a deficiency does exist, it causes a lack of normal growth and dry scaly skin.

Polyunsaturated fatty acids tend to lower the level of blood cholesterol and thus help prevent atherosclerosis, coronary artery disease, and strokes.

oil, and in salad dressings made from these oils. Exceptions to this rule are coconut and palm oil, which are high in saturated fatty acids. Other sources include walnuts and special margarines.

Hydrogenated fats

When hydrogen gas is bubbled through a polyunsaturated fatty acid, hydrogen atoms are added to the vacant spaces in the carbon chain, thus changing the fatty acid from the unsaturated to the saturated form. This makes the fat more solid and also makes it more resistant to turning sour or rancid. This process is known as hydrogenation and the fatty acids that result are called hydrogenated or partially hydrogenated fatty acids. Hydrogenation is used commercially to change the less expensive plant oils to more expensive margarine or shortening. Nearly 3 billion pounds of hydrogenated fats are consumed each year in the United States.

Hydrogenation also decreases the amount of linoleic acid present in the fat. Linoleic acid is the

Monounsaturated fats in olive oil reduce the blood cholesterol level.

Regular exercise will help you to increase your HDL level.

Cholesterol

Cholesterol, a yellowish, wax-like substance closely related to fat, is obtained ONLY from eating animal products. It is a normal part of all our body cells and is especially abundant in the brain and nervous system.

It is also present in large amounts in the liver and adrenal glands. The body produces about 1000 mg of cholesterol a day, while the average American diet supplies another 500 to 900 mg. This is two or three times more than should be eaten. The amount of cholesterol you eat every day should be no more than 300 mg at the very most. Even if there were no cholesterol in our diet, the liver, and to a lesser degree the body cells, would produce sufficient cholesterol for all of the normal body functions. Cholesterol is well-known for its connection with the buildup of waxy plaques in the walls of the arteries. When these plaques grow large enough to seriously interfere with the necessary flow of blood to vital structures, suchas the heart and brain, the result is heart attacks and strokes. If the plaques obstruct the arteries supplying blood to the intestines, severe abdominal pain may result.

Functions

Less well-known to most people are cholesterol's important and, in fact, indispensable functions. Much of the cholesterol in our body is used to help in the formation of bile salts, Vitamin D, and several of the adrenal and sex hormones. It is also an essential part of every cell membrane.

While cholesterol is found only in animal products, the amount present varies greatly, depending on the type of food eaten. Some common foods and their cholesterol content are given in Table 1.

Causes of high cholesterol

While persons with high levels of cholesterol in their blood are more prone to develop atherosclerosis, other factors also play an important part. Some of these are:

- Cigarette smoking.
- Lack of proper exercise.
- Emotional stress.
- Obesity.
- A diet high in saturated fatty acids.
- Heredity.
- Coffee drinking.
- Sugar—high intake of sucrose.
- Diabetes.

Cholesterol content of common measures of selected dairy and animal foods

FOOD	Cholesterol Amount	(in mg.)	FOOD	Cholesterol Amount	(in mg.)
Milk, skim, fluid or reconstituted powdered milk	1 cup	5	Clams, halibut, tuna	3 oz. cooked	55
Cottage cheese, uncreamed	½ cup	7	Chicken or turkey, light meat	3 oz. cooked	67
Lard	1 tbs.	12	Beef, pork, lobster, chicken or turkey, dark meat	3 oz. cooked	75
Cream, light	1 fluid oz.	20	Lamb, veal, crab	3 oz. cooked	85
Cottage cheese, creamed	½ cup	24	Shrimp	3 oz. cooked	130
Cream, half and half	¼ cup	26	Heart, beef	3 oz. cooked	230
Ice cream, regular, about 10% fat	½ cup	27	Egg	1 yolk or 1 egg	250
Cheese, Cheddar	1 oz.	28	Liver (beef, calf, pork, or lamb)	3 oz. cooked	370
Milk, whole	1 cup	34	Kidney	3 oz. cooked	680
Butter	1 tbs.	35	Brains	3 oz. raw	over 1700
Oysters, salmon	3 oz. cooked	40			

From Fats in Food and Diet. Agricultural Information Bulletin No. 361, 1974. Washington, D.C., U.S. Department of Agriculture.

Table 1

- Age and sex.
- High blood pressure.

Lipoproteins

Since cholesterol is insoluble in water, it must be attached to a protein in order for it to be carried in the blood. This combination of cholesterol linked to a protein is called a lipoprotein. Some lipoproteins contain a large amount of protein and are called high-density lipoproteins (HDL). Others contain a large amount of cholesterol and are called low-density lipoproteins (LDL). There are other groups of lipoproteins, but most of the cholesterol in the blood is in one of these two forms. In fact, about 25 percent of the blood cholesterol is HDL. Persons who have high levels of HDL have less coronary artery disease than those who have high LDL. It is, therefore, very important not only to determine the amount of total cholesterol in the blood but also the relative amounts of HDL and LDL. Persons who have a normal or low total cholesterol level may still have a high risk of coronary heart disease if they have a low level of HDL. In order to increase your HDL level, you should stop smoking, get regular exercise, and maintain a normal weight.

Cottage cheese is a good source of calcium and is also low in cholesterol.

Peanut butter contains monounsaturated fatty acids that help to reduce the level of damaging low-density lipoproteins in the bloodstream.

Problems caused by high cholesterol

On the front cover of *Time* magazine of March 26, 1984 is a picture of a plate containing two fried eggs and a piece of bacon, with the caption "Cholesterol—And now the bad news...." The cover story, beginning on page 56 and entitled "Hold the Eggs and Butter," begins with the subtitle "Cholesterol is Proved Deadly, and Our Diet May Never Be the Same."

This article is summarized in the introduction as follows:

This year began with the announcement by the federal government of the results of the broadest and most expensive research project in medical history. Its subject was cholesterol, the vital yet dangerous yellowish substance whose level in the bloodstream is directly affected by the richness of the diet. Anybody who takes the results seriously may never be able to look at an egg or steak the same way again. For what the study found, after 10 years of research costing $150,000,000, promises to have a profound impact on how Americans eat and watch their health.

Among the conclusions:

• Heart disease is directly linked to the level of cholesterol in blood.

- Lowering cholesterol levels markedly reduces the incidence of fatal heart attacks.

Basal Rifkind, Project Director of the study, believes that research "strongly indicates that the more you lower cholesterol and fat in your diet, the more you reduce your risk of heart disease."

There are two other factors that seem to have an influence on blood cholesterol levels. The first of these is dietary fiber, which tends to lower blood cholesterol, and the second is coffee drinking, which tends to elevate it.

Value of fats in the diet

Considering the fact that a high fat diet has been linked with such ailments as coronary artery disease, generalized atherosclerosis, cancer of the colon, prostate, and breast, and obesity—which leads to strokes, high blood pressure, heart disease, diabetes, and kidney failure—does fat have any real value in the diet, and if so what are some of its most important functions and uses in the body? The body must have a certain amount of fat to survive, but the proper amounts and the right kinds of fat are very important. Some important uses of fat in the body are as follows:

- Energy: stored fat acts as concentrated forms of energy, which can be used in place of carbohydrates. Producing energy from fat, however, is complicated and carbohydrates are the best source.
- Fat is an essential part of every cell in the body.
- Since vitamins A, D, E, and K are fat-soluble, fat is necessary for their proper utilization in the body.
- The essential fatty acid, linoleic acid, is supplied abundantly in dietary fat.

- While not an essential function, fat does increase the palatability of many of our foods.
- The fat under our skin, called subcutaneous fat, provides insulation and helps our body maintain its proper temperature. About one-half of our total body fat is used in this way.
- The other half is used inside our body and forms a cushion around many of the organs to protect them against sudden blows.
- Fat is necessary for many of the body's metabolic functions.

Oats are known to reduce blood cholesterol levels.

Fat content and major fatty acid composition of selected foods*

FATTY ACIDS [†]						FATTY ACIDS [†]					
FOOD	Total Fat Percent	Total Total Saturated Percent	Total Monoun- saturated Percent	Polyun- saturated Percent	Lino- leic Percent	FOOD	Total Fat Percent	Total Total Saturated Percent	Total Monoun- saturated Percent	Polyun- saturated Percent	Lino- leic Percent
Salad and cooking oils						**Fish, raw**					
Safflower	100	9	12	74	73	Salmon, sockeye	9	2	2	5	1
Sunflower	100	10	21	84	84	Tuna, albacore	8	2	2	3	0.5
Corn	100	13	25	58	57	Mackerel, Atlantic	10	2	4	2	0.5
Soybean, unhydrogenated	100	14	24	57	50	Herring, Atlantic	6	2	2	1	0.5
Cottonseed	100	26	19	51	50						
Sesame	100	15	40	40	40	**Nuts**					
Soybean, hydrogenated [‡]	100	15	43	37	32	Walnuts, English	63	7	10	42	35
Peanut	100	17	47	31	31	Walnuts, black	60	5	11	41	37
Palm	100	48	38	9	9	Brazil	68	17	22	25	25
Olive	100	14	72	9	8	Pecan	71	6	43	18	17
Coconut	100	86	6	2	2	Peanut butter	52	10	24	15	15
						Peanuts	48	9	24	13	13
Vegetable fats											
shortening, household	100	25	44	26	23	**Egg yolk**	33	10	13	4	4
Table spreads:						**Avocado**	15	2	9	2	2
Margarine, first ingredient on label:						**Milk fats**					
Safflower (liquid)-tub	80	13	16	48	48	Human		46	46	8	7
Corn oil (liquid)-tub	80	14	30	32	27	Goat		62	32	6	5
Corn oil (liquid)-stick	80	15	36	24	23	Cow		50	23	3	2
Soybean oil (hydrogenated) -stick	80	15	46	14	10						
Butter	81	50	23	3	2	**Cereal oils**					
						Rye		16	14	70	62
Animal fats:						Wheat germ		16	25	59	52
Chicken	100	32	45	18	17	Whole wheat flour		15	34	51	47
Lard (pork)	100	40	44	12	10	Oatmeal		22	36	42	40
Beef tallow	100	48	42	4	4	Rice		17	45	38	37
Lamb tallow	100	52	43	5	3	**Cocoa butter (chocolate)**		57	41	2	2

* Modified from U.S. Department of Agriculture: Bulletin No. 361, *Fats in Food and Diet.* Washington, D.C., U.S. Government Printing Office, 1977, and from Keys, Ancel, and Keys, Margaret: *Eat Well and Stay Well*, New York, Doubleday, 1963.

† Total is not expected to equal "total fat." ‡ Common salad and cooking oil for commercial and household use. < less than.

Table 2

Foods that are high in saturated fats should be limited to occasional treats.

Ways of reducing your fat intake

The amount of fat in some of our common foods is shown in Table 2. Some general rules to guide you in your use of fat are as follows:

- Reduce your total intake of fat. All fats, whether saturated or unsaturated, contain the same number of calories, 9 per gram, which is more than twice the number in carbohydrates and proteins.

- Eat more foods containing unsaturated fatty acids and fewer foods with saturated fatty acids.

- Omit high cholesterol foods, especially meat, and lower your consumption of eggs to no more than two a week.

- Stay alert for hidden fats. Read the food labels. Don't forget that hidden fat accounts for two-thirds of the total fat you eat.

- Be on your guard against foods containing coconut or palm oil or completely hydrogenated vegetable oils. These foods contain large amounts of the unhealthful saturated fatty acids.

In summary, while a certain amount of fat in our diet is essential, recent scientific data makes it clear that an excessive intake of fat is directly connected to heart disease and cancer, the No. 1 and 2 killers in the United States. It would only seem to make good sense then, to shift the main emphasis of your eating to a more plant-oriented diet of fruits, vegetables, and whole grain products.

Olives are a good source of monounsaturated fats.

Protein

Foods for tissue growth and repair

Proteins are very complex substances that contain the same three basic elements as carbohydrates and fat—carbon, hydrogen, and oxygen—but in addition protein contains about 16 percent nitrogen. Sulfur is also present in many proteins, and other minerals such as iron, copper, iodine, and phosphorus, are present in smaller amounts. The word protein is derived from a Greek word meaning "to be in first place," and thanks to a strong advertising and public relations effort, the majority of Americans have been led to believe that they must eat large amounts of animal protein each day in order to have sufficient strength to do their work, especially if this work includes hard physical labor. The average American now consumes approximately 100 grams of protein a day.

Legumes such as soybeans are a good source of protein.

Amino acids

The individual units, or building blocks, which join together to form a protein molecule, are called amino acids. There are about 22 different kinds of amino acids. A small protein molecule may consist of only about 50 amino acids, while a large protein molecule may contain hundreds or even thousands. For each particular protein, the amino acid "building blocks" are always present in exactly the same arrangement. Any variation from this arrangement results in a different protein. There are about 30,000 different proteins in the body, but only a very small percentage of these have been identified. A single liver cell contains nearly 1000 different enzymes and each one of these is comprised of a different protein.

When a protein is ingested, it is broken down in the intestinal tract into its individual amino acids. These then enter the large body "pool" of amino acids. From this "pool" each body cell selects the specific amino acids it needs to build a particular protein for its own special use.

Nonfat dry milk is the cheapest source of complete protein available.

Types of amino acid

Amino acids are divided into two groups—*essential* and *nonessential*. Essential amino acids are those that must be provided in our food. There are nine essential amino acids. All the others, the 13 nonessential amino acids, can be manufactured in the body so they do not have to be supplied in the diet.

The amino acids are the really meaningful part of the protein. So it is not unreasonable to divide proteins into two main groups, depending on the presence or absence of the essential amino acids.

Complete proteins

Complete proteins, sometimes referred to as high quality proteins, contain all the essential amino acids in sufficient quantity to support the growth of new tissue. These include all the proteins of animal origin except gelatin.

Nonfat dry milk is probably the cheapest source of complete protein. Complete proteins contain about 33 percent essential amino acids, compared to 25 percent in the less complete proteins.

Incomplete proteins

In less complete proteins, also called incomplete or low quality proteins, one or more of the essential amino acids is present in an insufficient amount to supply our needs. Proteins in plants are considered to be less complete and in general this is true, especially for fruits and vegetables (except legumes), which contain very little protein. Legumes, however, contain proteins rated nearly as high as those found in animal products. Soybeans, lima beans, navy beans, pinto beans, kidney beans, chick peas (garbanzos), black-eyed peas, and peanuts are all legumes.

The quality of protein available in peanuts is nearly as good as animal protein.

Vegetable proteins in sesame seeds can be combined with legumes or rice.

Complementary proteins

Nuts, seeds, and grains, while not as high in protein as the legumes, contain some amino acids that are either lacking or present in only small quantities in the legumes. For instance, legumes are rich in the essential amino acid lysine, but they are low in another one,

methionine. Just the opposite is true for grains, nuts, and seeds, which are rich in methionine but low in lysine. These two groups of less complete proteins complement each other; that is, when they are eaten together, an adequate supply of all the essential amino acids is provided for the body to use.

Some examples of this complementary activity are beans, peas, or lentils eaten with rice, a peanut butter and whole wheat bread sandwich, or corn and lima beans. Complementary proteins need not be eaten during the same meal, but should be eaten the same day, so that the amino acids will be available for use by the body at approximately the same time. Combinations of plant protein sources that can be combined with each other to produce high quality protein are shown in Table 1. The best way for vegetarians to be certain of getting enough complete protein is by eating a large variety of plant foods daily from the three groups: grains, legumes, and nuts and seeds.

Protein and the body

All body cells and tissues contain protein, even bone, hair, and nails. Protein comprises about 20 percent of the total weight of the body and about 50 percent of the body's dry weight. The muscles and liver contain large amounts of protein. In fact, nearly one-half of the protein in the body is located in the muscles. The only components of the body that do not contain protein are bile and urine. There is constant renewal of the cells in the body, but the rate of renewal varies greatly among the

Combining vegetable proteins

Combine LEGUMES With
Barley Corn Oats Rice Sesame seeds Wheat

Combine RICE With
Legumes Sesame seeds Wheat

Combine WHEAT With
Legumes Rice and Soybeans
Soybeans and Peanuts
Soybeans and Sesame seeds

Table 1

different tissues. For example, the cells that line the intestinal tract are replaced by new ones every few days, the red blood cells every 120 days, the cells that make up the muscles take even longer, while the cells in the brain are rarely replaced. When tissue breaks down, amino acids are released from the cells and added to the large pool of amino acids that are available in the body for the building of new protein.

Approximately 33 grams of protein are lost each day by the average adult male and must be replaced. The body has no means of storing amino acids, so the reserves are depleted in only a few hours. That is why we should try to eat some complete protein at each meal. If no protein is supplied in the diet, the body will continue to use up its protein in order to maintain all the vital body functions.

Rice and beans are classic complementary proteins and this dish is a staple traditional food in many cultures.

Protein in the diet

The diet of the average American contains two or three times the required daily amount of protein, and 60 to 70 percent of this is obtained from animal sources. Unlike some of the developing countries, where 70 to 80 percent of the protein in the diet is from cereals, protein deficiency in the United States is almost unheard of, even in those who follow a vegetarian diet. The protein requirement of the body is at its highest during infancy and childhood, the time of greatest growth.

A rough measurement of the daily requirement of protein in grams can be obtained by dividing your body weight in pounds by 3. A more accurate way is to multiply your weight in kilograms (Kg.) by 0.8. If you do not know your weight in kilograms, it can easily be found by dividing your weight in pounds by 2.2. The result (in Kg.) is then multiplied by 0.8 to obtain the daily requirement of grams of protein. For example, a 150-pound man would weigh about 68 Kg. This multiplied by 0.8 gives 54 grams of protein as his daily requirement. Additional protein must be supplied to growing children under the age of 18, following severe burns, hemorrhage, surgery, or serious illness, during pregnancy and lactation, and in the elderly. However, a person doing hard physical labor uses no more protein than the office worker, despite the many rumors to the contrary. Increasing the amount of protein in the diet does not mean that the body will make more protein if it already has a sufficient supply. Any excess protein in the diet is either burned for energy or stored as fat. In order for this to occur, however, nitrogen must first be removed from the protein. This nitrogen is changed to a waste

An acre of farmland used to feed cattle will result in 50 pounds of animal protein.

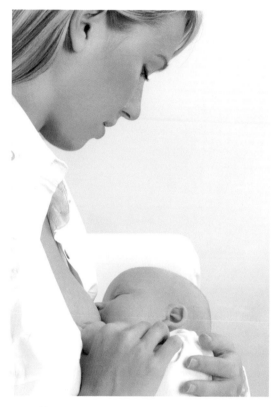

Mothers need extra protein during pregnancy and lactation.

of the protein is finally available to humans in the form of meat, milk, and eggs. It takes about 10 pounds of feed to produce 1 pound of beefsteak and about 6 pounds of feed to produce 1 pound of turkey protein.

Uses of protein

Protein has many important uses, as follows:

- It is essential for the growth, repair, and maintenance of all body tissues.
- It takes part in the production of enzymes and hormones, which help to regulate nearly every important function in the body.
- Proteins regulate the body's water and acid-base balance; they also help to maintain the body fluids in their normal, slightly alkaline state.
- Protein is essential in the formation of antibodies, which are the first line of defense against disease.
- They are a supplementary but very expensive source of energy, particularly when they are obtained from meat or meat products.

product, urea, in the liver and is then excreted in the urine. This places an extra workload on the kidneys.

Protein is an expensive food and only in affluent industrialized countries are such large amounts of animal protein consumed. Following are some examples that illustrate the excessive use of plant protein that is necessary to provide food for those who believe they must have meat to eat. One acre of farmland will produce enough soybeans to yield 500 pounds of protein; however, if this same acre is used to grow feed for cattle, only 50 pounds of animal protein will result. Only about 15 percent

Beans and whole grain toast are a good example of complementary proteins.

Mineral Elements in the Body

Micronutrients for good health and body function

The following is a list of the essential mineral elements normally found in the body. All of these minerals are bountifully supplied to us in natural foods, if they are not lost or destroyed during meal preparation. All of the bodily functions are operating continuously and must be supplied by the essential minerals found in foods. Natural minerals, especially, are needed for the purifying, cleansing process.

Macrominerals are those needed in the diet in amounts exceeding 100 mg per day. Microminerals are also called "trace elements," because they are needed in only very minute amounts. If all the minerals in the body were collected and weighed together they would make up only 4 percent of the body weight. Oxygen, hydrogen, carbon, and

Essential minerals

Macrominerals	Microminerals	
Calcium	Iron	Molybdenum
Phosphorus	Iodine	Chromium
Potassium	Zinc	Fluorine
Sulfur	Selenium	Silicon
Sodium	Manganese	Vanadium
Chlorine	Copper	Nickel
Magnesium	Cobalt	Tin

nitrogen, the elements in carbohydrates, fats, and protein, comprise 96 percent of the body weight and contribute 99 percent of all the atoms that are present in the body. If the body was completely burned, there would be about five pounds of minerals remaining. About one-half of this five pounds would be calcium and another 25 percent would be phosphorus, the two major minerals that are in the bones.

Essential minerals

About 60 different minerals have been identified in the body, but so far only those in the list above have been found to be essential. An essential mineral, like an essential amino acid, is one that must be supplied to our body in the food we eat. It performs a function that is necessary for the maintenance of life, for growth, or for reproduction. Minerals are necessary both for regulating body processes and for building tissue.

In comparison with the two and a half pounds of calcium in the body, all the trace elements (microminerals) together weigh only about one

Green leafy vegetables such as broccoli are packed with minerals.

ounce. But they are just as necessary to the proper functioning of the body as those elements that are present in larger amounts. Cobalt, the mineral associated with vitamin B_{12}, is present in only two parts per trillion of body weight. A large amount of research is in progress, and with new techniques it is possible to isolate elements in tissue that are present in very tiny quantities, about one part per billion; therefore, other trace elements will probably be discovered.

Mineral inhibitors

Minerals are widely distributed in our food. They are found in whole grains, nuts and seeds, dark green leafy vegetables, fruit, milk and milk products. There are substances in plants that combine with some minerals to form insoluble salts, rendering them less available for absorption into the body. For example, some of the iron, zinc, and magnesium we eat is made unavailable to the body by combining with phytates in whole grain. Calcium is rendered insoluble by oxalates that are found in some of the green vegetables. Minerals are not readily affected by acid or alkaline solutions nor by heat or oxygen. But, although minerals cannot be destroyed they can be dissolved in cooking water and then discarded. Moreover, nearly all the minerals are removed during the processing of refined flour and sugar.

There are three minerals that tend to be low in the average American diet: calcium, iron, and zinc.

Acid and alkaline

Some minerals are acid-forming when they are in solution, while others are alkaline. Those that are acid-forming are chlorine, sulfur, and phosphorus. These minerals are found mostly in meat, fish, poultry, cheese, cereals, prunes, plums, cranberries, rhubarb, cocoa, tea, and certain nuts (Brazil nuts, peanuts, and walnuts). Those minerals that are alkaline-forming are calcium, sodium, potassium, and magnesium. They are found in fruits, vegetables, milk, olives, almonds, coconuts, and chestnuts.

The body functions best in a neutral or a slightly alkaline medium and if too much acid is present, as it is in diets that are high in meat and animal products, it is given off by the lungs as carbon dioxide and is also excreted in the urine. Several other mechanisms are built into the body that maintain the proper acid-base balance. Various minerals contribute to this important function.

Cereals contain chlorine, sulfur, and phosphorus: acid-forming minerals.

Calcium

When a wide variety of food is eaten, an adequate supply of most minerals is obtained. But because dairy foods contain the largest amount of calcium, those on a strict vegetarian diet (vegans, who eat no meat or animal products) should be sure they get an adequate supply of calcium from other sources. Calcium is the most abundant mineral in the body, accounting for roughly two percent of the total body weight. Ninety-nine percent of the calcium is located in the bones and teeth and most of the remainder is in the blood. One eight-ounce cup of milk will provide about one-third of the daily calcium requirement. To get an equal amount by eating whole wheat bread, you would need to eat 18 slices.

It is not so much the quantity of calcium that we eat that is important; what really counts is the amount that is absorbed from the intestines and utilized by the body. Although calcium absorption varies under different circumstances and in different people, as is true of many of the other mineral elements, on the average only 20 to 40 percent of the calcium we eat is absorbed from the intestines. The absorption of calcium is increased by the following.

- Adequate amounts of vitamin D in the diet.
- Lactose (milk sugar) in the diet, which increases the calcium absorption by as much as 20 percent.
- An adequate supply of fluorine.
- Proper exercise.
- An acid environment of the upper intestinal tract.
- Periods of need, such as rapid body growth or low body stores of calcium.

The less calcium there is in the diet, the greater will be the percentage absorbed.

The absorption of calcium is hindered or decreased by the following.

- Oxalic acid in some foods unites with calcium and prevents its absorption. Some foods with high levels of oxalic acid are rhubarb, spinach, beet greens, peanuts, parsley, Swiss chard, and cocoa. But the oxalic acid in these foods binds only the calcium in that particular food and does not interfere with calcium from a different food that is eaten at the same meal. Thus, the overall effect of oxalates on calcium absorption is probably quite small.
- Phytic acid, a form of fiber found in the outer coats of grain, also binds calcium; however,

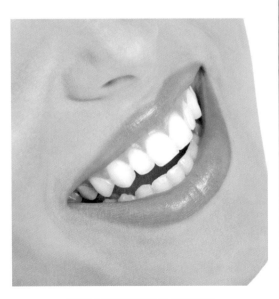

Calcium is important for strong, healthy teeth.

Children need calcium for healthy bone development.

under most circumstances this has little effect on the overall calcium absorption.

- A high protein diet causes increased excretion of calcium, so the body cannot use it. Eating too much protein also inhibits calcium absorption.
- Lack of exercise. Anyone that is immobilized for a time, such as invalids or even astronauts.
- Emotional instability.
- Laxatives and medicines that cause the intestinal contents to pass rapidly through the body.

- Some antacids and diuretics cause decreased calcium absorption.
- Excessive phosphorus intake. Some soft drinks are high in phosphorus.

Recommended daily allowance 800 to 1200 mg. 1200 mg—teenagers and during pregnancy and lactation. 1500 mg—women over 52.

Uses
- Development and maintenance of strong bones and teeth. Protects against osteoporosis.
- Ensures proper clotting of the blood.
- Needed for the contraction and relaxation of muscles, especially the heart.
- Needed for the proper utilization of iron.
- Acts as an enzyme activator.
- Assists in the absorption of vitamin B_{12}.
- Helps to regulate cell permeability.
- Helps to maintain the neutrality of the body fluids.
- Possibly helps in lowering the blood pressure.
- May help ward off colon cancer.

Sources
- Dairy products, including yogurt. These provide 75 to 85 percent of the calcium in the average American diet. There is about 300 mg of calcium in one eight-ounce cup of milk.
- Legumes; dark green vegetables such as broccoli, collards, kale, mustard, and turnip greens.
- Enriched cereals.
- Citrus fruits, figs.

Drinking herbal tea helps to retain calcium intake.

Osteoporosis

Osteoporosis, which literally means "porous bones," is a painful and potentially crippling disease caused by a loss of calcium from the bones. This loss results in thinning and softening of the bones with frequent fractures of the spine, hips, and wrists, loss of body height, and the formation of a "dowager's hump." About 150,000 persons in the United States, mostly women, suffer from hip fractures each year due to osteoporosis and 40,000 of these people will be dead within one year of the fracture. Osteoporosis affects 15 to 20 million people in America for an annual health bill approaching $4 billion. One of every four women will eventually become a victim of this largely preventable disease. Its greatest incidence is in women past the menopause or in those women who have lost the normal estrogen production of their ovaries, usually as the result of surgery. The loss of estrogens leads to decreased intestinal absorption of calcium and an increased loss of this important mineral through the kidneys. The average age for the menopause is 52 years and the average life expectancy for women in the United States is now a little over 78 years. Fifty percent of women over the age of 75 suffer from the symptoms of osteoporosis. While osteoporosis is far more common in women than in men, elderly men may also suffer from this condition. It is also more common in whites and Asians than in blacks. Vegetarians have been shown to have a lower incidence of osteoporosis than those who eat meat, probably due to a lower intake of protein and phosphorus.

A healthy lifestyle and proper treatment can go a long way towards the prevention of osteoporosis. Without a doubt, the ideal way to get all the calcium you need is from your food, but if a calcium supplement becomes necessary it should preferably be taken as calcium carbonate, the form in which calcium is most readily absorbed. Taking part at least 3 times a week in some form of weight-bearing exercise, such as walking, jogging, tennis, bicycling, jumping rope, etcetera, helps to maintain the normal bone structure. Cigarettes, alcohol, and excessive caffeine intake should be eliminated. Recent studies have shown that taking

Staying active and taking weight-bearing exercise such as tennis helps to maintain bone density throughout life.

low dosages of estrogen together with a 1500 mg daily intake of calcium is much more effective in preventing bone loss in postmenopausal women than when large amounts of calcium are taken by itself. In fact, the number of fractures due to osteoporosis after the menopause has been shown to be just about the same in those who take only calcium supplements as in those who do not.

If you have a tendency to form kidney stones, you should consult your family doctor before taking calcium supplements. Anyone taking calcium supplements should be sure to drink at least 8 cups of fluid a day.

Calcium supplements usually come in the following forms:

Percent calcium per 1000 mg

Calcium carbonate	**40%**
Calcium citrate	**22%**
Calcium lactate	**18%**
Calcium gluconate	**9%**

Dolomite, bone meal, or oyster shells are sometimes used, but the first two are not recommended because they may contain lead or other toxic substances. Read all labels carefully to see what form of calcium you are taking. For instance, a 1000 mg tablet of calcium carbonate contains 400 mg of calcium, while a 1000 mg tablet of calcium gluconate has only 90 mg of calcium.

Calcium content of some common foods

Dairy Product	mg	Fruits	mg
1 cup Yogurt*	415	5 medium Figs	126
1 cup Milk, nonfat	303	1 large Orange	96
1 cup Milk, low fat (2%)	314	4 large Prunes	45
1 ounce Swiss cheese	259	4 ounces Raisins	45
1 cup Cottage cheese, low fat	154	Vegetables	
1 cup Soymilk, fortified	150	1 cup Collards, cooked	152
1 cup Soymilk, regular	55	1 cup Turnip greens, cooked	139
Breads and Cereals		1 cup Mustard greens, cooked	138
1 cup Total, General Mills	200	1 cup Kale, cooked	125
1 cup Oatmeal, inst. Quaker	120	1 cup Rhubarb, cooked	105
1 each Buckwheat pancake, 4"	99	1 cup Spinach, cooked	83
1 cup All-Bran, Kellogg's	70	1 cup Broccoli, cooked	66
1 6-inch Tortilla, com	60	1 cup Rutabagas, cooked	59
1 cup Cream of Wheat, inst.	40	1 cup Artichoke, cooked	51
1 piece Cornbread, enriched	28	Legumes and Nuts	85
1 cup Oatmeal, rolled	21	1 cup Boston baked beans	73
1 slice Whole wheat bread	17	1 cup Soybeans	50
1 cup Cream of Wheat, reg.	13	1 cup White beans	48
Miscellaneous		1 cup Kidney beans	38
1 tbsp. Molasses, blackstrap	116	12-15 Almonds	38
Vegetarian Meat Analogs			
1 each Stakelet (Worthington)	80	1 each Grillers (Morningstar Farms)	67
1 each Griddle Steaks, frzn (Loma Linda Foods)	67	2 each Breakfast Patties (Morningstar Farms)	45

*Note: The amount of calcium in yogurt varies from brand to brand and also depends on whether it is plain or fruit-flavored.

In order to know if you need additional calcium, either in the form of food or supplements, you must first know about how much you already consume each day in your diet. The above chart gives several common food sources that are high in calcium and the amount of calcium each contains.

Notice the difference in calcium content between instant and regular Cream of Wheat and oatmeal: the instant varieties have calcium added.

While many other foods contain calcium, these are the best sources. Be careful about depending on multivitamin/mineral supplements to give you an adequate calcium supply. Most of them contain only small amounts of calcium. Check the label to find out the exact amount.

Many antacids contain calcium. For example, one regular Turns tablet contains 500 mg of calcium carbonate, which provides 200 mg of calcium.

It is extremely important to include adequate calcium in the diet during the growing years when the bones are developing. They will then be able to store a large amount of calcium that can be used later in life to help prevent osteoporosis. After about the age of 35 there is a gradual reduction in bone calcium that apparently cannot be prevented by any form of treatment. As mentioned in the preceding paragraphs, this loss accelerates considerably in women after the menopause. If you eat a well-balanced diet containing a good supply of calcium in early life and also form the habit of regular exercise, your bone mass will be increased and bone loss will be slowed during the middle and later years of life.

Dairy products such as milk are high in the micronutrient calcium.

High quantities of calcium are present in many green leafy vegetables, such as kale.

During times of growth it is particulary important to eat foods high in calcium.

Teenagers in particular need to be taught why it is especially important for them to eat a good diet, including foods high in calcium, because so many in this age group frequently substitute soft drinks for milk, one of our best sources of calcium. The greatest benefits of following a healthy lifestyle are obtained by those who develop good habits of eating and exercise early in life.

In a recent study of thousands of people around the country by the National Center for Health Statistics, it was found that teenage girls from 12 to 17 were eating an average of only 692 mg of calcium a day instead of the recommended 1200 mg. From 18 to 24 years of age, the calcium consumption was even lower. Girls and young women in these age groups who are not getting an adequate supply of calcium are not building up a good calcium reserve in their bones and are thus placing themselves in jeopardy for later developing osteoporosis. It cannot be emphasized too strongly that it is the adolescent years that are the most critical for building good strong bones. About one-half of the bone structure in an adult is formed during the rapid growth spurt of adolescence. This is not a matter of "What you don't know won't hurt you," for what you don't know (and do something about) may hurt you very much.

Another especially important period in which to get an abundant supply of calcium is during pregnancy and lactation, in order to promote good mineral formation of the infant's bone structure and baby teeth. The most critical period is during the last three months of pregnancy and the first few months of lactation, when bone development and growth is at its maximum. During the time of pregnancy and lactation, calcium intake should be 400 mg per day more than normal, or a total of about 1200 mg. If the mother is not getting enough calcium for the infant's needs, it will be withdrawn from the mother's bones, possibly leading to bone disease at some time in the future.

It should also be remembered that smoking, alcoholic beverages, and excessive intake of caffeine in coffee and soft drinks all seem to contribute to the development of osteoporosis.

Phosphorus

Next to calcium, phosphorus is the most abundant mineral in the body, comprising one percent of the total body weight. About 90 percent of the phosphorus is located in the bones and teeth and the rest is distributed in the cells throughout the body. No deficiency of phosphorus has been observed, for not only is it widely distributed in our food, but 50 to 70 percent of the phosphorus we ingest is absorbed. The average daily intake of phosphorus in the United States is 1500 to 1600 mg. If Amphogel, an antacid containing aluminum hydroxide, is taken with meals, it will react with the phosphorus and prevent some of it from being absorbed. Antacids containing aluminum hydroxide are not recommended.

Recommended daily allowance 800 to 1200 mg.

Uses

- Development of strong bones and teeth.
- A component of enzyme systems in the cells that govern the release and storage of energy.
- Part of the RNA and DNA in cells that controls protein production and the pattern of our genes.
- Transportation of fatty acids to various parts of the body.
- Helps to maintain the neutrality of the body fluids.
- Enzyme formation.

Sources

- Whole wheat grains.
- Nuts, legumes.
- Dairy products, eggs.
- Phosphate additives in carbonated drinks.

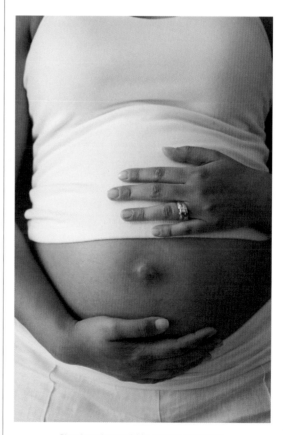

Phosphorus is essential for a baby's development.

Potassium

The word potassium comes from "potash," which is the ash that remains following the burning of vegetable substances. The average American diet contains 2000 to 6000 mg of potassium every day and it is readily absorbed from the intestines. The excess is excreted by the kidneys. A deficiency of potassium occurs in some illnesses in which there is prolonged vomiting and diarrhea. Certain medicines, such as diuretics, may cause a potassium deficiency. Poor circulation and constipation may indicate a lack of potassium. Foods that are high in potassium should be used in abundance in female troubles. A dietary deficiency of potassium occurs only rarely.

Recommended daily allowance 1825 to 5625 mg.

Uses

- Release of energy from the cells.
- Manufacture of glycogen and protein.
- Regulates fluid balance.
- Helps to regulate acid-base balance.
- Transmission of nerve impulses.
- Important in maintaining normal heart beat.
- Muscle contraction.

Sources

Widely distributed in a large number of foods. Especially good sources are bananas, dried fruit, potatoes, avocados, milk, whole grains, dark molasses, broccoli, and legumes.

Sulfur

Some sulfur is present in every cell of the body. It is a part of several amino acids, B vitamins, insulin, and other essential body compounds. It is found most abundantly in our hair, nails, and skin.

Recommended daily allowance
None known.

Uses

- Maintains healthy hair and nails.
- Needed in eliminating blood diseases.
- Helps to eliminate skin diseases such as acne.
- Stimulates the liver and increases the flow of bile.
- Important in maintaining normal body metabolism.

Bananas are an excellent source of potassium.

- Detoxifies some poisons in the body.
- Part of some enzyme systems.

Sources
- Protein foods.
- Cabbage and members of the cabbage family—cauliflower, broccoli, and Brussels sprouts.

Sodium

Sodium is one of the two elements that make up salt (sodium chloride), which is one of the oldest known chemical preservatives. Regular table salt contains 40 percent sodium. About two-thirds of the sodium is in the body fluids outside of the cells. The other one-third is in the bones. There is rarely a deficiency of sodium in the diet unless it is self-imposed by a person that is on a very low salt diet. In fact, the average diet has two or three teaspoons of salt each day, more than twice the amount needed. The amount of sodium in the body may be lowered by servere diarrhea or by excessive sweating.

About 18 percent of the population has high blood pressure. In about one-half of these the blood pressure rises as the sodium intake is increased. In the other half eating sodium seems to have little effect on the blood pressure.

Recommended daily allowance 1500 to 2500 mg.

Uses
- Maintains normal fluid balance.
- Transmission of nerve impulses.
- Muscle contraction.

Strawberries are a source of sodium, needed to maintain fluid balance.

- Increases the permeability of the cell wall.
- Helps to regulate and maintain osmotic pressure and acid-base balance.
- A good supply of sodium should be available in those who have rheumatism, hardening of the arteries, kidney stones, gallstones, stiff joints, acidosis, and diabetes. It should be restricted in those with high blood pressure and heart disease.

Sources
- Table salt.
- Processed foods, baking powder, baking soda.
- Milk, cheese, egg white.
- Strawberries, apples, huckleberries, gooseberries, cucumbers, carrots, beets, okra, cauliflower, spinach, asparagus, celery, Romaine lettuce, and watermelon.

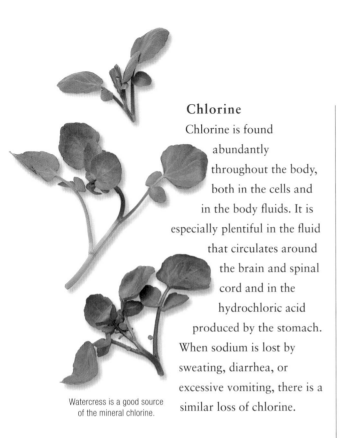

Watercress is a good source of the mineral chlorine.

Chlorine

Chlorine is found abundantly throughout the body, both in the cells and in the body fluids. It is especially plentiful in the fluid that circulates around the brain and spinal cord and in the hydrochloric acid produced by the stomach. When sodium is lost by sweating, diarrhea, or excessive vomiting, there is a similar loss of chlorine.

Recommended daily allowance 1700 to 5100 mg.

Uses

- Helps to maintain water balance, acid-base balance, and osmotic pressure.
- Increases the capacity of the blood to carry carbon dioxide to the lungs for excretion.
- Produces the normal acid environment in the stomach. This aids in the absorption of iron and vitamin B_{12}.
- Helps cleanse the intestines and body of toxins.

Sources

- Watercress, raw white cabbage, spinach, lettuce.
- Tomatoes, radishes, asparagus, celery, cucumbers, parsnips, carrots, onions and turnips.
- Pineapple.

Magnesium

There is a total of about one ounce of magnesium in the body. Sixty percent of this is located in the bones, and the rest is in muscle, blood, soft tissues, and cells. Between 30 and 70 percent of ingested magnesium is absorbed by the small intestine, depending on the amount eaten. The amount that is absorbed is decreased by the presence in the intestines of calcium, phytates, and fat. It is increased by vitamin D and lactose.

Recommended daily allowance 300 mg.

Uses

- Helps to form strong bones and teeth.
- Helps to regulate muscle relaxation and contraction.
- Proper function of the nerves.
- Activates enzymes controlling metabolism.
- Acts as a laxative.
- Foods containing magnesium are helpful in people who suffer from constipation and autointoxication and may be of help in stiff joints.

Sources

- Green leafy vegetables.
- Nuts, seeds, whole grain cereals. During refining of the grain, about 80 percent of the magnesium is removed.
- Soybeans, peas, green beans, brown rice, apples, cherries, figs, raisins, prunes, lemons, alfalfa, and celery.
- Milk.

Baby foods are fortified with iron to prevent nutrient deficiency during early childhood.

Iron

If it were possible to collect all of the iron in our body into one place and weigh it, it would weigh about as much as a penny. About two-thirds of this iron is located in the hemoglobin of the red blood cells and the rest of it is in the liver, spleen, bone marrow, and muscles.

The most widespread nutrient deficiency of early childhood in the United States is not a lack of vitamins or protein, but rather a lack of iron. Nearly 10 percent of toddlers in the United States have been found to be iron deficient. Milk is a poor source of iron, even mother's milk, and a baby is born with only enough iron to last for about six months. Iron-fortified formulas and infant foods are therefore necessary, starting when cow's milk is substituted for breast milk or at about 4 months of age for breast-fed infants.

Cow's milk has less than 1 mg of iron per quart, and of that amount only 10 percent or less is absorbed. Other groups of people who may develop iron deficiency anemia are preschool and adolescent children, women during their childbearing years, women who are pregnant, and for two or three months following delivery. For these groups, an iron supplement in the form of ferrous sulfate or ferrous gluconate may be required. Because of its possible effects on the intestinal tract of nausea, constipation, and diarrhea, the iron should be taken either an hour before or with meals. Start with one pill daily and increase to several. Do not take them all at the same time, but spread them throughout the day. Iron supplements will turn the stools a very black color, which should not be mistaken for blood.

Cooking food in a cast-iron pot increases its iron content.

Another caution about taking iron is that it can be dangerous or even fatal if taken in large doses. It is the fourth most common cause of poisoning in children below the age of five years, so it must be kept well out of their reach.

Ordinarily only about 5 to 10 percent of the iron we eat is absorbed. But if for some reason the body needs more iron, as much as 30 to 35 percent can be absorbed. The body keeps using the iron that it has and very little is excreted, perhaps 1 mg a day in men and 1.5 mg in women. Men are able to store about 1000 mg of iron but women can store only about 300 mg.

Cooking in the old time cast-iron pots and kettles gave a good supply of iron, especially when acid foods were being cooked. The longer the food was allowed to simmer in the iron pot, the higher the iron content became in the food.

The absorption of iron is increased by:
- The presence of vitamin C (ascorbic acid) taken at the same meal. Vitamin C has no effect on the absorption of iron supplements.
- The hydrochloric acid in the stomach.
- The form of iron that we eat.
- An increased need of iron by the body.
The absorption of iron is hindered by:
- The presence of tannic acid, found in tea, cola drinks, and coffee. Drinking tea with a meal or within an hour after a meal may reduce the iron absorption by as much as 87 percent.
- Phytic acid, found in grain and fiber.
- Excess phosphorus and calcium in our diet.
- Phosvitin, present in egg yolk.
- Some antacids that contain calcium and phosphate salts.
- Inorganic iron. This is the form of iron in all plants and eggs and about half of the iron in meats. Only 3 to 5 percent of this kind of iron is absorbed, but this amount can be increased two to three times by eating a good vitamin C source at the same time as the other foods.

Recommended daily allowance 10 mg for males. 18 mg for females.

Uses
- Iron is a vital part of the hemoglobin that carries oxygen to the tissues.
- Iron is part of the enzyme system present in all cells that is responsible for energy production and release.
- An important constituent of the muscles.

An ounce of bran will provide the daily allowance of iron for women.

Sources

- Whole grain cereal products.
- Nuts, legumes, raisins, molasses.
- Green leafy vegetables, yellow vegetables, potatoes.
- Dried fruits.
- Boiled lentils or kidney beans.
- One ounce of any of the following Kellogg's cereals will provide 18 mg of iron, 100 percent of the recommended daily allowance of iron for women: Product 9, Fruitful Bran, Raisin Bran, Bran Flakes.

Iodine

About 15 to 30 mg of iodine is present in the body; about equal to the size of a match head. Sixty percent of this is in the thyroid gland and the rest is in the blood. Iodine is readily absorbed from the intestines and from the skin, where it is sometimes used on cuts as an antiseptic. About one-third of the iodine we eat is used by the thyroid gland; the rest is excreted in the urine.

If there is not enough iodine in the diet, the thyroid gland enlarges, causing a swelling in the neck. This enlargement is called a goiter. A goiter, which was treated with seaweed, was recorded as early as the year 3000 BC in Chinese literature. If the thyroid gland is too active, hyperthyroidism (Grave's disease) results. This causes a rapid pulse, weight loss, nervousness, excessive sweating, and protruding eyeballs.

Recommended daily allowance 150 micrograms.

Uses

- An important part of the thyroid hormone, thyroxine, that is responsible for metabolism.
- Essential for the function of the thyroid gland.

Sources

- Iodized salt.
- Food that is grown near the ocean.
- Kelp.

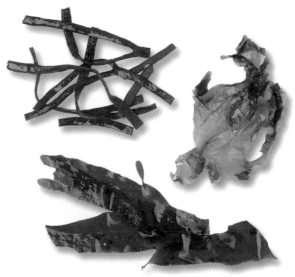

Seaweed is a good source of iodine, needed to regulate body metabolism.

Zinc

Of the body's total of two grams of zinc, about 70 percent is in the bones. The rest is distributed in the blood, hair, skin, and testes. About one-half of the zinc that is eaten is absorbed. The amount absorbed is increased when the supply in the body needs to be increased and also during pregnancy and lactation. Fiber and phytic acid, found in whole grains, decrease the availability of zinc for absorption, as does the taking of oral contraceptives. There are large areas in the United States where the soil is low or lacking in zinc and in these areas some people have been found with a possible zinc deficiency. Vegetarians also have a tendency to be deficient in zinc, so they must be sure to eat some foods with a high zinc content. Large doses of zinc can prevent the proper

Legumes are good sources of zinc, needed for growth and healthy skin.

absorption of copper and may lead to anemia. It also reduces the amount of good HDL-cholesterol in the blood.

Recommended daily allowance 15 mg.

Uses
- Proper growth of the body.
- Helps with the proper healing of wounds and maintains healthy skin.
- Needed in enzymes concerned with metabolism and digestion.
- Helps maintain proper sense of taste and smell.
- For utilization of vitamin A.
- Transportation of carbon dioxide.
- Carbohydrate metabolism.

Sources
- Whole grains.
- Legumes, nuts.
- Vegetables and fruits are poor sources of zinc.

Selenium

In 1957 it was discovered that selenium was an essential mineral and that certain diseases in animals, which were thought to be caused by a lack of vitamin E, could readily be cured by giving selenium. The amount of selenium in the soil and water varies considerably throughout the United States, as well as the entire world, and this in turn causes a variation in the amount of selenium in our food. The section of the country from which our food originates is probably more important in determining the amount of selenium we get than

Grains grown in areas such as Wyoming, Montana, and North or South Dakota are high in selenium.

the type of food we eat. But because the food we buy at the market comes from various parts of the country, the average American does not need to worry about obtaining enough selenium. The average diet contains 1.3 mg of selenium per day.

Several studies seem to indicate that in areas where there is an abundance of selenium in the soil, the rate of cancer is less. In an article published in the prestigious medical journal, *Diseases of the Colon and Rectum* in July 1984, Richard Nelson M.D. believes that a decreased consumption of selenium may be a cause for a recently noted change in the location of colon cancer in the United States and other western countries. This change has taken place gradually over the past 30 years. Whereas 30 years ago cancer was much more frequent in the last 10 or 12 inches of the colon, it is now becoming more common in the first part of the colon, which is located in the right side of the abdomen.

An investigation into the possible causes for this change suggested that it was not only the result of decreased selenium consumption, but also that an increased intake of zinc and fluoride may play a part by opposing the action of selenium.

When colon cancer was experimentally produced in rats, a 90 percent reduction in right-sided colon cancer was noted if the rats were given a selenium supplement. This did not occur if the selenium supplement was withheld.

It has been noted for some time that people living in areas with a deficiency of selenium in the soil have an increase in the amount of cancer in general, but especially of colon and breast cancer.

Cereals are a good source of the antioxidant selenium.

Why should there be a deficiency of selenium?

- During the past 30 to 40 years there has been a gradual increase in the consumption of meat at the expense of grains and vegetables. The amount of selenium in meat is quite low compared with the amount in whole grain cereals. There is strong evidence that an increased rate of colon cancer is associated with a high consumption of meat and beef fat and a decreased intake of dietary fiber.

- Meat is also very high in zinc, which prevents the utilization of selenium. The zinc in plant foods is bound to phytates and excreted in the stool, but all the zinc in meat is available for absorption. Increased zinc levels in the blood have been associated with colon and breast cancer.

- The artificial fluoridation of water supplies may be linked to an increase in right-sided colon cancer. Fluoride is also a potential selenium antagonist.

Cancer is the second most common cause of death after heart disease, and cancer of the colon is the second most frequent cause of cancer deaths. Cancer of the colon is next in frequency only to lung cancer in men and to breast and lung cancer in women. The lifetime risk of developing a cancer of the colon is about 4 percent, and 6 million Americans now living will die of colon cancer if the present trend continues.

The *FDA DRUG BULLETIN* of August 1984 reported 12 cases of toxic overdose of selenium that occurred when it was discovered that some selenium tablets contained 182 times the amount indicated on the label. The estimated doses that were taken ranged from 27 to 2310 mg.

Symptoms of a toxic overdose consisted usually of nausea and vomiting, nail changes, fatigue, and irritability. Less commonly experienced were loss of hair and nails, diarrhea, abdominal cramps, dry hair, sensory changes on the skin, and garlic odor on the breath.

Recommended daily allowance .05 to 0.2 mg (over age seven years).

Uses

- Selenium, along with vitamin E, protects the body tissues from oxidative damage. This is especially true of the cell membranes.
- Helps to protect normal body cells against radiation damage.
- Assists in the prevention of cancer.
- Required by the body for maximum immune response.
- Retards the rancidity of unsaturated fatty acids.

Sources

- Grains, nuts, cereals. Eighty percent of selenium is lost in the refining and processing of food.
- Foods grown in high-selenium areas, such as the Dakotas, Montana, and Wyoming.

Manganese

Most of the 10 mg of manganese that we have stored in our body is in the liver, pancreas, bones, and kidneys. About 30 to 50 percent of the manganese in our food is absorbed into our body, but calcium and iron inhibit the absorption of manganese from the intestines. No deficiency of manganese has been reported in humans.

Recommended daily allowance 2.5 to 5.0 mg.

Uses

- Necessary for the normal development of bones and connective tissue.
- Part of the enzyme systems involved in fatty acid, cholesterol, and carbohydrate synthesis.
- Maintenance of normal reproductive functions.

Sources:

- Whole grain cereals, nuts, rice.
- Green vegetables.
- Kelp.

Green vegetables contain manganese, needed for healthy development.

Tomatoes are a source of silicon, which stimulates growth.

Copper

Almost half of the copper in the body is found in the bones and muscles, but the most concentrated source is in the liver. Vitamin C and phytic acid both act to hinder the absorption of copper.

Recommended daily allowance 2 to 3 mg.

Uses
- Prevents anemia.
- Energy and connective tissue metabolism.
- Part of the tissue that acts as a covering for the nerves.

Sources
- Widespread in most foods.
- Nuts, dried peas and beans, dried fruit, whole grains, leafy vegetables.

Cobalt

In 1948 it was discovered that cobalt is an essential part of vitamin B_{12}, the vitamin that is necessary for the prevention of pernicious anemia.

Recommended daily allowance None determined.

Uses
- Necessary for the formation of vitamin B_{12}.

Sources
- Widespread in food. No deficiency has ever been reported.
- Grains, seeds, green leafy vegetables.

Molybdenum
Recommended daily allowance .15 to 0.5 mg.

Uses
- Component of essential enzymes.

Sources
- Legumes, cereal, yeast.
- No deficiency in the diet has been recognized.

Chromium
Recommended daily allowance .05 to 0.2 mg.

Uses
- Essential for the maximum utilization of glucose.
- Synthesis of cholesterol and fatty acids.
- An essential part of other enzyme systems.
- May help to prevent atherosclerosis.

Sources
- Whole grains. Much of the chromium is lost during the refining of grain.
- Brewer's yeast.

Fluorine

In the early 1930s it was noted that many children living in Colorado and some of the adjoining states had a very dark, mottled discoloration of their teeth. It was also found that these teeth had far fewer cavities. Further studies showed that this was due to the high content of fluorine in the drinking water. Mottling of the teeth did not occur unless there was more than 2.5 parts per million of fluorine in the water. Since that time, many communities in the United States have added small amounts of fluorine to the drinking water supply in amounts of 1 part per million. This has reduced the incidence of dental cavities from 50 to 60 percent in children. Although no definite harmful effects have been noted, there is still much controversy over whether this mineral should be added to the public water supply.

Adding fluoride to water is a controversial practice and may discolor teeth.

Recommended dally allowance 1.5 to 4.0 mg.

Uses

- The main function of fluorine appears to be the prevention of cavities and to help build strong teeth.
- Recent studies have shown that fluorine may help to prevent osteoporosis.

Sources

- Fluoridated water.
- There are not many good food sources.

Silicon

Recommended daily allowance Not known. Because of its widespread distribution, a deficiency is rare.

Uses

- Promotes the formation of connective tissue.
- Hardens teeth and bone.
- Stimulates growth of the body.

Sources

- Whole grain cereal.
- Green vegetables, tomatoes, figs.

Vanadium, Nickel, Tin

These minerals have been found to be essential for the normal growth and development of animals. Their exact function in humans has not been determined at the present time but a deficiency is not likely, since they are widely available in foods.

Vitamins

More micronutrients for good health and body function

Discovery of vitamins

Hundreds of years ago it was found that some foods could prevent or even cure certain diseases, such as scurvy, beriberi, rickets, and pellagra. Even in ancient Greece, Hippocrates gave liver as a treatment for night blindness without realizing that he was using a good source of vitamin A. It was not until the twentieth century, however, that the substances in food that were capable of producing these cures were discovered, isolated, and produced in the laboratory. Dr. Casimir Funk, in 1912, gave these compounds the name of "Vitamine," or vital amine. He wrote the first book on *Vitamines* in 1914. Later on, in 1920, after it was discovered that not all of these compounds were amines, the "e" was dropped from the end of the word. The name vitamin, now a household word, has been used ever since.

The last vitamin to be discovered was vitamin B_{12} in 1948. Perhaps others will be discovered some day.

What are vitamins?

In general terms, all vitamins are body regulators. They are complex organic substances that are essential for growth, reproduction, maintenance of health, and regulation of nearly all metabolic processes in the body by their association with enzymes and coenzymes.

The total weight of all the vitamins in the body is only about one-fourth of an ounce. An average person eats two to three pounds of food a day and in this amount of food the vitamins weigh only about 1/150th of an ounce. Vitamins cannot be produced in the body so they must be supplied as they are used up or eliminated. When several vitamins are needed for the proper operation of a certain function in the body, this function is impaired if even one of the necessary vitamins is lacking.

Vitamins are made by plants. Humans get their vitamins either by eating the plants or by eating meat after the animals have eaten the plants and incorporated the vitamins into their own bodies. Vitamin supplements can be purchased nearly anywhere. The total amount of money spent on vitamins yearly in the United States is about $1.2 billion, and this is increasing at the rate of about 10 percent a year. The FDA estimates that 40 percent of the U.S. population aged 16 or over takes vitamin and mineral supplements.

Who should take supplements?

There are some groups of people in the United States that most likely should be taking vitamin and mineral supplements. These include the following.

- Those who are not eating an abundant and well-balanced diet; such as the elderly, especially those living alone, or teenagers and others eating out a lot and not taking care to get a good variety of foods.
- Women who are pregnant or breast-feeding.
- Those recovering from a severe illness or surgery.
- Alcoholics.
- People who eat a lot of refined or processed foods.
- Those in low income groups where a wide variety of food from the different food groups cannot be obtained.

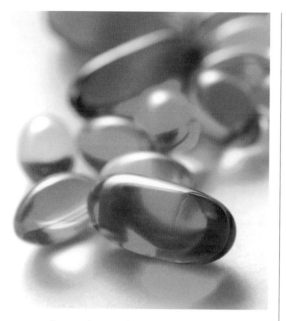

Some people may need to take vitamin supplements.

A fresh supply of vitamin C is needed daily as it is not stored in the body.

- Those who are suffering from severe debilitating diseases of various kinds.

Several recent surveys of thousands of American families showed that there were some deficiencies in the average diet. The vitamins that were found to be low were vitamins A, B_6 (pyridoxine), and C, while the minerals that tended to be deficient were iron, calcium, and magnesium.

Types of vitamin

Vitamins can be separated into two groups depending on whether they are soluble in fat or in water. While some characteristics are common to each group, they are not related chemically nor do they have similar effects on the bodily functions.

Fat-soluble vitamins A, D, E, and K:

- Soluble in fat but not in water.
- Stored in the body. Because there is no good mechanism for their excretion, taking large doses over a prolonged period of time may result in toxic symptoms and can even prove fatal. This is true of vitamins A, D, and K, but not of vitamin E.
- They are stored mainly in the liver, where the supply is sufficient to last for several months.
- They are absorbed from the intestines in the same way as fat.
- They are not easily lost by cooking or storage, but are destroyed by rancidness.
- Symptoms due to a deficiency of these vitamins appear slowly.
- Mineral oil in the intestines hinders absorption.

Water-soluble vitamins B complex and C:

- Soluble in water but not in fat.
- Not stored in the body so a fresh supply is needed daily.
- Easily destroyed by heat, cooking, and storage.
- Any excess beyond the amount that is needed by the body is excreted in the urine.
- Deficiency symptoms develop rapidly.

Fat-Soluble Vitamins

VITAMIN A (Retinol)

Vitamin A deficiency is common throughout the world in underdeveloped, overpopulated countries. It is estimated that worldwide, 80,000 children a year become blind as a result of vitamin A deficiency and about one-half of these children die.

Vitamin A is present in our food in two forms. In food of animal origin it is found as the active vitamin (retinol), while in plant foods it is found as provitamin A carotenes, a precursor of vitamin A. Carotene is an orange-yellow pigment that is present in green vegetables, but is masked by the green color of the chlorophyl in the leaves.

Vitamin A is important for a child's healthy growth and development.

A precursor, or provitamin, is a substance that is changed in the body to a vitamin. Only a portion of the carotene that we eat is changed to vitamin A. This takes place in the wall of the small intestine. The amount that is changed varies between 30 and 70 percent, depending on the type of food and the form in which it is eaten. Carotene itself is not active in the body.

In most of the food we eat about half of the vitamin A is in the form of retinol and the other half is provitamin A. The liver stores about 90 to 95 percent of our vitamin A, enough to last months or perhaps even years under normal circumstances.

Functions
- Gives the ability to see in dim light.
- Maintains normal skin.
- Needed for growth and development of strong bones and teeth.
- Needed for the secretion of mucus by the cells lining the respiratory, urinary, and intestinal tracts that helps keep them moist and healthy.
- Aids the normal reproductive processes.
- Needed for carbohydrate metabolism in the liver.
- Essential for proper smell, hearing, and taste.
- Aids in the prevention of certain types of cancer.
- Beta carotene is a non-toxic antioxidant and helps prevent disease by neutralizing free radicals.

Deficiency
- Poor vision in dim light (night blindness).
- Dry, scaly, itching skin.
- Increased susceptibility to infections, especially in the respiratory tract.

- Changes in the eyes that may lead to blindness. The eyes become dry, swollen, and infected. This condition is called xerophthalmia.
- Slow wound healing.
- Poor bone growth in children.
- Defective enamel on teeth and an increased number of cavities.
- Loss of taste and smell.
- Stunting of body growth.

Toxicity

Because vitamin A cannot be excreted from the body in any significant amount, toxicity results from prolonged daily doses in excess of 50,000 IU in adults and less in children. The symptoms of an overdose are nausea, diarrhea, headache, dizziness, loss of hair, bone pain, dry itching skin, drowsiness, and cessation of menstruation. These symptoms will clear up in a few days if the excess intake is stopped. Toxicity only occurs with retinol and not with carotene. An excess intake of carotene will cause the skin to turn yellow. This can be seen in those who drink large amounts of fresh carrot juice.

Sources

- Deep yellow vegetables such as carrots, pumpkin, sweet potatoes, winter squash, yellow corn, tomatoes.
- Dark green vegetables such as broccoli, chard, spinach, beet greens, collards.
- Yellow fruits such as apricots, cantaloupe, peaches, persimmons, oranges, mangoes.
- Watermelon.

Dosage

5000 IU (1000 RE): males 11 years and over.
4000 IU (800 RE): females 11 years and over.
5000 IU (l000 RE): during pregnancy.
6000 IU (1200 RE): during lactation.

Since 1974 the designation RE (retinol equivalent) has been the preferred method for indicating the dose of vitamin A. Most food value charts at the present time give both the IU (International Units) and the retinol equivalent.

Stability

Very little vitamin A is lost during cooking or processing. It is stable to heat and alkali, but not when it is exposed to acids, light, or oxygen.

Carotene, a form of provitamin A, is present in dark green vegetables.

VITAMIN D (Calciferol)

Vitamin D, the "sunshine vitamin," is produced by the ultraviolet rays of the sun reacting with a cholesterol-like chemical that is naturally present in the skin. But the older one gets, the less vitamin D can be made in this way. The skin of a person in his or her eighties can only make about one-half the vitamin D of a 20-year-old. Over a period of several days this chemical is changed to vitamin D by the liver and kidneys. Recent studies suggest that exposing only your arms, hands, and face to the noonday sun for 10 to 15 minutes twice a week will allow enough vitamin D production to meet the average requirements. Fog, smog, clouds, clothing, and skin pigment are effective in filtering out part of the ultraviolet rays and thus reducing the amount of vitamin D that is produced. Window glass and sun-blocking agents with a protective factor over 8 totally stop vitamin D production. For the most part, vitamin D is stored in the liver, but it is found also in the bones, skin, brain, and fat. There is no good way for the body to eliminate an excess amount of this vitamin.

Egg yolk is one of the best food sources of vitamin D.

Functions

- Regulates the absorption and metabolism of calcium and phosphorus to produce strong bones and teeth.
- Necessary for the proper absorption of calcium and phosphorus from the intestine.
- Maintains normal blood levels of calcium and phosphorus.

Deficiency

- Rickets in children. The bones become soft and bend easily, causing bowed legs and knock-knees. The teeth make their appearance late and they decay easily. The chest is usually deformed and the growth stunted.
- Osteomalacia in adults. The bones lose their strength and tend to become painful and may even break.

Toxicity

Because the body does not excrete excess vitamin D, toxicity is not uncommon. Symptoms consist of failure to grow normally, kidney stones, high blood pressure, weight loss, loss of appetite, irritability, vomiting, excessive thirst, diarrhea, and weakness.

Toxic symptoms may be caused by amounts of 2000 IU in children or 75,000 IU in adults, taken daily over a long period of time. The amount necessary to produce these symptoms of toxicity varies considerably from person to person.

Exposure to sunlight promotes vitamin D production in the skin.

Sources

- Vitamin D is the least available vitamin in food. Fruits, vegetables, and grains are poor sources of this vitamin. The best sources are egg yolk, milk, butter, and cheese.
- Formed in the skin when exposed to sunlight.

Dosage

400 IU to age 18 (10 micrograms of cholecalciferol).

200 IU in adults (5 micrograms of cholecalciferol).

200 IU added to the usual dose during pregnancy and lactation.

Stability

Vitamin D is stable to heat, storage, oxidation, acid, and alkali but is sensitive to light.

VITAMIN E (Tocopherols)

Vitamin E was first recognized as essential in 1922, when it was found to be necessary for normal reproduction to take place in laboratory animals. Eight natural forms of vitamin E are found in food and alpha-tocopherol is the most active form.

Approximately 40 to 60 percent of vitamin E in our diet is stored in the fat, muscles, and liver.

Functions

- A strong antioxidant. Vitamin E neutralizes free radicals, preventing them from producing disease by injuring the normal cells in our body.
- Protects vitamins A and C and unsaturated fatty acids from undergoing oxidation.
- Protects the red blood cells from destruction.
- Regulates the release of energy from glucose and fatty acids.
- Takes part in the reproductive process by helping to prevent recurrent spontaneous abortions.
- Slows down the aging process.
- May be useful in treating persons exposed to air pollution.
- Useful to those who develop pain and cramps in the legs while walking.
- Helpful in cases of sterility, impotence, decreased sexual drive, heart disease, psychiatric disorders, and to increase the performance of athletes.
- May help to prevent the formation of nitrosamines, some of which cause cancer.

Savoy cabbage is a good source of vitamin E, a powerful antioxidant.

Deficiency

- A deficiency has sometimes been found in premature babies, causing a special type of anemia, and in persons who have deficient fat absorption over a long period of time.
- In general, deficiency is not a problem. However, to help prevent damage from free radicals 150 to 400 IU should be taken as a daily supplement.

Toxicity

None has been identified. Large doses have been reported to interfere with the action of vitamin K, causing an increased tendency toward bleeding.

Sources

- Wheat germ and wheat germ oil are the richest sources.
- Soybeans.
- Whole grain cereal, legumes, corn, nuts, seeds. Up to 90 percent of the vitamin E in cereals is lost during the refining process.
- Green leafy vegetables, peppers, carrots.

Dosage

15 IU in males (10 mg alpha-tocopherol equivalents).

12 IU in females (8 mg alpha-tocopherol equivalents).

Stability

Vitamin E is not affected by normal cooking, acid, alkali, or heat. Deterioration of vitamin E occurs with exposure to light or oxygen, and it is also caused by rancidity. Deep fat frying destroys vitamin E because of the long periods of high temperature, which results in the fat turning rancid. The freezing of vegetables may cause considerable loss of vitamin E. This is not true of any of the other vitamins, which show no appreciable loss during the freezing process.

Alfalfa sprouts are high in vitamin E.

VITAMIN K (Menadione)

Vitamin K is the last of the four fat-soluble vitamins. Like the other fat-soluble vitamins, it is not a single entity but a group of chemically related substances that, in the case of vitamin K, are called quinones. These include both the naturally occurring vitamin K that is in plant and animal foods, and also the synthetic vitamin K (menadione).

Functions

• Necessary for the proper clotting of blood.

Deficiency

• There is normally a deficiency of vitamin K in newborn babies, since vitamin K cannot reach the baby in any significant amount while it is still in the uterus. Furthermore, for the first few days after birth vitamin K cannot be produced in the intestine of the newborn baby, because no bacteria are present. This results in a condition called hemorrhagic disease of the newborn. Therefore, to prevent this from occurring, all newborn infants are routinely given vitamin K.

• In adults a deficiency of vitamin K is always due to a lack of absorption. This may be due to various diseases, including any condition that causes chronic diarrhea or bile duct obstruction. Certain drugs may also result in deficiency.

Toxicity

Toxicity only results from an excess of the synthetic forms of vitamin K, and may result in jaundice and anemia in infants.

All newborn babies are given vitamin K to prevent deficiency.

Sources

• Dark green leafy vegetables.
• Cauliflower, alfalfa, peas, and cabbage.
• Cereal.
• Soybean oil and other vegetable oils.
• Synthesis by bacteria in the intestines.
• Both cow's milk and mother's milk are low in vitamin K.

Dosage

10 to 20 micrograms: newborn to one year.
15 to 100 micrograms: increasing dose from one to eleven years.
70 to 140 micrograms: adults.

Stability

Vitamin K is destroyed by light, some oxidizing agents, acids, and alkali. It is stable to heat, air, and ordinary cooking.

Water-Soluble Vitamins

Vitamin B Complex

Several different vitamins compose what is commonly known as vitamin B complex. These vitamins are different from all the others vitamins, in that they all contain nitrogen in addition to carbon, hydrogen, and oxygen. Two of the B complex vitamins, thiamine and biotin, also contain sulfur, and vitamin B_{12} contains cobalt and phosphorus.

The B complex vitamins are very closely associated in their functions in the body and they all tend to be found in the same food groups. If there is a deficiency in one of these vitamins, the others in the group will not function properly. They are all concerned with the proper functioning of some of the coenzyme systems in the body. Perhaps the most important of the group are thiamine, riboflavin, and niacin. When these three are present in adequate amounts in the diet, there

Thiamine is found mostly in the outer layer (the bran layer) of rice.

is not likely to be a serious deficiency of vitamin B. During the milling process, cereals lose nearly all of their vitamin B as well as other important nutrients. Enriched cereal has thiamine, riboflavin, niacin, and iron added.

VITAMIN B_1 (Thiamine)

The first description we have of a disease resembling vitamin B deficiency is found in ancient Chinese writings dating as far back as 2600 BC. A lack of this vitamin results in a disease called beriberi, which means "I can't, I can't." It was apparently called this because those who had a severe thiamine deficiency that affected their nervous system eventually were unable to move.

Little is then recorded of beriberi until about the middle of the nineteenth century, when refined grains and cereals came into common use. This is especially true in some countries where rice was the main food. During the 1800s many Japanese sailors developed beriberi and many of them died. When fish, meat, and vegetables were added to their diet, the disease immediately disappeared. In Java a Dutch prison physician noted that chickens fed with polished rice left over from the prisoners' meals developed a disease with symptoms that were very similar to those in beriberi. He found that this disease was cured by feeding the chickens whole rice instead of the polished rice that the prisoners were eating. Later it was thought that beriberi was caused by some unknown factor that was present in the outer coat of grains and beans, but was lacking after the grain was milled. This finally led to the discovery of thiamine as well as

Whole grain bread contains thiamine, needed for energy production.

other members of the vitamin B complex family.

Even with the knowledge that we now have available, beriberi is still a problem in some countries such as the Philippines, where a large percentage of the rice that is eaten is highly polished and not enriched. Additional vitamin B_1 is also lost during the washing and cooking of the rice.

Raw fish is frequently eaten in some countries, and it is interesting to note that there is an enzyme present in certain raw fish that divides the vitamin B_1 molecule, making it unavailable for use by the body. This, however, usually does not result in a vitamin B_1 deficiency, since this enzyme is destroyed by cooking the fish.

The body stores enough vitamin B_1 to last for about one or two weeks, and any excess is excreted in the urine.

Functions

- Necessary for energy production.
- Stimulation of the appetite.
- Essential as part of the coenzyme system for carbohydrate metabolism.
- For proper functioning of the nervous and cardiovascular systems.
- Prevention of beriberi.

Deficiency

A lack of this vitamin results in beriberi. In infants of two to five months of age, this may be a rapidly fatal disease unless treated immediately with thiamine. This occurs more often in breast-fed babies.

Beriberi was first noted when polished rice was eaten in place of brown rice. Now we know that since thiamine is located mostly in the outside layer of the rice (the bran layer), it was being removed during the milling process.

The nervous system is severely affected in cases of beriberi because it depends upon glucose for its normal function and thiamine is intimately involved in glucose metabolism. Symptoms that may occur are fatigue, depression, irritability, moodiness, inability to concentrate, confusion, headaches, leg cramps, numbness and tingling in the feet, problems with walking and finally paralysis of the legs.

The gastrointestinal system may also be involved with loss of appetite, constipation, nausea, and weight loss.

Heart failure may occur with accumulation of fluid in the tissues. This is known as "wet beriberi."

In the United States, beriberi is seen mainly in chronic alcoholics.

Steamed vegetables retain water-soluble vitamins such as vitamin B complex.

Toxicity

None known.

Sources

- Wheat germ, whole grain bread and cereal.
- Dried peas and beans, peanuts and peanut butter, legumes.
- Nuts.
- Green leafy vegetables.
- Protein-rich foods are generally good sources of vitamin B_1.

Dosage

0.5 mg per 1000 calories in the diet. The total amount of thiamine should not be allowed to fall below 1.0 mg per day in adults.

Stability

Since this is a water-soluble vitamin, cooking must be done with care. Use as little water as possible at as low a temperature as possible and for as short a time as possible. Reuse the water, since much of the thiamine is leached out into the water. Alkali, such as in baking soda and some antacids, destroys thiamine. The destruction of thiamine begins at temperatures over 100°C. The smaller the pieces of food that are being cooked, the greater will be the loss of this vitamin. Although vitamin B_1 is stable in the dry state, in the wet state it is the most unstable of all the vitamins except for vitamin C.

RIBOFLAVIN (Vitamin B_2, Vitamin G)

Recent studies have shown that between 6 and 26 percent of persons in America have either a definite or borderline deficiency of this vitamin. This is especially true among those who drink little if any milk. Other groups in which there is an inadequate intake of riboflavin are alcoholics, the aged, women during pregnancy and lactation, and women taking oral contraceptives. An increased intake of this vitamin is needed during periods of growth or physical stress.

One quart of milk a day supplies all the necessary riboflavin. Milk in general supplies about 40 percent of all the riboflavin consumed by Americans. The safest course, if you use milk, is to sterilize it by sufficient boiling.

Functions

- Production of energy.
- Tissue growth, maintenance, and repair.
- Red blood cell production.

A quart of milk supplies the required daily dose of riboflavin.

Deficiency

Cracks appear at the corners of the mouth. The lips become inflamed and also split and crack. The tongue becomes smooth and purplish-red in color and the skin gets dry and scaly. The eyes become very sensitive to light, water easily, and become irritated. There is impairment of vision, diminished reproductive capacity, and the general growth pattern of the body is retarded.

Toxicity

None known.

Sources

- Wheat germ.
- Leafy vegetables, nuts, legumes.
- Whole grains.

Dosage

1.2 mg—women.
1.4 mg—men.
A minimum dose of 1.2 mg per day should be taken by everyone.

Stability

Riboflavin is slightly soluble in water. It is stable to heat, acid, and oxidation, and only a small amount is lost during ordinary cooking. It is destroyed by sunlight, ultraviolet light, and alkaline solutions.

It was discovered that when milk in clear glass bottles was delivered on the doorstep by the milkman and allowed to sit in the sun, 50 to 70 percent of the riboflavin was lost in 2 hours.

Avocados contain niacin, needed for healthy skin.

NIACIN (Nicotinic acid, vitamin B$_3$)

Niacin is the only vitamin that can be manufactured in the body, where it is made from tryptophan, an essential amino acid, in the presence of other nutrients. Sixty mg of tryptophan gives about one mg of niacin.

It was not until 1937 that niacin was found to be the cure for pellagra. This deficiency disease was widespread in the United States in the early part of the twentieth century. It was common in some cities in the south, where many people lived largely on a diet of corn (maize), molasses, and salt pork.

Niacin occurs both as nicotinic acid and nicotinamide. Neither one should be confused with nicotine, which occurs in tobacco.

Functions

- For proper functioning of the nervous and digestive systems.
- Energy metabolism.
- Maintains a healthy skin.
- Production of fatty acids, steroids, and cholesterol.

Deficiency

Pellagra's symptoms are the "four D's"—diarrhea, dermatitis, depression, and dementia or death.

Skin. A reddish rash appears on the skin of the feet, hands, and face. This rash becomes much worse when exposed to the sun.

Nervous system. Headache, confusion, irritability, dizziness, delusions, severe depression, and sometimes death.

Gastrointestinal tract. Sore mouth and tongue, mild intestinal upset, loss of appetite and weight, diarrhea.

General symptoms of fatigue, weakness, backache, and anemia may also be present.

Toxicity

None has been reported for nicotinamide.

Nicotinic acid in large doses produces flushing, stomach upset, dizziness, and nervousness.

Sources

- Legumes, peanut butter.
- Whole grain or enriched bread and cereals.
- Seeds and nuts.
- Broccoli, potatoes, tomatoes, collards.
- Avocados, figs, prunes, bananas.

Dosage

13 niacin equivalents (NE) per day.

Stability

Niacin is stable to heat, acids, alkali, light, and oxidation. It is lost in the water to some degree during cooking.

PYRIDOXINE (Vitamin B_6)

Pyridoxine has been used in large doses in the treatment of many conditions. It has attained some success in the treatment of nausea that occurs commonly during the early months of pregnancy and also in the reduction of dental cavities, if the pyridoxine is sucked in the form of lozenges.

Functions

- Active in the metabolism of protein, glucose, and fat.
- Red blood cell production. Synthesis of hemoglobin.
- Aids in the manufacture of niacin from tryptophan.
- Normal functioning of the nervous system.
- Production of antibodies.
- Production of regulatory substances.

Deficiency

Many people in this country have a borderline or low intake of pyridoxine. The symptoms of pyridoxine deficiency consist of anemia, nausea, sore mouth, smooth red tongue, kidney stones, dermatitis around the eyes and at the corners of the mouth, poor growth, vomiting, abdominal pain, depression, and confusion. In infants there are sometimes convulsions.

Toxicity

Usually none. People taking extremely large doses have had symptoms of difficulty in walking, tingling sensation in the hands, lips, and tongue, numbness in the feet, and clumsiness.

Sources

- Whole grain cereals, yeast, nuts.
- Legumes, bananas, potatoes, green vegetables, yellow corn.
- Wheat germ, seeds, avocados.

Dosage

2.2 mg per day in males.
2.0 mg per day in females.
This dose should be increased during pregnancy and lactation, in the elderly, in alcoholics, and in women taking oral contraceptives.

Stability

During the milling process of wheat 75 to 90 percent of the pyridoxine is lost. It is stable to heat and acid, but destroyed by oxidation and light.

Nuts and seeds contain B vitamins, essential for nervous system function.

FOLACIN (Folic acid)

Functions

- Formation of hemoglobin and red blood cells.
- Normal growth and reproduction.
- Protein metabolism.
- Treatment of sprue and pernicious anemia.
- Prevents neural tube defects in the fetus.

Deficiency

A deficiency of folacin is common throughout the world, even in the United States, but is found mostly in the tropics. There is an increased need for folacin during infancy, pregnancy, and in conditions where the food is not properly absorbed. A folacin deficiency leads to pernicious anemia. Symptoms of diarrhea, weakness, and fatigue are noted. The tongue and mouth become sore and the tongue itself appears smooth and reddish in color. The daily needs of an adult male could be supplied for 6 years by only one teaspoon of folic acid.

Toxicity

None known.

Sources

- Green leafy vegetables, broccoli, asparagus, okra, parsnips, cauliflower, Brussels sprouts.
- Nuts, legumes, whole grain cereals, yeast.
- Oranges, carrots, cantaloupe.

Dosage

400 micrograms (0.4 mg).

800 micrograms during pregnancy.

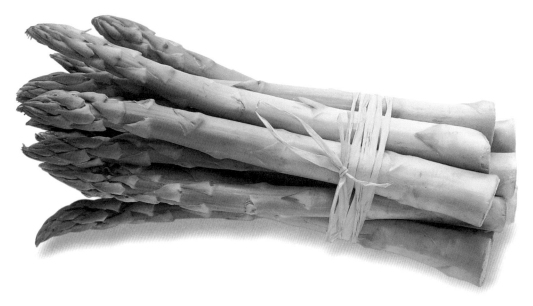

There is an increased need for folacin (found in vegetables such as asparagus, and nuts and legumes) during pregnancy to prevent defective fetal development.

500 micrograms during lactation.
During her childbearing years, every woman should take 0.4 mg Folacin daily.

Stability
Folacin is destroyed by processing, light, and improper cooking and storage of foods.

COBALAMIN (Vitamin B$_{12}$)
This vitamin was synthesized in 1948, the last of the B complex vitamins. The crystals are a bright red color, so vitamin B$_{12}$ is sometimes referred to as the "red vitamin." Plant foods contain none of this vitamin. In order for vitamin B$_{12}$ to be absorbed from the intestine, it must be united with a special protein in the gastric juice called "intrinsic factor." The average person absorbs about 30 to 70 percent of vitamin B$_{12}$ in the diet. Persons who are deficient in the "intrinsic factor" are not able to absorb this vitamin properly and subsequently develop pernicious anemia. Strict vegetarians (vegans), who eat no animal products of any kind, may also develop a vitamin B$_{12}$ deficiency. Some of this vitamin is made in the human intestinal tract, but this occurs in the colon where no absorption of the vitamin can take place.

Functions
- Normal functioning of all the body cells.
- Proper functioning of the nervous system.
- Normal growth.
- Protein, carbohydrate, and fat metabolism.
- Production of red blood cells.

Deficiency
Pernicious anemia, with a sore mouth and tongue, loss of appetite and weight, weakness, difficulty in walking, mental disturbances.

Vitamin B$_{12}$ is found only in animal foods; therefore, those on a total vegetarian diet, who eat no meat or animal products of any kind, should take a supplement or eat some type of vitamin B$_{12}$ fortified food such as fortified soybean milk.

In adults a rather large amount of vitamin B$_{12}$ is stored in the liver. This is sufficient to last for several years with no further intake. Children, however, will show a deficiency of this vitamin after two to three years, since their storage capacity is low. The stores of the vitamin in the liver seem to increase with age.

Toxicity
None.

Sources
- Animal products only.
- Dietary supplements.

Dosage
3 micrograms per day over age seven.
The average diet contains about 5 to 15 micrograms per day.
Adults take a B$_{12}$ (50 micrograms) tablet once a week.

Stability
Destroyed by alkali. About 30 percent of vitamin B$_{12}$ is lost in normal cooking.

PANTOTHENIC ACID

This vitamin, once called vitamin B_5, is present in every cell in the body and is a component of all living matter.

Functions

- Metabolism of protein, fat, and carbohydrate.
- Synthesis of hemoglobin, hormones, and cholesterol.
- Energy metabolism.
- Production of antibodies.
- Essential for numerous chemical reactions in the body.

Deficiency

An actual deficiency of pantothenic acid is difficult to document, but persons who are found with low values seem to have a decreased resistance to infection and an inability to withstand stressful situations.

Experimental deficiencies have been produced that show symptoms of tiredness, headache, insomnia, nausea and vomiting, abdominal pain, numbness and tingling in the hands and feet, and muscle cramps.

Toxicity

None.

Sources

- Yeast, green leafy vegetables.
- Broccoli, whole grain cereals and bread, legumes, yams.

Dosage

4 to 7 mg per day.

Stability

Only a small amount is lost during cooking.

VITAMIN C (Ascorbic acid)

Nearly everyone who completed a high school or college history course remembers studying about the events concerning British sailors, scurvy, and lime juice that took place during the seventeenth and eighteenth centuries. The story goes back much further than this, however, and descriptions of a disease resembling scurvy have been found on papyrus tablets in the city of Thebes, dating back as far as 1500 BC. Hippocrates, in 450 BC, described symptoms resembling scurvy in Greek soldiers. Scurvy was also noted during the time of

Yams are a good source of pantothenic acid.

Vitamin C is present in peppers and is essential for collagen formation.

regularly supplied on all British ships. This is why the British sailors were called "limeys," a name that has persisted to this day. As recently as the American Civil War, some soldiers died from scurvy, and even today there are still areas in the United States where the intake of vitamin C is borderline or inadequate. This is especially true among the lower income groups.

At the present time fresh fruits and vegetables contribute over 90 percent of the vitamin C in the American diet.

the Crusades, particularly in the winter when fresh fruits and vegetables were not available. In 1497 when Vasco de Gama sailed around the Cape of Good Hope, almost two-thirds of his crew died from scurvy, and Magellan lost many of his crew when he sailed around Cape Horn in the 1520s. This disease was particularly prevalent among British sailors during this time, and usually appeared about three months after the ship had left the home port. In 1753 Dr. James Lind published his experiments on British seamen, showing that giving them oranges or lemons prevented scurvy. Even though those in positions of responsibility in the British Navy at that time seemed to officially ignore the results of these experiments, when Captain Cook made his long voyage in 1775, he stocked his ship with as much fresh fruit and vegetables as possible and replenished them at every port where such supplies were available. None of his crew came down with scurvy. It actually takes only one-tenth cup of orange juice a day to prevent scurvy. By 1795 lime juice was

Functions

- Essential for collagen formation. Collagen is the protein material that binds the tissue cells together and is necessary for healthy teeth, bones, skin, and tendons.
- Increases the absorption of iron and calcium from the intestines.
- Promotes the healing of wounds.
- Converts the inactive form of folic acid, a vitamin of the B complex group, to the active form.

Grapefruit juice contains vitamin C, needed for wound healing.

- Protects the body from infections.
- Regulates many essential body processes.
- Essential for the integrity of the blood vessel walls.
- The synthesis of red blood cells and some hormones.
- An antioxidant vitamin.

Deficiency

A deficiency of vitamin C results in scurvy, probably the oldest recognized vitamin deficiency disease. When this vitamin is totally eliminated from the diet, the symptoms of scurvy begin to appear in about 90 days and consist of dryness of the skin, bleeding into the skin around the hair follicles, bleeding in the eyes, loss of hair, bleeding and swollen gums, fatigue, pains in the bones and joints, cavities in the teeth, sore mouth and gums.

The antioxidant vitamin C is present in many fruits such as strawberries.

If vitamin C is not completely eliminated from the diet, but the amount is less than adequate, the symptoms of scurvy take a longer time to develop and may be somewhat different. These symptoms are irritability, listlessness, swollen and tender joints, loss of appetite, weakness, fatigue, restlessness, bleeding under the skin and in the mouth around the gums, and in children a failure to grow normally.

Those requiring a greater than normal intake of vitamin C are smokers, women taking birth control pills, and elderly people.

Toxicity

No toxic effects have been noted with doses moderately over the recommended allowance. With sustained high doses, there is an increased risk of kidney stones developing due to the conversion of excess vitamin C to oxalic acid. There may be some interference with the normal metabolism of vitamin B_{12}, and symptoms of anemia, skin rash, diarrhea, and low blood sugar have occasionally been reported.

Sources
- Citrus fruits and juices, either fresh, frozen, or canned.
- Green peppers, broccoli, brussels sprouts, tomatoes and tomato juice, cabbage, greens, potatoes, yams, cauliflower, asparagus, and cabbage.
- Strawberries, cantaloupe, guava, mangoes, papaya.
- Rose hips, acerola (a West Indian cherry).

Vitamin C is rapidly lost upon exposure to air.

Dosage

35 to 50 mg to age 14.

60 mg over age 14.

80 mg during pregnancy.

100 mg during lactation.

Stability

Vitamin C is the *most unstable* of all the vitamins. When exposed to air, vitamin C is rapidly lost. The loss is not as great if the foods are stored in a refrigerator. It is easily destroyed by alkali, so baking soda should not be used while cooking vegetables. Other methods of preserving vitamin C are as follows.

- Avoid excess chopping and cutting of foods.
- Cook the vegetables in a steam pressure cooker or use as little water as possible.
- Cook potatoes with the skin on.
- Don't use copper cooking utensils.
- Add the food to be cooked to water that is already boiling.
- Keep the pot covered.
- Vitamin C is preserved by freezing.

Microwave cooking preserves slightly more of the vitamin C than cooking with steam pressure. Both of these methods preserve about twice as much of the vitamin as boiling the vegetables in water.

Water

Your body's transport system

The best six doctors anywhere,
And no one can deny it,
Are sunshine, water, rest and air,
And exercise and diet
These six will gladly you attend,
If only you are willing.
Your ills they'll mend
Your cares they'll tend,
And charge you not a shilling.

Lettuce has a very high water content.

Water is the most abundant of the essential nutrients in our body, the total amount being about 45 quarts. Between 50 and 75 percent of our total body weight is water; fatter people have proportionately less water than thin people. Water is present in all the tissues of the body as well as in every cell. Even our bones are made up of nearly one-third water, while our muscles and our 10 to 12 billion brain cells contain 71 percent water.

It is possible to live for several weeks without food, but we can survive for only a few days without water. Next to oxygen, it is the most essential substance for the preservation of life. None of the nutrients we eat would be of any value without the presence of water. Thirst occurs when we lose only about one percent of our total water; if we lose as much as 20 percent, death results.

About two-thirds of the body's water is located inside the cells, and the remainder is outside the cells in the tissues. Water, as well as nutrients and waste material, continually passes in and out through the cell walls by a process called osmosis.

Functions of water

The two most important functions of water are: (1) to act as a solvent for the essential nutrients, so that they can be used by the body; and (2) the transportation of nutrients and oxygen from the blood to the cells and the return of waste material and other substances from the cells back to the blood so they can be removed from the body. Other important functions are:

- To give shape and form to the cells.
- To regulate the body temperature.
- As a lubricant in joints and other areas.

Water loss		Water intake	
Skin	550 cc	Liquids	1500 cc
Lungs	440 cc	Solid foods	750 cc
Urine	1550 cc	Produced in the body	400 cc
Stool	150 cc		
Total	2650 cc	Total	2650 cc

1000 cc equals 1 quart   500 cc equals 1 pint   240 cc equals 1 cup

Table 1

Water content of various foods

Food	Percent Water	Food	Percent Water
White sugar	0.5	Chicken	63
Nuts and dry cereals	2-3	Veal	66
Crackers	5	Bananas	75
Gelatin	13	Cottage cheese	79
Butter	15	Potatoes	80
Dried fruits	25	Oranges, apples	86
Bread	36	Milk	87
Cheese, Cheddar	37	Fruit juice, vegetables	90
Beef	47	Lettuce	96

Adapted from Adams, C.: *Nutritive Value of American Foods*, USDA Handbook No. 456, Washington, D.C. 1975.

Table 2

- To cushion certain body organs.
- As a body builder, and to maintain peak physical performance. A loss of only 5 percent of our body water results in a 30 percent decrease in work performance.

Maintaining water balance

The intake and output of water must balance each other, and in the normal person the body has wonderful ways of maintaining this important balance. Most of our water comes from what we eat and drink, although some of it is made in the body. We eliminate water normally through our lungs, skin, urine, and intestines. Table 1 gives the approximate amount of water gained and lost from each of these sources every day.

Some foods contain large amounts of water while others have very limited amounts. Table 2 gives the water content of various foods.

We should drink six to eight eight-ounce glasses of pure water daily. This will provide enough water for all of the essential bodily functions and will help to maintain normal elimination.

Here is a helpful suggestion for the millions of Americans who are troubled with constipation; perhaps it is caused by not including enough roughage and liquid in the diet, or sometimes because the colon becomes lazy from the overuse of laxatives. Shortly after rising, drink some lukewarm water. Start by drinking half a glass or less and over a week or two slowly increase the amount until you can take two glasses without your stomach rebelling. It is best not to use ice water at this time of day, since energy is needed to warm it to body temperature and also because cold water tends to slow down the emptying time of the digestive tract. Two additional glasses of water (not warm) can be taken between breakfast and lunch and two more between lunch and dinner.

Drinking several glasses of water a day will maintain normal body function.

Fresh Air, Exercise, and Sleep
More of life's essentials

Through the lungs, the body receives life-giving air. One may live for many days without solid food and for several days without any liquid, but death comes in a few minutes without air. The capacity for using air can be greatly increased by properly exercising the lungs, as has often been demonstrated in the treatment of those with tuberculosis (consumption).

What is air?

Air is a mixture of numerous gases, but it is composed chiefly of oxygen and nitrogen. Life is more dependent upon the regular and adequate supply of oxygen than upon any other element. Fortunately for us, the nitrogen in the air dilutes the oxygen, for in an atmosphere of pure oxygen we would be so overactive as to be very short-lived. Experiments have shown that prolonged inhalation of air in which the proportion of oxygen is much greater than that in which it naturally occurs in the atmosphere causes such disturbance in the body metabolism that death finally results. Therefore, we know that the mixture called air did not happen accidentally, but has been perfectly formed for the needs of human beings as well as for those of animals and plants.

The water vapor present in the air is necessary to enable the lungs to use the oxygen readily, as is shown by the fact that dry oxygen is not as readily absorbed as that which contains the proper amount of moisture.

Blood and the lungs

A very important change takes place in the blood as it passes through the lungs. The blood is returned in the veins from all parts of the body to the right side of the heart. At this point the blood has a dark purplish color because it is low in oxygen and contains a large amount of carbon dioxide and other impurities. Next it is pumped through the pulmonary arteries to the lungs. In the lungs, the pulmonary arteries carrying the impure blood keep branching and getting smaller and smaller until they are only about the width of one red blood cell. When they reach this size, these very tiny blood vessels are surrounded by the air sacs in the lungs so that the red blood cells are able to give off their carbon dioxide and take on a fresh supply of oxygen. There are about 300 million of these tiny air sacs (alveoli) in the lungs, and if we could lay them out on a flat surface they would cover an area roughly 700 square feet in size.

When the blood leaves the lungs with a fresh supply of oxygen it flows back to the left side of the heart and is pumped all through the body. It is then a bright red color, due to the increased oxygen. The oxygen is taken up by the hemoglobin in the red blood cells, and is supplied to every part of the body.

Red blood cells

There are about 25 to 30 trillion red blood cells in our bodies, but each one lives only about 120 days. This means that in order to provide an adequate supply of oxygen to the many millions of tissue cells, 2.5 million new red blood cells must be produced every second. In adults, these new cells are manufactured mainly in the bone marrow.

As the blood passes through the tiny capillaries— the smallest channels that carry blood to every tissue in the body—each red cell gives up a portion of its oxygen, takes in carbon dioxide, and returns to the lungs to be cleansed again. The blood is slightly cooled and loses some of its water as it passes through the lungs. The amount of carbon dioxide that is released by the blood while digestion is taking place is greatly diminished by the use of such items as stimulating foods, sugar, animal foods, and even more by wine, rum, beer, ale, cider, tea, and coffee. Strenuous exercise increases the removal of carbon dioxide gas up to six times the ordinary amount.

Improving lung capacity

The lungs are greatly improved by regular exercise. When the lungs are not exercised and expanded to their limit on a regular basis, they lose their elasticity. In many persons there is almost a total loss of the power to really expand the chest.

Forming the habit of deep breathing will make you sleep better, think more clearly, have better circulation, and make you feel better all over because of the increased supply of oxygen that will be provided to every organ in your body.

Plants help to sustain levels of fresh air by taking in carbon dioxide and releasing oxygen into the atmosphere.

Deep breathing exercise

The following exercise is most beneficial when it is done in the fresh air.

- Stand straight, placing your hands along your lower ribs, with the fingers pointing down and inward.
- Take in a slow deep breath through your nose, making sure you feel the lower ribs move outward.
- When you have filled your lungs with as much air as possible, force yourself to take another sniff of air. If your ribs have not moved outward, give them a slight tug by hooking your fingers beneath them.
- Now let the air out slowly through your mouth, keeping the lips partly closed so there will be some resistance. When you feel like all the air has been let out, push the lower ribs in with your hands to force out the last little bit.

Start doing this exercise once three times a day and gradually work up to four or five deep breaths three times a day.

You may vary this routine by breathing in rapidly and exhaling slowly or vice versa. Musicians and public speakers often benefit by taking these deep breathing exercises, as it helps them to develop better breath control. When a person feels weary and exhausted from sedentary employment, the practice of deep breathing in the manner just described, with the body erect and the chest well expanded, will prove very refreshing and will help induce a restful sound sleep. The great advantage of an abundance of lung exercise can be seen from the fact that professional singers suffer less from lung disease than others and their chests are always better developed than are those of most other persons.

Health effects of breathing impure air

The detrimental effects of breathing impure air, especially in a room where there are several people, are headache, nervousness, dullness, and aggravation of all diseases pertaining to the lungs. Current scientific studies show that there is an increase in lung cancer in nonsmokers who are constantly subjected to an atmosphere polluted with cigarette smoke. It is interesting to note that the cells that are the most sensitive to a lack of oxygen are the cells of the brain. The headaches with which school children are sometimes afflicted are often caused by breathing foul air. Tuberculosis (consumption) is most frequent in those whose habits, vocations, or occupations are sedentary, as they usually spend much time in an atmosphere of impure air.

An old army surgeon, who was in charge of large hospitals during World War I, related a very interesting experience illustrating the importance of providing the sick, especially persons suffering with fever, with an abundance of pure air. He said that in a large hospital he had 320 cases of measles at one time during the winter season. The hospital caught fire and burned to the ground, and the patients had to be placed outdoors in tents. All but one or two recovered. He said he had no doubt but that the number of deaths would have been thirty or forty at least, if the patients had remained in an indoor environment.

Walking is an enyoyable way of increasing your oxygen intake and a very popular form of exercise suitable for all ages.

Exercise and oxygen intake

Walking increases the inhalation of oxygen threefold and has recently become one of the most popular forms of exercise in the United States. Regular exercise in the open air is one of the most important factors for the preservation of health and the prolongation of life. The greater the degree of activity, the larger the amount of oxygen taken into our bodies. In cold weather we get a larger supply of oxygen than in hot weather. This makes us more active, both mentally and physically. Outdoor life in the cool fresh air of temperate zones helps us to develop a strong constitution and increases our resistance to disease.

Proper exercise in the open air and sunshine gives good form and strength to the physical body and—all other health habits being equal—is one of the surest safeguards against disease and premature death. It gives buoyancy and strength and maintains a healthful mental balance, free from the extremes that result from artificial living.

Oxygen, the elixir of life, is one of the best blood purifiers and one of the most effective nerve tonics. Useful work in the open air will bring new strength and vitality, and produce a happy and cheerful attitude of mind. If the poisonous waste matter that should be thrown off by the lungs is retained, the blood becomes impure and not only the lungs but the stomach, liver, and brain are affected. The digestion is retarded, the skin becomes sallow, the brain clouded, the thoughts confused, the heart depressed, and the whole system inactive and very susceptible to disease.

Well-ventilated houses

Every room, and especially every sleeping room, in the house should be well-ventilated throughout the year, both day and night. Have plenty of light, sunshine, and air in your houses to make you strong, healthy, and happy.

Addendum The statements about the bad effects suffered from breathing impure air in enclosed quarters is certainly medically and scientifically correct today. Consider the following item that appeared in a leading science journal.

The men who built the beige and brick one-story house in rural Mount Airy, Maryland, boast that they can heat the whole place with a hair dryer. It is a veritable fortress against the loss of energy. There are leakproof, triple-glazed windows, a weather-stripped, magnetically sealed front door, and plastic sheets in the walls, floors, and ceilings that keep the home's living space as airtight as the inside of a sandwich bag.

The herb valerian has been used for thousands of years to promote sleep.

But a funny thing happened when these conservation-minded men from the National Association of Home Builders Research Foundation bottled things up so tightly. Without the drafts of fresh outside air typical in most homes, the indoor air went bad. Investigators found high levels of formaldehyde gas throughout the house and they detected indoor radioactivity more than 100 times the natural outdoor background level.

The Mount Airy house dramatically demonstrates an environmental problem that has only lately attracted governmental and scientific attention. The problem is indoor air pollution.

In the new breed of energy-efficient homes, as well as in more typical "leaky" homes around the United States, recent air sampling has established that pollutants are more concentrated indoors than out. In some residences—both old and new—these pollutants exceed national health limits. (Michael Gold, "Indoor Air Pollution," *Science*, Vol 80, March/April, 1981, p. 30.)

Getting a good night's sleep

The usual causes for a lack of sleep are pain, headache, cold feet, painful stomach or colon, nervous tension, worry, lung congestion, emphysema, mental illness, and inability to relax.

The following suggestions will help you get a good night's sleep.

1 Engage in some form of physical activity during the day, but not just before retiring. Don't take a midday nap.

2 The room should be dark, but not necessarily pitch black.

A comfortable bed will help you to get a good night's sleep.

3 A comfortable bed; if the bed is too soft, it may produce various muscle aches, and especially may cause or increase back pain.

4 Usually the quieter the better. Some people get used to sleeping with certain noises such as traffic, trains, music, clocks, etcetera, and have a hard time going to sleep if these sounds that they are used to are not present.

5 Relaxation is very important. Before going to bed, try reading or listening to some soothing music for an hour. One of the best positions for relaxing tense muscles is lying on the back with pillows under the head, arms, shoulders, and knees. Try to think of each muscle group. Tighten the muscles and then purposely relax them, starting with the toes and working up to the head. Be sure the facial muscles, including the eyelids and jaws, are all relaxed.

6 Try to have your stomach empty. Your evening meal should be light and should be eaten 3 to 5 hours before you retire. Avoid any drinks with caffeine, especially coffee, tea, colas, cocoa, or chocolate. If you really feel you need something to drink, take warm herb tea.

7 Take a warm bath for 10 to 20 minutes immediately before retiring. The temperature of the water should not be over 95°F. If the water is too hot, it will have a stimulating effect and keep you awake. If your feet are still not warm, use a heating pad or hot water bottle.

8 Don't smoke cigarettes before going to bed; the nicotine acts as a stimulant.

9 The best temperature in the bedroom for most people to sleep is 60° to 70°F.

Your Foods

Fruits

Valuable sources of micronutrients

God planned in the beginning that fruit should form a large part of our diet, and if we would follow that plan today, it would add much to our health. While it is true that fruit, like other things, has deteriorated significantly since creation, yet if we would take care of the trees and eat fruit in the proper way, it would prove an untold blessing today.

In the beginning, man was told to dress the trees. This was for a purpose. Every tree should be pruned and dressed so that the sun will shine on the fruit for at least part of the day, if not all day. If there are too many limbs and leaves, and the fruit grows completely in the shade, it will have much less food value, flavor, and life-giving properties. The seed of fruit and vegetables grown in the shade for two or three years will not germinate. It will, to a great extent, lose its quality and life-giving properties. Therefore, all fruit trees should be pruned so that sun and air have free access to the branches.

Another thing that should be remembered is that fruit, before it is ripe, is in the starchy state, and while in this condition it has but little food value and is hard to digest. But as fruit ripens it turns into grape sugar, especially when ripened in the air and sun, and is very easily digested. Fruit that is grown in the shade or is picked before it is ripe is better eaten cooked than raw. A great deal of the fruit that is shipped is picked before it is ripe. While it does ripen to some extent after it is picked, it is never the same as when it ripens on the tree.

Selecting fruit

If fruit is picked before it is fully grown, it is practically worthless as far as real food value is concerned, except perhaps for the banana, which is a very peculiar fruit. It can be picked green and will continue to ripen and develop its sugar.

Fruit has always been an important part of the diet, being a source of carbohydrate, water, vitamins, and minerals.

Trees should be pruned so that sun shines on the fruit for part of the day to maximize flavor, food value, and life-giving properties.

It should never be eaten until every particle of green has disappeared, the outer skin begins to turn brown, and the pulp has become mellow. Most bananas are eaten altogether too green while they are still in the starchy state. When the banana is fully ripe, it contains twenty-five percent grape sugar, which requires very little or no digestion. Any infant or invalid can eat mashed ripe bananas.

Some time ago I was in a fruit store looking for a bunch of bananas that suited me. The storekeeper said: "I like bananas, but I cannot eat them. Yesterday about eleven o'clock I got very hungry and ate two bananas, and they made me so sick that I had to go to bed." I asked him to point out what kind he had eaten. He had eaten bananas that were in the starchy state, and had probably not masticated them properly. Without proper mastication, bananas will form gas, putrefy, and cause trouble.

In buying prunes, buy a large size, since the large prunes have practically no larger pit than the small ones. The smaller the prunes, the less fruit you have, and the more pit. A large prune, when soaked overnight in cold water, can be eaten without any cooking and is very delicious. You can do the same thing with figs, apricots, or peaches when you get a good grade. When you do cook them, only very little cooking is needed.

Fresh figs can be eaten without any cooking required.

Unripe grains are the opposite of unripe fruits. The grain before ripening is in the milky state, or the grape sugar state, and can be digested without any cooking. That is the way grain was eaten in the beginning and no doubt that is the way the disciples and Jesus ate it. But when it ripens, grain turns into starch. Therefore, ripe grain should be thoroughly cooked before it is eaten.

The juice of oranges, grapes, pineapples, and grape fruit may be taken when ripe with no sugar added. These juices can be used to quench the thirst with good results if they are used as a drink between meals.

Citrus fruits in particular, but also strawberries, cantaloupes, and cherries, are high in vitamin C. All the yellow colored fruits are also high in vitamin A. Dried fruits, such as apricots, prunes, and raisins, contain little if any vitamin C but they are extremely rich in minerals, especially iron.

Eating food in its natural state

There are several reasons why we should not eat so much soft food or drink with our meals. First we hear so much about alkaline foods and that they are all right to eat, but the fact is that the saliva is more alkaline than any of these foods. Another fact is that if we eat our food in its natural state and thoroughly mix it with saliva before we swallow, it will alkalinize the system more than all of the known alkaline foods combined. When the food reaches the stomach, it is mixed with the digestive juice known as the gastric juice. In order for the gastric juice to do its work properly, it needs the help of the saliva. The food leaves the stomach in a semi-liquid form and in the small intestine it mixes with the pancreatic juice and the bile, which cannot perform their functions satisfactorily without the prior work of the saliva and the gastric juice.

If many of these little points were observed, you would see a marvelous improvement in your health. When you take so much fluid and soft foods with your meals, it dilutes these various digestive juices so that they become weak and do not have the proper power to digest the food as God had planned they should. There is perfect law and order in our system, and when we violate these principles we suffer the consequences.

Many years ago when we made tests on these things, we found that half a good-sized lemon would destroy typhoid germs in a glass of water; the healthy gastric juice in the stomach is four times as strong as lemon juice. Here is where the Scripture is fulfilled, that when we eat or drink any deadly thing, it shall not hurt us. Of course, I would not advise anyone to take carbolic acid or any concentrated poison and think they would be protected by what the Scripture says and that our digestive fluids would counteract the impurity. But nevertheless it is true that if you see to it that your bloodstream is pure and you eat the foods that make your digestive fluids pure or normal, then your system will be better able to resist typhoid, diphtheria, smallpox, tuberculosis, and other deadly germs.

God has provided still further preventive, nonpoisonous, remedies like gentian root, calamus root, valerian root, black currant juice and leaves, and many others. These are God's harmless preventives and anyone can take them in abundance. God never intended that man should take any poisons that are Satan's production. God cannot answer our prayers for recovery when we continue to use poisonous remedies that always do the system harm. God's remedies never leave a harmful effect on the system.

Nature is God's physician for suffering humanity, healing without money and without price. There is no law against anyone being his own doctor and going into the garden and eating the right fruit and then plucking some of the leaves and making a tea of them and drinking it.

Dried fruits are low in vitamin C but have a high iron content.

Grapes are best eaten in season fresh from the vine.

diet for a week or so is beneficial to the system. I have known people who thrived on eating the entire grape: skin, seeds, and all. But those who have weak digestion, and others with whom this would not agree, should not swallow the skin or seeds. In cancer cases grape juice is particularly recommended.

A grape drink may be made as follows: two-thirds cup grape juice, one-third cup water, and one heaping teaspoon of soybean flour. This is very nourishing.

Grapes and grape juice

I have experimented with grape juice a great deal, with gratifying results. Combining grape juice with a nut milk, about half-and-half, quickly furnishes the system with new blood of the purest kind. It is an excellent remedy for anemia.

Much of the grape juice found on the market is not good because it is adulterated. But good grape juices are available that are pure and unadulterated and are good medicine. The best way is to make your own, drinking it immediately after it has been squeezed. Then you know it is pure and you lose nothing of the flavor or food value. If it stands for any length of time after being squeezed, it loses something of the flavor and food value. The same rule applies to all fruit juices—drink them at once after squeezing. If left standing, they undergo a change. You may also can your own fruit juices.

The very best way is to eat the grapes fresh from the vine when they are in season. A grape

Freshly squeezed oranges have the highest vitamin and mineral content.

Oranges

The orange is one of Nature's finest gifts to man. Orange juice contains predigested food in a most delicious and attractive form, ready for immediate absorption and utilization. The amount of food value contained in a single large orange is about equal to that found in a slice of bread. But orange juice differs from bread in that it needs no digestion, while before bread can be used for energizing and strengthening the body, it must undergo digestion for several hours. A glass of orange juice has more vitamin A, thiamine, niacin, vitamin C, and more iron and potassium than a glass of milk. This is the reason oranges are so strengthening and refreshing to invalids and feeble persons, as well as to those in good health.

Orange juice is rich in salts, especially in lime and alkaline salts that counteract the tendency to acidosis. In such serious diseases as scurvy, beriberi, neuritis, anemia, or any condition in which the tissues are bathed in acid secretions, the alkaline mineral salts of fresh fruits will be of great benefit. The orange, lemon, and grapefruit are invaluable.

Orange juice has a general stimulating effect on the peristaltic activity of the colon. It should be taken about one hour before breakfast.

Orange juice is perfectly suited to those who are suffering from a fever. Four to six quarts of liquids should be taken daily to relieve and quench the fever's fire and to eliminate poisons through the skin and the kidneys, as fever is Nature's effort to rid the body of accumulated poisons. Acid fruits satisfy the thirst; and the agreeable flavor of

The sweeter an orange is, the greater its food value.

orange, lemon, and other fruit juices makes it possible for the patient to obtain the large amount of liquid needed.

Orange juice is indispensable for feeding bottle-fed babies. The use of orange juice will help prevent scurvy, pellagra, and rickets.

The acid and sugar in the orange aid digestion and stimulate and increase the activity of the glands in the stomach.

Orange juice is capable of serving more useful purposes in the body than any of the other fruit juices. The sweeter the orange the greater its food value. As people become better educated in nutrition, oranges will be much more freely used and appreciated.

Lemons

Medicinally, lemons act as an antiseptic—an agent that will prevent infection or putrefaction. They are also anti-scorbutic, which means a substance that will prevent scurvy. They also assist in cleansing the system of impurities. The lemon is a wonderful stimulant to the liver and is also a solvent for uric acid and other poisons. It liquefies the bile and is very good in cases of malaria. Sufferers from chronic rheumatism, rickets, tuberculosis, and gout will benefit by taking lemon juice, as will those who have a tendency to bleed or have uterine hemorrhages. During pregnancy it will help to build strong bones in the child. The lemon contains certain elements that help to build a healthy system and then to keep that system healthy. The lemon, owing to its potassium content, will nourish the brain and nerve cells. Its calcium strengthens the bony structures and makes healthy teeth.

The minerals found in lemons have an important part to play in the formation of plasma—the fluid portion of the blood. A single average-sized lemon contains phosphorus, 16 mg; sodium, 2 mg; calcium, 26 mg; potassium, 138 mg; vitamin C, 53 mg; and iron, 0.6 gm. Lemons are useful in treating asthma, biliousness (gas), colds, cough, sore throat, diphtheria, influenza, heartburn, liver complaints, scurvy, fevers, and rheumatism.

Traditional remedies

- For diphtheria, use pure lemon juice every hour, or more often if needed. Use either as a gargle or swab the throat with it. Swallow some until it cuts loose the false membrane in the throat.
- For sore throat, dilute lemon juice half-and-half with water and gargle frequently. It is better to use it full strength if possible.
- A slice of lemon tied over a corn overnight will greatly relieve the pain.
- A slice of lemon tied over a whitlow will not fail to bring the pus to the surface where it can be easily removed.
- To relieve asthma, take a tablespoon of lemon juice one hour before each meal.
- For liver complaints, the juice of a lemon should be taken in a glass of hot water one hour before breakfast every morning.
- To break up influenza, take a large glass of hot water with the juice of a lemon added, while at the same time keeping the feet in a deep bucket

Lemons cleanse the body of impurities and are used in traditional remedies.

or other vessel of hot water. Have the water deep enough so that it comes almost to the knees. Keep adding water as hot as the patient can stand it for about 20 to 30 minutes, or until the patient is perspiring freely. Be sure there is no draft on the patient while this is being done. The patient should be near the bed so he can get into bed without moving around, thereby avoiding any danger of getting chilled. If it is convenient, a full hot tub bath would be good in place of the foot bath. The lemon water should be taken every hour until the patient feels that all symptoms of the cold are gone.

- A teaspoon of lemon juice in one-half glass of water will relieve heartburn.
- Lemon juice is an agreeable and refreshing beverage in fevers if the bowels are not ulcerated.
- For rheumatism, one or two ounces of lemon juice freely diluted should be taken three times a day, one hour before meals and at bedtime. In cases of hemorrhage, lemon juice diluted and taken as cold as possible will help stop it.
- Scurvy is treated by giving one or two ounces of lemon juice diluted with water every two to four hours. In excessive menstruation, the juice of three or four lemons a day will help check the bleeding. It is best to take the juice of one lemon at a time in a glass of cold water.

The question may be asked: "How can one with an inflamed or ulcerated stomach partake of lemon juice? Would not a strong acid like that of the lemon act as an irritant?"

That would depend on how it was taken. If in quantity—yes, but if taken very weak at first,

diluted with water, it will eventually cease to burn. The sufferer afflicted with an ulcerated stomach has to use great perseverance to effect a cure, but it can be cured if care and patience are used.

The gastric juice in the stomach is four times as strong as lemon juice.

I wish that humanity would understand the real value of the lemon and learn to make a real medicine of it. It should be especially remembered that it is a wonderful remedy for colds, influenza, and all kinds of fever. Always take without sugar.

Household uses

There are many uses for lemons. For example, lemon juice will sour sweet milk, making it suitable for cooking. Add a few drops or a small teaspoonful to each cup of milk. The addition of 1 teaspoon of lemon juice to a quart of very hot soybean milk will make it curd to make soybean cheese.

- Lemon juice is excellent to use in the place of vinegar. Use it just as you would use vinegar.
- The addition of a little lemon juice and some of the grated lemon rind adds greatly to the flavor of dried fruits, figs, prunes, peaches, etcetera. Add while stewing the fruit.
- To bleach linen or muslin, moisten with lemon juice and spread in the sun.
- For the hands, after washing dishes and to remove vegetable stains, rub them well with lemon juice. It will keep the hands white and soft, and will also remove any strong odor, such as onions.

To remove ink stains, iron rust, or fruit stains, rub the stain well with lemon juice, cover with salt, and put in the sun. Repeat if necessary.

Vegetables
More sources of minerals and vitamins

Nutritional worth

Vegetables, along with fruits, are a wonderful source of vitamins and minerals, and at the same time they are low in calories. One-half cup of such vegetables as broccoli, tomatoes, green beans, and carrots, among many others, has only about 25 calories.

According to the *U.S. News and World Report*, December 8, 1980, the amount of fresh vegetables consumed per person in the U.S. decreased 1.2 percent between 1960 and 1979 to 144.3 pounds, while the percentage of processed vegetables increased 29 percent to 65.0 pounds. The same magazine in its February 4, 1985 issue gives the total vegetables consumed per person as 207 pounds, up from 187 pounds in 1963. Such items as fruit, grains, meat, fish, and poultry also showed an increase in consumption while coffee, milk, and eggs decreased.

A survey reported in the Summer 1985 Newsletter of the American Institute for Cancer Research showed that the percentage of fruits and vegetables consumed by Americans over the past 3 years increased by 25 percent. Strangely enough, however, 21 percent of American households reported eating no potatoes, 22 percent no fresh fruits, 23 percent no canned fruits or vegetables, and 72 percent no dried fruits or vegetables.

Color and nutrients

As a general rule, the darker the color of the vegetable, the richer it is in nutrients. Leafy vegetables are exceptionally good sources of calcium, iron, vitamin A, vitamin C, and riboflavin. The leaves are the most active part of the plant and the greener the leaves the higher the vitamin and mineral content will be. The outer, darker-colored leaves of cabbage and lettuce contain much more nutrient value than the inner, lighter-colored leaves. Broccoli and cauliflower are also very good sources of minerals and vitamins. Broccoli, along with the other cruciferous vegetables, cauliflower, cabbage, and Brussels sprouts, may also play a part in the prevention of cancer. Broccoli is a member of the cabbage family and was brought to the United

Home-grown vegetables have the highest nutritional value.

States from Italy. It once was called "Italian Asparagus." One cup of cooked broccoli gives up to 300 percent of the daily needs of vitamin C for an adult, 4.5 grams of protein, only 50 calories, and hardly any fat. One stalk of broccoli, if properly cooked, contains 30 percent more vitamin C than an eight-ounce glass of orange juice. In addition broccoli contains significant amounts of pantothenic acid, folic acid, thiamine, niacin, riboflavin, potassium, phosphorus, iron, and calcium.

While the calcium in some dark green vegetables, such as spinach and beet greens, is rendered largely unavailable to the body because of a high level of oxalates, the oxalic acid level in broccoli is low, making it a much better source of calcium. Of course, you don't have to worry about the high oxalates in some vegetables interfering with the absorption of calcium from other sources, such as other high calcium foods, when they are eaten at the same meal.

Vegetables begin to lose their nutrients as soon as they are exposed to air.

The dark-orange vegetables, such as carrots, yams, and winter squash, are a rich source of vitamin A and the deeper the color the more vitamin A is present. Light yellow vegetables like corn and wax beans are not as high in vitamin A.

Home-grown vegetables

Growing your own vegetables is the surest way to get the most nutritional value, provided they are prepared properly. The sooner vegetables are eaten after being picked the more nutrients will be present. If you let vegetables or fruit sit around the house at room temperature for a few days after bringing them home from the market, there will be a large loss of vitamins A and C due to the action of destructive enzymes. In fact, 50 percent of the vitamin C can be lost from some vegetables after only one day. What you do purchase should be kept cool and away from light and air. The best place for them is in the refrigerator in a plastic bag.

Brightly colored vegetables such as carrots are high in vitamin A.

Starchy vegetables such as parsnips are a good source of carbohydrate.

Eating a wide variety of vegetables daily is best, including at least one serving each of a yellow and a green leafy vegetable.

Starchy and starchless vegetables

Starchy vegetables include potatoes, lima beans, peas, corn, parsnips, winter squash, pumpkin, and yams. Even these starchy vegetables have only about 100 calories in half a cup.

Starchless vegetables are carrots, young beets, celery, cucumbers, tomatoes, soybeans, squash, turnips, onions, okra, Brussels sprouts, and artichokes. Starchless and sugarless vegetables are lettuce, spinach, all greens, tomatoes, celery, radishes, string beans, cabbage, cauliflower, eggplant, endive, and asparagus.

Another advantage of eating an abundance of vegetables and fruits is the presence of fiber, which helps to keep the digestive tract functioning properly and is an excellent aid to prevent constipation. See "Fiber," following.

Causes of vitamin loss

Many people are concerned about the effect that processing has on the nutritive value of vegetables, and rightly so. Freshly picked vegetables, of course, are most nutritious, with frozen next and canned last. There may not be much difference between these methods of preparation. Vitamin A losses are minimal during processing and one study showed 44 percent of vitamin C remaining in freshly cooked peas, 39 percent in frozen, and 36 percent in canned. The best way to be sure of getting a good supply of nutrients from vegetables, if you can't always get fresh ones, is to eat as wide a variety of fresh, canned, and frozen vegetables as you can.

During the cooking process, minerals as well as the water-soluble vitamins B complex and C are lost to varying degrees in the cooking water. This water should be saved and used in soups, stews, and the like. Heat, light, and exposure to air are other causes for the loss of vitamins while preparing vegetables. These

Starchless vegetables such as cucumber have very few calories.

losses affect vitamins A, C, E, K, and many members of the B complex family of vitamins. In order to preserve as much of the nutrient value as possible, the suggestions for cooking given in the chapter on Food Preparation should be followed as closely as possible.

Potatoes

We hear so much about mashed potatoes not being good to eat. It is true that the ordinary mashed potatoes that are eaten everywhere are a very unwholesome product. When potatoes are peeled, boiled, and then mashed with a large piece of butter or other fat, they become unwholesome food. When potatoes are peeled there is practically nothing left but starch. The alkaline part of the potato is cut away when they are peeled, and the starch is acid-forming.

The Irish potato is a very valuable food, but not after it has been peeled and boiled in a quantity of water that is drained down the sink, leaving the potato lifeless, without minerals, and acid-producing. The eyes and the peeling of the Irish potato contain its life-giving properties. When the skin of the potato is not eaten, the best part of it is lost. Also, when the skin is baked too brown, the life-giving properties are destroyed.

How to cook potatoes

Baking is the ideal way to cook a potato, but it must be properly baked. The skin should be a little crisp, but not too dark brown or black. Before putting potatoes in the oven to bake, scrub them thoroughly and prick the skin all over with a fork. This causes some of the moisture to evaporate, and helps to make the potatoes dry and mealy.

Another excellent way to prepare potatoes is to steam or pressure-cook them. All vegetables may be excellently prepared in the steam pressure cooker under a low temperature, as the original food flavors are then preserved in an economical way. They can also be improved by placing them in a warm oven and allowing them to dry out for a few minutes after pressure cooking. Many who have found it impossible to eat potatoes prepared in any other way are able to eat them when they are prepared in this way.

A properly cooked baked potato retains all its nutrients.

Fiber

A natural aid to regular digestion

A great deal has been written during the past several years about fiber in the diet, both in scientific journals and in lay publications. Plus, people who are interested in their health, which includes most of us, want to know more about fiber; what it is, what it's good for, where to get it, etcetera. Even several well-known cereal manufacturers are promoting the large amount of fiber that is contained in some of their products. Drugstore counters display many bulk and fiber-type laxatives, and there are even high-fiber cookies and wafers to "help keep you regular."

Fiber is found in the outer covering of the grain (the bran).

Sometime you may hear the term "bulk" or "roughage" used, but these really mean essentially the same thing, so we will refer to them all as fiber. Fiber is the tough, structural part of plants, such as the stems, leaves, coverings of the seeds and fruits, etcetera, that undergoes little if any digestion as it passes through the intestinal tract. This is because humans, unlike some animals, do not possess the enzymes necessary to break down fiber to any degree.

Benefits of fiber

The beneficial effect of fiber is nothing new. About 2400 years ago, Hippocrates said, "wholesome bread clears up the gut and passes through as excrement." Dr. John Harvey Kellogg, a vegetarian who founded the famous Battle Creek Sanitarium in Michigan in the late 1800s, was one of the early American advocates of a high-fiber diet. His brother, W. K. Kellogg, established the world-famous cereal company based on Dr. Kellogg's corn flakes, which he had developed for the patients at the sanitarium.

The average American diet contains only about half the fiber that it should. The reason is quite simple. Most Americans eat large amounts of refined food, especially refined cereals and bread from which the bran has been removed during the milling process. The bran, which is the outer covering of the grain, is where the fiber is located. We also eat a lot of overcooked vegetables and drink a lot of fruit juices instead of eating the fruit raw.

The benefits of a diet containing adequate fiber are no longer in doubt. At the top of the list would probably be the help received by those who are

Popular breakfast cereals have had the bran removed when the grains are milled.

troubled by chronic constipation. According to some recent statistics, this would include a large percentage of those living in Western countries. Walk down the aisle of nearly any drugstore and see for yourself how many preparations are available for the treatment of constipation—pills, oils, powders, liquids, granules, suppositories, and enema kits, to name but a few. Most people have found it necessary to take a laxative at some time during their lives and this does no harm. It is, however, entirely possible to become "addicted" to some types of laxatives and after using them daily over a period of years, it becomes impossible for the bowels to move normally by themselves.

When eating the average Western-type highly-refined diet, it takes the food about three days to pass completely through the intestinal tract. This results in a small, hard stool that requires much straining and therefore develops a very high pressure in the colon in order for the bowels to move. This increased pressure is responsible for other problems in the colon and elsewhere, which we shall mention shortly.

Diverticulosis

Diverticulosis is a very common disorder of the large intestine that is found in Western countries. In fact, it is present in nearly half the population over the age of 50 years. Diverticula are pockets that are found on the outside of the colon when the high pressure in the colon forces apart the lining of the colon through a weak place in the wall. Everyone has these areas of weakness. They are located where the small blood vessels that nourish the intestine pass through the wall. These pockets, which look like bubbles on the outside of the colon, may connect with the colon by a rather narrow opening. The pockets may be large or small, few or many, and are one of the most common causes of bleeding from the intestines. They are most numerous in the portion of the colon that is located in the left lower abdomen, but they do not occur in the rectum. Diverticulosis is rarely seen in some parts of the world, such as Africa, where a high-fiber diet and large stool volume are typical.

Raw fruit is high in fiber, needed to maintain regular digestion.

How does fiber help?

In the first place it increases the bulk of the stool and this makes it pass through the digestive tract in about half the time. The increased bulk results in decreased pressure buildup in the colon. Fiber also attracts and holds water like a sponge, making the stool much softer and easier to pass, and this also contributes to a lowering of the pressure. If you are one of the millions who suffer from constipation, following are some helpful suggestions.

- Increase the amount of fiber in your diet.
- Drink one or two glasses of water in the morning about 30 to 60 minutes before breakfast. Use the water as it comes out of the tap or try heating it slightly. Take your time. Don't gulp the water down in a hurry. Your stomach, like your body, requires a daily morning bath.
- Eat lots of fresh fruits and vegetables.
- Drink six to eight glasses of water a day between meals.
- Exercise daily for at least 30 minutes. Walking is good.
- Use whole grain bread and cereals.
- Do not resist the natural urge for your bowels to move.

Other problems related to lack of fiber

Besides constipation, there are many other physical problems that appear to be related to a low-fiber diet. Dr. Dennis Burkitt of London, England, is the person who has done more than anyone else in recent years to investigate and promote the use of fiber in the diet. He had this to say: "There is now a fairly well-defined list of diseases that are recognized as characteristic of

Drinking plenty of water will help to keep your digestion running smoothly.

modern Western culture. All of them have their minimum presences in economically more developed countries and are rare in rural communities in the Third World....These diseases include ischemic heart disease, gallstones, diabetes (Type II), obesity, varicose veins, deep vein thrombosis, hiatus hernia, colorectal cancer, appendicitis, diverticular disease, and hemorrhoids....There is evidence to suggest that all the diseases in this list are diet-related. The reduction in intake of dietary fiber, and in cereal fiber in particular, is the diet change that has been predominately, incriminated in the increased prevalence of certain gastrointestinal diseases, in Western countries mainly, during the past half-century." (From "Fiber as Protective Against Gastrointestinal Diseases," Dennis Burkitt, C.M.G., F.R.S., M.D., F.R.C.S., *The American Journal of Gastroenterology*, April 1984, pp. 249-252.)

Most people who have diverticula never develop any serious problem, although some may have a lower abdominal pain, cramps, or constipation. Some may have a "spastic" or "irritable" colon. In about 20 percent of persons with diverticulosis, an infection with an abscess or even a perforated diverticulum may occur. If this should happen, the term diverticulitis is used, and it may develop into a life-threatening situation where surgery is needed. There are usually fever and severe pain in the left lower abdominal region. About 200,000 persons are hospitalized each year in the United States with diverticulitis. It has been shown that not only will a high-fiber diet prevent the formation of diverticula, but it will also improve the symptoms of diverticulosis.

Sunflower seeds have a high fiber content.

Appendicitis

Appendicitis has also been linked with the amount of fiber we eat. Dr. Burkitt, who spent 20 years as a physician in Uganda, Africa, states that he rarely saw a case of appendicitis during this entire time. When African children were sent away to school in Europe, however, and started eating a Western-type diet low in fiber, the incidence of appendicitis began to increase dramatically. Those children that remained at home and ate their customary diet had no trouble with appendicitis.

Colon cancer

Colon cancer now causes about 60,000 deaths each year in the United States. It is one of the most common cancers. More evidence is accumulating daily that it is not only related to the amount of fat but also to the amount of fiber in the diet. A diet high in fiber helps to protect against colon cancer because the fiber speeds up the passage of the stool through the colon, which decreases the amount of time for the potentially cancer-causing toxins to come in contact with the lining membrane of the colon.

Hemorrhoids

A very common and irritating affliction of Western society is hemorrhoids. These dilated veins frequently become painful and irritated, and often bleed. They are very frequently seen in those with chronic constipation and are thought to be caused by excessive straining while attempting to move the bowels. Hemorrhoids are rarely seen in those who regularly eat a high bulk diet. As an interesting sidelight, Dr. Burkitt mentions that "the Emperor

Eat brown bread to increase the amount of fiber in your diet.

Napoleon was suffering from hemorrhoids during the battle of Waterloo, and it is interesting to cogitate on whether the outcome of the battle might have been different had he been given bran sometime before the conflict, in which case his attention might have been more on the battle and less on his bottom!"

How to increase your fiber intake

The amount of fiber in the average American diet is about 15 to 20 grams a day. This should be increased to 30 to 40 grams. This can be accomplished quite readily by observing a few simple rules, as follows.

- Read the nutrition labels on bread and eat only bread that is made from 100 percent whole grain.
- Eat breakfast cereals that are high in fiber content, such as All Bran, Fiber 1, Shredded Wheat, oatmeal, Wheatena, or add a few spoonfuls of unprocessed oat bran to your favorite cereal.
- Use brown instead of white rice.
- Eat fruits fresh instead of cooked canned, or juiced whenever possible. Also eat the skin whenever possible.
- Cook vegetables as little as possible.
- Eat legumes such as beans, lentils, and garbanzos (chick peas) often.
- Sunflower seeds and most nuts are high in fiber content. Use nuts moderately, however, as they are high in fat.

There are some precautions to observe when starting to increase the fiber in your diet.

- Drink plenty of liquid; 6 to 8 glasses a day is best.
- Increase the amount of fiber in the diet gradually over a period of several weeks.
- Some gas or bloating may occur as the amount of fiber is increased, but this will slowly improve over a period of several months.

Bran muffins are a good source of dietary fiber.

Legumes such as lentils should be consumed often.

Rich sources of food fiber

4 grams or more per serving. Foods marked with an * have 6 or more grams of fiber per serving.

Breads and Cereals	Serving	Legumes (Cooked portions)	
All Bran*	⅓ cup-1 oz.	Kidney beans	½ cup
Bran Buds*	⅓ cup-1 oz.	Lima beans	½ cup
Bran Chex	⅔ cup-1 oz.	Navy beans	½ cup
Corn Bran	⅔ cup-1 oz.	Pinto Beans	½ cup
Cracklin' Bran	⅓ cup-1 oz.	White beans	½ cup
100% Bran*	½ cup-1 oz.	Fruits	
Raisin Bran	¾ cup-1 oz.	Blackberries	½ cup
Bran, unsweetened*	¼ cup	Dried prunes	3
Wheat germ, toasted, plain	¼ cup-1 oz.		

Table 1

Fiber content of foods

The following list of rich and moderately rich sources of fiber was originally published by the National Cancer Institute. NCI advises that to increase the amount of fiber, choose several servings of foods from this list. The dietary fiber content of many foods is still unknown, so this is not a comprehensive list. Also, with regard to cereals, the brand name products listed are representative of the fiber content of similar types of cereal products. Other cereal would be expected to have similar amounts of dietary fiber.

Moderately rich sources of food fiber
1 to 3 grams of fiber per serving.

Breads and Cereals	Serving	Vegetables	Serving	Fruits	Serving
Bran muffins	1 medium	Artichoke	1 small	Apple	1 medium
Popcorn (air-popped)	1 cup	Asparagus	½ cup	Apricot, fresh	3 medium
Whole wheat bread	1 slice	Beans, green	½ cup	Apricot, dried	5 halves
Whole wheat spaghetti	1 cup	Brussels sprouts	½ cup	Banana	1 medium
40% Bran Flakes	⅔ cup-1 oz.	Cabbage, red and white	½ cup	Blueberries	½ cup
Grapenuts	¼ cup-1 oz.	Carrots	½ cup	Cantaloupe	¼ melon
Granola-type cereals	¼ cup-1 oz.	Cauliflower	½ cup	Cherries	10
Cheerio-type cereals	1-¼ cup-1 oz.	Corn	½ cup	Dates, dried	3
Most	⅓ cup-1 oz.	Green peas	½ cup	Figs, dried	1 medium
Oatmeal, cooked	¾ cup	Kale	½ cup	Grapefruit	½
Shredded wheat	⅔ cup-1 oz.	Parsnip	½ cup	Orange	1 medium
Total	1 cup-1 oz.	Potato	1 medium	Peach	1 medium
Wheaties	1 cup-1 oz.	Spinach, cooked	½ cup	Pear	1 medium
Wheat Chex	⅔ cup-1 oz.	Spinach, raw	½ cup	Pineapple	½ cup
		Summer squash	½ cup	Raisins	¼ cup
Legumes (cooked) and Nuts		Sweet potato	½ medium	Strawberries	1 cup
Chick peas (Garbanzo beans)	½ cup	Turnip	½ cup		
Lentils	½ cup	Bean sprouts (soy)	½ cup		
Peanuts	10 nuts	Celery	½ cup		
Almonds	10 nuts	Tomato	1 medium		

From *FDA Consumer*, June 1985, page 32

Table 2

Oatmeal

The ideal basic food

Common oatmeal, which can be purchased in every grocery store in the land, is a most wonderful food. However, it is not properly prepared by many and is terribly abused by the majority of people. It is one of the finest foods for growing children that we have, but the way the oats are eaten many times spoils the real quality of the oats, when milk and sugar are put on the oatmeal, they cause it to ferment in the stomach and thus its benefit is lost. There also is a great misunderstanding among some people about steel-cut and finely flaked quick-cooking oats. There is not a hair's breadth of difference between the steel-cut oats and the finely flaked oats as far as food value or life-giving properties are concerned.

"The chemical analysis of rolled oats and steel-cut oats is identical, because quick-cooking rolled oats is nothing more than steel-cut oats run

Flaked oats are quick to cook and easy to digest.

through heavy rollers revolving at a great rate of speed. We guarantee a minimum of 15 percent protein and of 7.5 percent fat, and a maximum of 1.9 percent fiber, 66 percent nitrogen free extract, and 77 percent carbohydrate.

Rolled oats is one of the few—if not the only—cereal food that carries the germ of the grain, and that is important."

The above is taken from a letter by G.M. Hidding, General Manager of the Purity Oats Co., of Keokuk, Iowa, May 27, 1936.

Benefits of eating oatmeal

Flaked oats are much more easily handled by most people because they digest quicker and take less time to cook. The steel-cut oats ought to cook at least four hours in a double boiler, while the finely flaked oats take only three minutes—a great saving in fuel and a great saving to our old weak stomachs. A fine way to prepare oats is just the

The food value in one cup of cooked rolled oats

Calories			148
Protein			5.4 grams
Fat			2.8 grams
Carbohydrate			26.0 grams
Fiber (crude)			0.5 grams
MINERALS		*VITAMINS*	
Sodium	1 mg	Thiamine (B$_1$)	0.17 mg
Potassium	130 mg	Riboflavin (B$_2$)	0.07 mg
Calcium	21 mg	Niacin	0.5 mg
Magnesium	0 mg	Ascorbic Acid	0 mg
Phosphorus	158 mg	Iron	1.7 mg

Table 1

way it is given on the package. I eat it just that way with some zwieback and some nice soybean butter on the zwieback. I enjoy it very much, more so than many years ago when I used milk and sugar on it. Something dry, like zwieback or some whole wheat crackers should be eaten with the oatmeal, so that plenty of saliva is produced to mix with it.

Cook the oatmeal this way to increase the fiber in your diet: combine equal parts of steel-cut oats and sterilized bran with water according to the directions on the package. Cook six to ten minutes, then set aside five minutes before serving. A considerable part of this will be imperfectly cooked; therefore, it is not readily acted upon by the saliva and intestinal juices, but passes on into the colon where it will aid in the destroying of putrefactive poisons caused from the decomposition of proteins and other foods.

Oatmeal can be used in many ways. When oatmeal is not spoiled in the preparation or used in wrong combinations, it is one of the finest foods we have to prevent disease. I read in a daily paper many years ago that the Great Northern Railroad had a very urgent piece of road to make. They hired a big crew of men and worked them fourteen hours a day. Instead of giving them ordinary water to drink, they gave them oatmeal water and the paper stated that not one man was laid off on account of sickness. It stated that never before had there been such a wonderful experience in the history of railroads.

Oatmeal water should be more frequently used than it is. It is a very good medicine for the sick. To make oatmeal water, use the finely flaked oats and put two heaping teaspoonfuls in a pan with a quart of water. You can make it stronger or weaker to suit your taste. Put it on the stove and let it simmer for half an hour. Then beat it with a spoon or eggbeater and strain it through a fine sieve. This makes an excellent drink for anybody, especially the sick. If desired, you can add just a pinch of salt and a little soybean milk.

Another recipe for making oatmeal water is: take a heaping tablespoonful of oatmeal to a quart of water and let it simmer for two or two and a half hours in a tightly covered pan, and, then strain it. This makes a very refreshing, cooling drink after it is cooled off in the icebox.

All oat foods are whole grain products even if milled fine.

I quote the following from *Diet, The Way to Health*, by R. Swinburne Clymer, M.D.: Oats, steel-cut or Scotch: silicon 24.0; phosphorus 18.2; potassium 13.6; magnesium 5.2. Oats is one of the richest silicon carriers known and if properly combined with fruit or vegetable eliminants, is the ideal basic food for children during the winter months to prevent infection from all zymotic diseases.

Oatmeal, if combined with other foods so as to prevent congestion and the formation of toxins and acids due to the acid reaction, would do more to prevent contagious diseases than all the serums thus far invented. Oatmeal is neither artificial nor a substitute. It is a natural agent that supplies those elements that, by their antiseptic properties, help to combat contagious infections.

Oats are rich in phosphorus, essential for healthy growth.

Besides this antiseptic quality, oats are rich in phosphorus, which is required for the formation of strong bones and teeth and also for brain and nerves—tissues required by the mind in study.

Wherever a large amount of silicon is required, prescribe oatmeal, or if this is not practical due to digestive disturbances, then use the extract, "Avena Sativa."

The following are extracts from a letter dated April 21, 1936, from F. L. Gunderson, biochemist in the Nutrition Laboratory of the Quaker Oats Co., Chicago, Illinois.

We are very glad to enclose a description of the manufacturing process for both standard and quick-cooking tolled oats flakes. Many people have the erroneous idea that the hulls of the oat grain are comparable to the bran of wheat. That is not correct. The hulls (or flowering glumes) of the wheat grain envelop the whole kernel rather loosely and consequently go into the straw stack at threshing time. In contrast, the glumes of the oat grain are wrapped a bit more securely around the kernel, and remain on the oat kernel as an individual wrap until they are removed in the rolled oats mill. After removing the hull from the oats, the kernel from which rolled oats are made possesses all of the bran, middlings, endosperm, and germ portion natural to the grain. Whole oat kernels (oat groats), steel-cut oats, large or "standard" type rolled oats flakes, and small or "quick" type rolled oats flakes are all whole grain products. In the sense that "refined" is sometimes used as an antonym for "whole grain," there are no refined oat foods. The very botanical and

To get the best quality, oats should be harvested as soon as they are ripe.

physical structure of the oat grain together with the universal oat milling processes are such that all oat foods are whole grain products. The composition of steel-cut oats, large flaked oats, and small flaked rolled oats is identical if made from the same type of grain.

With regard to the vitamins in oats, our own tests, as well as those of other well-known research people, indicate that there is no destruction in the manufacturing process.

Manufacturing Processes for Oats

Description Flaked oats made from the best quality of large oats with the hulls removed.

Method of manufacture The oats go through an extensive cleaning process in which corn, wheat, barley chaff, and wheat seeds are removed. The oats are then carefully sized to uniform diameter by grading in special machines, the light oats, double oats, and pin oats being removed for feed. The oats are again graded to uniform length, about five grades being obtained. The clean, graded oats are roasted and partially dried, after which they are cooled and passed to a large burr stone where the hulls are torn from the groats. The oats mixture is next bolted to remove any flour and the hulls are then removed in special machines and the cleaning process is continued until the groats are free of hulls and unhulled oats.

For production of "quick" rolled oats, the groats are at this stage steel cut. The clean groats pass to the steaming chamber, where they are partially cooked with live steam and from which they pass to the rollers, where the groats are formed into flakes. The rolled oat flakes are cooled in a current of air to about 110°F, following which the product is immediately weighed and packed by automatic mechanical equipment.

Nuts

High-calorie, high-protein foods

Nuts take the place of meat in nearly every respect. With the exception of the peanut (which is really a legume) and chestnuts, the average nutritive value of nuts is about 160 to 200 calories per ounce. This is double the value of an equal quantity of sugar or starch. The large amount of fat in nuts and seeds makes them very high in calories. They have a relatively large amount of protein and are good sources of iron and the B vitamins. All nuts except walnuts, peanuts, and filberts produce an alkaline reaction in the body.

Nuts should be purchased in the shell when possible. In this form they are probably fresher, since the shell protects the nut, and they are very likely to be cheaper, depending on the quantity purchased. Of course, shelling the nuts takes time. Brazil nuts are particularly difficult, but the task may be made easier by soaking these nuts in water anywhere from 30 minutes to 2 hours before shelling them. If you do elect to purchase nuts already shelled, buy them whole and break them up yourself. Don't forget that salted nuts turn rancid much faster than unsalted ones and that shelled nuts should be kept in the freezer in a plastic bag away from light, heat, and moisture.

Types of nut

Almond One-fifth of the weight of the almond consists of protein and it is of the very finest quality. The almond yields a most delicious oil, which is highly digestible. Almond butter can be made into a milk or cream which, with the addition of a little sweetening, resembles cow's milk in appearance and in nutritive properties.

The freshest nuts are those that are still in the shell—these will keep for up to a year if refrigerated.

Hickory nut A pound of hickory nut meat is equal in nutritive value to more than four pounds of average meat. Two-thirds of the weight of the hickory nut is easily digested oil.

Pecan The pecan is a valuable nut, high in nutrition.

Walnut One pound of black walnuts contains more than 100 percent more protein than the same quantity of Salisbury steak. The English walnut differs slightly from the black walnut in that it contains more fat and less protein.

Butternut The butternut also contains more fat than the black walnut, but has the same amount of protein. The butternut is low in carbohydrates; therefore, it is very valuable for persons suffering from diabetes.

Peanut When thoroughly dried, the peanut contains 50 percent or more protein than the best beef steak. Further, half of its weight is an excellent oil. Emphasis must be placed on the fact that salted roasted peanuts are over-roasted and indigestible. Unroasted peanut butter is easily digested and highly nutritious. The protein of the peanut is nearly equal to the protein of milk and eggs as a tissue-building element. A very fine milk can be made from peanut butter. Peanuts are also used extensively in malted nuts and vegetable meats.

Coconut A most excellent substitute for butter can be prepared as follows: cut the meat of the coconut

For a creamy butter substitute, soak grated coconut in warm water.

in strips, grate or grind it with a meat grinder. Soak it in several times as much warm water as you have coconut and let it sit for 2 or 3 hours. A rich cream will rise to the top. Skim off the cream and work it into a butter with an ordinary butter ladle. Coconut oil is high in saturated fatty acids, so it should be avoided.

It is better to eat nuts in an emulsified form such as nut butters. Otherwise they must be thoroughly masticated, so that no little hard pieces enter the stomach.

Small particles of such concentrated foods cannot be acted upon by the digestive juices and often pass undigested through the alimentary canal.

Nut butters prepared without roasting are superior in nutritive and hygienic value to the best cuts of meat and to dairy butter and cheese.

The protein of nuts is of greater value for the renewal of the body cells than the protein derived from the muscular tissues of a dead animal with all its waste products.

The pecan, filbert, English walnut, almond, hickory, and chestnut are abundant in growth-promoting vitamins. Chestnuts should never be eaten raw because of their tannic acid content.

The nut should not be used as a dainty but as a staple article of diet. The popular idea that nuts are hard to digest has no foundation as long as they are thoroughly masticated when eaten. The habit of eating nuts at the end of a meal, when in all probability more food of a highly nutritious nature has been eaten than is necessary, is very injurious. It is an equally injurious habit to eat nuts between meals. Improper mastication is a common cause of indigestion from the use of nuts.

Peanuts should be heated slightly to remove the skin. Other nuts may be blanched and crushed without roasting. Over-roasting makes the nut very difficult to digest.

Nuts should be eaten as a part of every heavy meal, and made a part of the bill of fare. But because nuts are so highly concentrated, only a few ounces should be eaten at a time.

Nutritive value of nuts
(usual serving—100 grams or 3½ ounces)
VITAMINS (MG) MINERALS (MG)

	ALMONDS	BRAZIL NUTS	BUTTERNUTS	CASHEWS	CHESTNUTS	COCONUT	FILBERTS (HAZEL NUTS)	HICKORY NUTS	MACADAMIA NUTS	PEANUTS	PECANS	PISTACHIOS	SUNFLOWER SEEDS	WALNUTS, ENGLISH
CALORIES	54.1	65.9	61.2	48.2	4.1	34.7	62.4	62.4	71.6	44.2	73.0	53.7	47.3	64.4
FAT GRAMS	19.6	11.0	8.4	27.0	–	14.0	16.7	12.8	15.9	23.6	13.0	19.0	19.9	15.0
PROTEIN GRAMS	18.6	14.4	23.7	18.5	2.9	3.4	12.6	12.6	7.8	26.9	9.4	19.3	24.0	15.0
CARBOHYDRATE GRAMS	597	646	629	578	377	359	634	673	691	559	696	594	560	654
POTASSIUM	–	660	–	–	–	–	–	–	–	337	300	–	–	225
IRON	4.4	3.4	6.8	5.0	3.8	2.0	3.4	2.4	2.0	1.9	2.4	–	7.1	2.1
PHOSPHOROUS	475	693	–	428	373	98	337	360	161	393	324	–	6	380
CALCIUM	254	186	–	46	27	21	209	TR.	48	74	74	–	120	83
NIACIN	4.6	–	–	2.1	.6	.2	.9	–	1.3	16.2	.9	.7	5.4	1.2
B_2	.67	–	–	.19	.22	.10	–	–	.11	.13	.11	.11	.23	.13
B_1	.25	.08	–	.63	.22	.10	.46	–	.34	.30	.72	.22	1.96	.48

Table 1

Nuts contain more iron than other foods; they also contain a high content of calcium, particularly almonds, Brazil nuts, and filberts. Nuts are high in fat, but contain no cholesterol. Most nuts have an alkaline reaction on the system except for peanuts, walnuts, and filberts, which are acid-forming.

Addendum The statement that "A pound of walnuts contains almost 50 percent more protein than the same quantity of beef" is not accurate. At the time this statement was made (in the 1930s), there were no specific nutritive values assigned to edible foods by the United States Department of Agriculture. But now such values are available and they show that one pound of black walnuts (chopped or broken kernels) contains about 86 grams of protein. The same weight (one pound) of oven-cooked relatively fat roast beef contains 85 grams of protein; one pound of oven-cooked relatively lean roast beef contains 112 grams of protein; one pound of broiled relatively lean and fat sirloin steak contains 100 grams of protein; and one pound of broiled relatively lean sirloin steak contains 144 grams of protein.

Nuts are very high in potassium and magnesium content.

The percentage of protein content of some nuts, dairy products, and meat, is as follows: peanuts, 26.9; walnuts, 15.0; turkey, 24.0; cured ham, 16.9; fresh ham, 15.2; beef (meaty and fat), 18.6; beef (regular hamburger), 16.0; cheddar cheese, 23.2; dried nonfat milk, 35.6.

Dairy products and meat are very high in cholesterol, which is now implicated as one of the

Nuts are high in potassium and magnesium and have no cholesterol.

major causes of heart attacks (coronary occlusion). Nuts have no cholesterol content.

It should be remembered that the statement, "Nuts perfectly take the place of meat" was written by my father in the 1930s. It is now a well-known fact that a total vegetarian diet (vegan) is lacking in vitamin B_{12}. This vitamin was not discovered until 1948, at least a decade after this book was first published. Therefore, persons on a total vegetarian diet must seek a vitamin B_{12} supplement.

The statement that "nuts contain more iron than any other foodstuff" is true for certain nuts, but not all of them. Parsley is extremely high in iron; however, an equal weight of black walnuts contains more iron than parsley. Most of the other nuts, however, including English walnuts, contain somewhat less iron than parsley does for an equal weight. These figures are from the USDA *Home and Garden Bulletin* #72, 1981.

Bread and Refined Flour
Food for fuel, fiber, vitamins, and minerals

Importance of bread

Bread is a most important health food. "There is more religion in a loaf of good bread than many think." (*Ministry of Healing*, p. 302.) Properly baked bread made from the right material, whole grain flours, has been the staff of life from the earliest Bible times, and has always been one of the principal foods that God gave to man; but it has indeed been made the staff of death by the modern invention of milling.

Bread made with milled white flour cannot impart to the system the nourishment that is found in whole grain bread. The use of refined flour aggravates the difficulties under which those who have inactive livers labor.

Most of the wheat breads purchased in the grocery stores are unhealthful, for they contain various percentages of white flour and are seldom thoroughly baked. Make sure that you purchase

Rye bread is wheat free and suitable for those with gluten intolerance.

100 percent whole wheat bread. Bread is more healthful if eaten when it is at least one day old. It should be baked clear through the center of the loaf so that no part of it is soft or gummy.

God never intended that wheat and other grains should be separated into their different parts, presented to the people as a wonderful invention, and then sold for a big price. Untold harm is done by the bakery goods that are found on the market today. They are baked just enough to stand up, but not enough to kill the yeast germ; nor are they baked enough so that the starch is changed to an easily digested form. The baking process was instituted by God Himself to prepare the grains and starchy foods so they could be eaten by humans and provide proper nourishment.

From the earliest times a great deal of unleavened bread was used; more, in fact, than leavened bread. The bread that Abraham's wife baked for the strangers who were angels was unleavened bread, for it took her just a short time to make this bread. In the sacrificial offering no leavened bread was ever used. Leaven was looked upon as a symbol of sin (Luke 12:1). If leaven or yeast of any kind is used in bread, it needs to be thoroughly baked so that the yeast germ is entirely destroyed.

Lately yeast has been widely advertised to be eaten raw as a stomach remedy, but yeast should never be eaten unless it is first cooked. Yeast is a highly nourishing and wholesome product when it is cooked until the yeast germ is destroyed. The analysis of yeast is just the same as the analysis of Vegex, which is sold for such a high price.

Whole grain breads retain essential vitamins and minerals, as well as fiber.

In recent times a myth has been spread that no one over the age of 35 or 40 years should eat bread. This is correct when applied to most of the bread that is sold on the market, as it should not be eaten by anyone at any time. But one can live very well on a diet of only whole wheat bread, whole rye bread, or whole barley bread, with vegetables and fruit added.

Oats also make an excellent bread. Delicious bread can be made by taking part whole wheat flour, whole corn flour, whole oat flour, and whole soybean flour. Add a little malt honey or Karo syrup. This will make a bread that anyone can live and work on by eating just a little fruit with it.

Before any of the grains are ripe, when they are still in the milky state, they can be eaten raw. They are then in the grape sugar state and are like the sugar that is found in thoroughly ripe fruit. After the grain ripens, it turns to starch, and before starch can be used by the body, the outer cellulose wall must be broken by grinding or cooking.

The baking process is very similar to the ripening of the fruit on the tree. Before it is ripe, fruit is in the starchy stage and unfit to eat, but after it ripens in the sun the starch turns to grape sugar. It is then ready for assimilation, and requires very little digestion. When bread is put in the oven, it goes through the same process. To a large extent, the prolonged baking gradually changes the starch into a form that the digestive juices in the body can properly act upon to renew the body.

Refined or milled flour

Unlike the refining of gold, which removes impurities and makes the product much more valuable, the refining of cereal grain (wheat, rice, corn) removes most of the valuable nutrients and makes the grain much less valuable from a nutritional standpoint. Perhaps instead of calling it refined flour, which to many people suggests improvement in the product, it should be called milled or devitalized flour. This type of flour has a definite advantage to all those who are engaged in the distribution, storage, and baking processes, since not only does refined flour not spoil and turn rancid, but it is also much less likely to be infested with insects. The real loser, then, is actually the consumer. Refining cereal, however, also removes phytates and phytic acid, which bind some of the iron, calcium, and zinc, resulting in a loss of some of these minerals to the body.

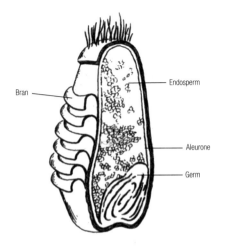

A kernel of wheat—the outer layer (bran) is rich in minerals and vitamins.

Effect of enrichment on wheat flour

Nutrient mg Per lb	Unenriched	Flour Enriched	Whole Grain
Iron	3.6	13.0	15.00
Niacin	4.1	16.0	19.70
Thiamine	0.28	2.0	2.49
Riboflavin	0.21	1.2	0.54
Calcium	73.00	73.0	186.00

Source: *Nutritive Value of American Foods in Common Units*, Agriculture Handbook No. 456, Agricultural Research Service, U.S. Department of Agriculture, Washington, D.C., 1975, p.274.

Table 1

All of the commonly used cereal grains are the seeds of grasses and each one has a structure somewhat similar to the grain of wheat shown left. Notice that the essential vitamins and minerals are located in the bran, aleurone, and germ layers; and that the endosperm, which is the portion remaining after the milling process, contains only starch and a little protein. Whole grain contains the entire seed except for the outer layer or hull, which is inedible and therefore discarded. It should be remembered that whole grain cereals and breads must be kept in the refrigerator since the fat, which is present in the germ portion, tends to turn rancid quickly.

Flour enrichment

The refining of grain began in the United States around the year 1910. Enrichment of refined white flour was made mandatory by the U.S. government during World War II. This enrichment program consisted of adding thiamine, riboflavin, niacin, and iron in sufficient quantity to bring the grain almost back to its original content of these four nutrients. The addition of calcium and Vitamin D was optional. Table 1 shows the effect of enrichment on three types of wheat flour.

Following World War II, the decision regarding the enrichment of grains was left to the states, and about 34 states now require the enrichment of bread and flour. It is very important, therefore, that consumers, especially those who do not live in states that require enrichment, read the labels on bread, cereals, pasta, rice, etcetera, to make sure they are enriched. It costs the manufacturer the paltry sum of less than 1/10 of a cent for the vitamins and minerals that are needed to enrich one loaf of bread. Even though approximately 90 percent of the bread sold in the United States is enriched, refined foods

Cereal grains such as wheat are seeds of grasses.

Whether or not refined white flour is enriched depends on the State.

still comprise approximately 50 percent of the American diet, and while the consumption of enriched bread and flour is decreasing, the consumption of nonenriched foods is increasing.

Another, and perhaps more important, fact to remember is that 17 other minerals and vitamins, as well as fiber, that are removed during the milling process are not replaced and are therefore absent even in enriched bread and flour. A list of these nutrients with the approximate amount that is lost is shown in Table 2 overleaf.

Nutrients lost during milling of wheat flour

Percentage Lost	Loss Replaced by Milling	by Enrichment	Percentage Lost	Loss Replaced by Milling	by Enrichment
Bran (fiber)	100%	–	Phosphorus	71	–
Vitamins			Magnesium	85	–
Thiamine (Vitamin B₁)	77	Yes	Potassium	77	–
Riboflavin (Vitamin B₂)	80	Yes	Sodium	78	–
Niacin	81	Yes	Chromium	40	–
Vitamin B₆ (Pyridoxine)	72	–	Manganese	86	–
Pantothenic acid	50	–	Iron	76	Yes
Folacin	67	–	Cobalt	89	–
Alpha-tocopherol (Vitamin E)	86	–	Copper	68	–
Choline	30	–	Zinc	78	–
Minerals			Selenium	16	–
Calcium	60	–	Molybdenum	48	–

Adapted from: Henry A. Schroeder, M.D., "Losses of Vitamins and Trace Minerals Resulting from Processing and Preservation of Food," *The American Journal of Clinical Nutrition*, Volume 24, pages 566-569, May 1971.

Table 2

Bread is not a particularly fattening type of food.

What happens to all the valuable minerals, vitamins, and bran that are removed during the milling process? These nutrients are used as animal food, mainly for cattle and hogs.

Bread and nutrients

Following is the nutritional information for frequently purchased loaves of "supermarket" bread. These figures are for an average serving size of two ounces, which is approximately two slices of bread.

The ingredients in a loaf of enriched white bread are as follows: enriched flour (barley, malt, iron, niacin, thiamine mononitrate, riboflavin), water, corn syrup, yeast, partially hydrogenated animal and/or vegetable shortening, (may contain lard and/or beef fat and/or soybean oil and/or cotton seed oil and/or palm oil), salt, wheat gluten, dough conditioners (contains one or more of the following: calcium, stearoyl lactylate, mono- and diglycerides, ethoxylated mono- and diglycerides, mono- or dicalcium phosphate), potassium bromate (soy flour, calcium sulfate, whey).

The ingredients listed on a loaf of *enriched wheat bread* are as follows: enriched flour (barley, malt, iron, niacin, thiamine mononitrate, riboflavin), water, whole wheat flour, sugar, corn syrup, partially hydrogenated animal and/or vegetable shortening (may contain lard and/or beef fat and/or soybean oil and/or cotton seed oil), yeast, salt, wheat gluten, soy flour, calcium sulfate, dough conditioners (contains one or more of the following: calcium stearoyl lactylate, mono-and diglycerides, ethoxylated mono- and diglycerides, mono- or dicalcium phosphate), potassium bromate (caramel color).

The ingredients listed on a loaf of generic *white enriched bread* are as follows: flour, water, corn syrup, salt, yeast, soy bean oil, calcium propiniate (preservative), mono- and diglycerides, lecithin, ethoylated mono- and diglycerides, barley, malt, ammonium sulfate, potassium bromate, niacin, azodicarbonamide, iron, fungal enzymes, thiamine mononitrate, riboflavin.

In comparison with these commercially available loaves of bread, the ingredients listed on two loaves of bread baked at the Loma Linda Market Bakery are as follows:

Sprouted Whole Wheat Bread—ingredients: sprouted wheat, whole wheat flour, water, yeast, salt, honey, soy oil, malt, and lecithin.

100% Whole Wheat Bread—ingredients: whole wheat flour, water, yeast, sugar, soy bean oil, malt, salt, and lecithin.

Salt is an important ingredient in bread.

As mentioned before, it must be remembered that since the last two loaves of bread listed above contain the entire grain of wheat, including the fat in the germ layer, they will become rancid if left in the open air for very long and therefore they should be kept in the refrigerator.

Bread is really not a particularly fattening item of food, as most people think. A slice of nearly any kind of bread contains about 70 calories, and an important point is that about 75 percent of these calories is supplied by the carbohydrates. Bread is low in fat. If you use 100 percent wholegrain bread, you will find it to be a good source of fiber, minerals, vitamins, and complex carbohydrates.

Meat and Vegetarianism
Different food philosophies

The problem with eating meat

Meats of all kinds are unnatural food. Flesh, fowl, and seafoods are very likely to contain numbers of bacteria that infect the intestines, causing colitis and many other diseases. They always cause putrefaction.

Research has shown beyond all doubt that a meat diet may produce cancer in some cases. I have treated patients who have suffered from severe headaches for many years. Every remedy had been tried without relief, but when meat was excluded from the diet they obtained most gratifying results.

Excessive uric acid

Excessive uric acid is caused by eating too much meat and may result in rheumatism, Bright's disease, kidney stones, gout, and gallstones. A diet of potatoes is an excellent way to rid the system of excessive uric acid.

Legumes such as peas are high in protein.

Increased uric acid comes from the following:

1 Uric acid taken into the body in meat, meat extracts, tea, coffee, etcetera. A pound of steak contains about 14 grains of uric acid. This accounts for the stimulant effect of eating a steak, since uric acid is a close chemical relative to caffeine.

2 Uric acid formed in the body from nitrogenous foods.

It is an established fact that meat protein causes putrefaction twice as quickly as vegetable protein. There is no ingredient in meat (except vitamin B_{12}) that cannot be procured in products of the vegetable kingdom. Meat is an expensive second-hand food material and will not make healthy, pure blood or form good tissues. The nutritive value of meat broths is practically nothing. They always contain uric acid and other poisons.

The argument that flesh must be eaten in order to supply the body with sufficient protein is unreasonable. Protein is found in abundance in beans, peas, lentils, nuts of all kinds, and soybeans.

Whereas, before the flood when no flesh was eaten, men regularly lived over 900 years; after the flood, when flesh was added to man's diet, the life expectancy soon decreased to a little over 100 years.

Toxins and chemicals

The meat we eat is composed mainly of part of a muscle from an animal, along with varying amounts of fat and other tissues such as nerves and blood vessels, as well as many toxic substances that we cannot see. At the time of slaughter, all the vital processes that were taking place in the animal came to an abrupt halt and the toxins that were in the tissues at the moment of death remained there. Some of these products are urea,

Protein is found in abundance in vegetarian sources such as soybeans and soybean products like tofu.

uric acid, creatinine, creatine, phenolic acid, adrenalin, possibly various bacteria and parasites, either alive or dead, various hormones, antibiotics, pesticides, herbicides, and other elements the animal had been exposed to or eaten while still alive.

Chemicals occasionally found in fish in some areas are lead, mercury, calcium, cadmium, zinc, antimony, and arsenic. Pesticides such as DDT are only very slowly degradable in the body, so it accumulates in the fat and muscles of animals. Meat, fish, and poultry contribute 13 times more DDT to the average diet than vegetables do.

Dr. Wynder of the American Health Federation stated: "It is our current estimate that some 50 percent of all female cancers in the Western world, and about one-third of all male cancers, are related to nutritional factors." As the consumption of animal fat and protein increases, the incidence of breast cancer increases in females and the incidence of colon cancer increases in both sexes. Women who eat large amounts of meat have a tenfold greater chance of developing breast cancer than those who eat little animal fat.

Increasing your intake of fresh fruit helps to protect against many diseases.

compounds, and a low-fiber (meat) diet promotes constipation and prolongs the contact of these toxic compounds with the lining membrane of the colon, in this way promoting the development and growth of colon tumors.

The fat content of chicken has more than doubled in 20 years because of modern production techniques. In 1960 raw chicken contained 5 grams (about one teaspoonful) of fat in every 100 grams of edible meat. By 1980 this had tripled to 15 grams of fat in every 100 grams of meat. During the same 20 years the consumption of chicken increased from 23 pounds per person per year to 56 pounds per year. Sixty-three percent of the calories in a fast-food chicken dinner, with extra crispy dark meat, deep fried, and with mashed potatoes, gravy, and coleslaw come from the high fat content. This is enough to supply the recommended amount of fat for an entire day. Dark meat contains two to three times as much fat as light meat. Most of the fat is just beneath the skin and should be removed along with the skin if this meat is eaten.

A one-pound charcoal-broiled steak, well done, contains 4 to 5 micrograms of benzopyrene, an amount equal to what a person would get from smoking about 300 cigarettes. During broiling, fat from the meat drips onto the charcoal, producing benzopyrene that distills back up onto the meat. Benzopyrene is one of the main cancer-producing agents found in tobacco smoke. In Iceland, where large amounts of smoked fish containing benzopyrene are consumed, there are large numbers of patients with cancer of the stomach and intestinal tract.

Food additives also add to the cancer danger. Nitrites, added to some meat to help it keep a healthy, fresh, pink color, may be changed to nitrosamines that are highly carcinogenic.

Animal proteins somehow alter the way that some bacteria act in our intestines. These bacteria change bile acids into potential cancer-forming

Effects of the American diet on health

The typical American diet with its high intake of fat and nearly twice the necessary amount of protein, has the following ill effects on the body.

- An increased risk of colon, breast, and possibly prostate cancer.
- Increases the formation of atherosclerosis in the arteries.
- Causes softening of the bones by increasing the excretion of calcium.

- Alters the normal immune mechanism.
- Decreases stamina and depletes energy reserves.
- A low-fiber diet results in constipation, diverticulosis, and hemorrhoids.
- Increases the blood cholesterol and triglyceridec levels.
- Toxins found in the animals before they are slaughtered are eaten with the meat.
- The risk of ingesting parasites, such as beef and hog worms, and bacteria.
- Possible allergic problems from substances added to the food.

In the 1940s most nutritionists felt that it was not possible to obtain a nutritionally adequate diet without the use of meat. They have now had to revise these ideas, since numerous scientific studies have verified the fact that a well-planned vegetarian diet can be nutritionally adequate, with a supplemental source of vitamin B_{12} needed by strict vegetarians who use neither milk nor eggs.

Since deficiency diseases have been found in those eating meat as well as in vegetarians, it is clear that a nutritionally adequate diet involves much more than whether or not a person eats meat. In America today, it is not difficult to obtain a diet with all of the needed nutrients without eating meat, provided that a wide variety of food is eaten. This is very important since the greater the variety of food that is used in the diet the more likely it is that all the necessary nutrients will be supplied.

There are many reasons why some people choose not to eat meat. Among these are religious, ethical, economic, and ecological reasons; but the main reason is to have better health.

A well-planned vegetarian diet will meet all your nutritional requirements.

Cattle need to be fed 21 pounds of protein in order to obtain one pound of protein in return.

The world food crisis

In 1974 the President's Science Advisory Committee stated: "The world food problem is not a future threat. It is here and now." At the time this report was given, many hundreds were starving daily in India, Africa, and other areas of the world. The full impact of this statement was not felt, however, until 1985, when the famine in Ethiopia and some surrounding countries, during which hundreds of thousands of children and adults starved to death, was dramatically brought to the attention of the entire world.

Land use and food production

It has been estimated that in 1974 there was about one acre of agricultural land for every person. This is far more than enough to provide an adequate food supply for a vegetarian, who requires only about one-fourth of an acre. Those who depend on animal protein for food, however, require about 3 acres of land per person. This is a very significant difference; about twelve times more land is needed to feed a meat-eater than a vegetarian. As the population of the United States increases, more and more good agricultural land is disappearing, as urban areas expand into the surrounding countryside.

Another way to look at it is this. If a man chooses to use his acre of land to feed cattle, he would be able to produce enough meat to supply his protein requirement for 77 days; if he used his acre to produce milk, his protein requirement could be met for 236 days; for 877 days if he grew wheat; and for 2,224 days if he used his acre to grow soybeans.

This comparison is emphasized even further when you realize that 21 pounds of protein must be fed to cattle in order to get one pound of protein in return. This difference between the amount of protein fed to cattle and the amount returned comes to 48 million tons, enough to meet 90 percent of the world's protein deficiency if it were fed to them as cereal.

Animal feed

At the present time, nearly one-half of all land that is harvested in the United States is planted in crops that are fed to animals. These crops include corn, oats, wheat, barley, soybeans, rye, and sorghum. Add to this a million tons of fish products, and you get some idea of the amount of our food resources that are used to produce meat. This is taking place at a time when millions around the world are either starving or are undernourished, and even though the vast majority of Americans get too much protein in their diet, starvation in the United States remains a daily threat for thousands.

Even though in Russia only 28 percent of their crops are used to feed animals, compared to 78 percent in the United States, their daily intake of protein is nearly the same as ours.

Is it any wonder, then, that the President's Science Advisory Committee states later in the same report that "the production of animal foods cannot be justified on an economic basis except in special cases."

Water

While the heart-rending pictures of children dying from starvation have been projected by television into millions of homes around the world, another substance that few people give much thought to, but that is just as essential for maintaining life, has also been gradually getting more scarce. That substance is water. While our population continues to grow, and there seems to be an endless need for more water for industry, agriculture, drinking, and other uses, more and more of our water supply is becoming contaminated and unfit for use.

But how is this connected with meat eating? Simply in this way: 2,500 gallons of water a day are required to provide food for a meat-eater, but only 300 gallons a day are needed for a vegetarian.

Water is a basic requirement for life but is becoming more and more scarce.

Those who eat eggs and milk are called lacto-ovo vegetarians.

The growth of vegetarianism

The name "vegetarian" was coined in 1842 by English vegetarians, and it was not very long ago that vegetarians were still looked upon as rather odd, even fanatical individuals. They were often called "grass eaters" and many other even less complimentary names. It was generally felt what was needed to do a "man's work" was lots of meat and potatoes.

Today more and more people, especially in the younger generation, are turning to a vegetarian diet. With nearly three-quarters of a billion vegetarians in the world and about 7 million of them living in the United States (1 in every 32 Americans), being a vegetarian no longer carries the stigma that it once did. More restaurants are now providing for those who do not choose to eat meat, but even so it can still be difficult in some areas to "eat out" and get a good vegetarian meal.

Types of vegetarian

There are many kinds of vegetarians, each eating a somewhat different type of meatless diet. The three most common groups are the following.

1 Lacto-ovo vegetarians, the largest group, who include eggs as well as milk and milk products in their diet.

2 The lacto-vegetarian, who does not eat eggs but uses milk and milk products in addition to plant food.

3 The total (pure) vegetarian, or vegan, who eats no animal products of any kind. Fewer people follow this type of vegetarian diet than the other two.

Vegetarians who eat eggs, milk, and milk products have no difficulty in obtaining all the components that are necessary for a nutritionally adequate diet. The vegan, on the other hand, must be much more careful in the foods he selects.

Food combining

The most practical way to make sure that our protein intake is adequate, not only in quantity but also in quality, is by supplementation of food proteins; that is, by combining foods so that all of the essential amino acids are present in sufficient amounts. It was thought at one time that in order to form a complete protein, all of the essential amino acids had to be eaten during the same meal. But now it is known that our systems can make up temporary deficiencies from the pool of amino acids that are present in the body. Combining the protein in eggs and milk with the protein from vegetable sources—grains, nuts, seeds, legumes, vegetables—raises the protein in the plant foods to a good biological value. With the vegan, however, supplementation of foods becomes more of a problem, but one that can and must be dealt with. For example, some grains such as corn, wheat, and polished rice, are high in the essential amino acid methionine but limited in lysine. These grains can be combined at the same meal with legumes such as lentils, beans, and peas that are low in methionine but high in lysine, and in this way good high quality proteins can be obtained.

Some other good supplementary food combinations for the vegan are as follows:
- Combining grains with legumes.
- Combining nuts and seeds with legumes.
- Combining grains with vegetables.
- Combining legumes with vegetables.

Grains combined with nuts and seeds may not furnish high quality protein.

Eating a variety of vegetarian foods will ensure that the essential amino acids are present in sufficient amounts.

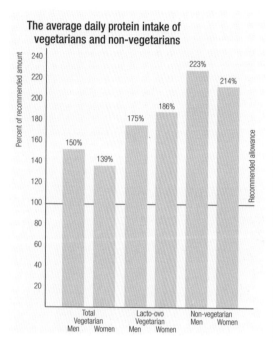

The average daily protein intake of vegetarians and non-vegetarians

Table 1

Eating more vegetables instead of meat improves health in general.

Protein consumption

In the United States today few cases of protein deficiency are seen. When they are found, they usually occur in those people who are not getting enough to eat. One problem with most American diets is that there is too much protein and not too little. The typical American eats about twice the amount of protein required by the body. The excess is either burned for fuel or stored in our body as fat. This places an increased workload on the kidneys and liver. A diet persistently high in protein and low in carbohydrates may cause permanent damage to the kidneys. It may also cause a loss of calcium from the bones resulting in osteoporosis (softening of the bones).

There has been a marked increase in the consumption of animal fat and protein, which now provides over two-thirds of the total protein consumption. In 1975 each person in the United States consumed 99 grams of protein a day. While it is true that animal foods in general provide a higher concentration of protein than plant foods, Table 1 clearly shows that even total vegetarians obtain more protein than the daily amount needed.

Special requirements for vegans

Vegans have to be especially careful to obtain enough of the following nutrients in their diet.

- **Calcium** Vegetarians in general need less of this mineral than those who eat meat, since less calcium is required when there is a reduced intake of protein. Calcium is present in dark green leafy vegetables; however, both spinach and chard contain oxalic acid, which combines with calcium to make it largely unavailable to the body. Soybeans, sesame seeds, dried fruit, citrus fruits, black strap molasses, and cauliflower are also good sources of calcium. Children may need to take fortified soy milk to be sure of developing strong bones and teeth.

- **Riboflavin** Found in green leafy vegetables. Also in mushrooms, squash, and almonds.
- **Vitamin D** This vitamin is obtained either by exposure of the skin to sunlight for 15 to 20 minutes each day or by drinking fortified soy milk if daily exposure to sunlight is not possible. Vitamin D increases the absorption of calcium and phosphorus from the intestinal tract.
- **Zinc** Found in legumes and whole grains. Wheat germ is high in zinc.
- **Iron** Iron is found in legumes, dried fruits, and green leafy vegetables. It is also present in whole grains, especially if eaten in yeast bread. The yeast destroys the phytates in the grain so that they cannot combine with the iron and zinc and render them unavailable to the body. The 10 mg of iron required daily in males is readily obtained in a vegetarian diet if a variety of foods high in iron is eaten. But the 18 mg of iron required by females is much more difficult to obtain without the use of fortified foods. An iron deficiency anemia is frequently found in women throughout the world. This may result from an inadequate intake of foods containing iron, the improper

absorption of iron from the intestines or from an increased blood loss. The increased fiber and phytates in a vegetarian diet may also result in the decreased absorption of both iron and zinc from the intestines: taking some vitamin C at the same meal increases the absorption of these two miners and tends to counteract the action of the phytates. Cooking in a cast-iron pot will also increase your iron intake. A recent study has shown that the iron nutritional status of vegetarians and meat eaters is essentially the same. Vegans must be sure to eat foods with a high iron content every day. If this is not possible, they should take an iron supplement. Others who may need an iron supplement are infants, women that have an unusually heavy menstrual flow, and women who are pregnant.

Vegetables such as cauliflower are a good source of calcium.

- **Vitamin B$_{12}$** The question of vitamin B$_{12}$ always comes up when vegetarianism is discussed. This is the vitamin of which we need the smallest amount—only three millionths of a gram per day. Vitamin B$_{12}$ is not found in plant sources. Only the total vegetarian has any difficulty in obtaining enough vitamin B$_{12}$, since large amounts are found in milk and eggs. Perhaps the best way for a vegan to obtain a sufficient amount is to take a B$_{12}$ supplement or use fortified soy milk, breakfast cereal, or meat analogs. Comfrey is also a source of vitamin B$_{12}$; twelve comfrey tablets a day are necessary, however, to fulfill the body's need. Miso, a fermented soybean product used as a flavoring agent, can also be used as a source of vitamin B$_{12}$. If children on a total vegetarian diet have difficulty

The herb comfrey is a source of vitamin B$_{12}$.

in eating enough of this type of food, soy milk that is fortified with calcium, riboflavin, and vitamins D and B$_{12}$ can be used. Some people who have been total vegetarians for 15 or 20 years are still found to have normal blood levels of vitamin B$_{12}$, while others have low blood levels after being on the same diet for only 3 or 4 years. The reason for this difference is not known, but it is known that vitamin B$_{12}$ may be stored in the liver for many years. It is also recognized that the reabsorption of vitamin B$_{12}$ from the intestines is very efficient.

Health benefits of vegetarianism

A recent study reported in the *New England Journal of Medicine* showed that a low protein, largely vegetarian diet could stop the advance of various kidney diseases in many persons. Such diseases included diabetes, high blood pressure, and chronic glomerulonephritis. Many persons with these diseases were saved from a kidney transplant operation or from renal dialysis treatments by using a nearly totally meat-free diet.

Research on the relation of diet to coronary artery disease, reported in the *Journal of the American Medical Association*, June 3, 1961, by Dr. W. A. Thomas, showed that a vegetarian diet can prevent 90 percent of clots from forming in arteries and veins and 97 percent of heart attacks.

Dietary fat and heart health

The American Heart Association in 1961 issued pa report on dietary fat and its relation to heart attacks and strokes. This report, which was updated in 1965, recommends the following.

- To eat less animal (saturated) fat.
- To increase the intake of unsaturated vegetable oils and other polyunsaturated fats, substituting them for saturated fats wherever possible.
- To eat less food rich in cholesterol.
- If overweight, to reduce caloric intake so that a desirable weight is achieved and maintained.
- To start to apply these dietary recommendations early in life.
- To maintain the principles of good nutrition that are important with any change in the diet. Professional nutritional advice may be necessary in order to assure that correct adherence to the diet will not result in any imbalance or deficiency.
- To adhere consistently to the above dietary recommendations, so that a decrease in the concentration of blood fats may be both achieved and maintained.
- To make sound food habits a "family affair," so that the benefits of proper nutritional practices—including the avoidance of high blood fat levels—may accrue to all members of the family.

Key benefits in brief

In summary, some of the important benefits of following a vegetarian diet are the following.
- Less colon, breast, and possibly prostatic cancer.
- Greater bone strength.
- Lower blood pressure.
- Lower serum cholesterol and triglyceride (blood fat) levels.
- Less obesity.
- Less expense.
- Less heart disease.

- Fewer problems with constipation, diverticulosis, and hemorrhoids.
- Less chance of developing varicose veins.
- Less exposure to toxins present in meat.
- Conservation of the world's food supply.
- No danger of ingesting parasites, bacteria, carcinogens, or other toxic substances found in meat.
- Vegetarianism doesn't require the cruel treatment and slaughter of animals.

Miso soup, derived from soybeans, is low-calorie and high in minerals.

Milk

Source of protein, calcium, other minerals, and vitamins

For many people, drinking cow's milk is like taking a poison. Half the invalids in the world suffer from dyspepsia and milk may be the cause. In some people, milk causes constipation, biliousness, coated tongue, and headache. All these are the symptoms of intestinal autointoxication. Soybean milk and nut milks are excellent substitutes and have practically the same nutritional analysis, but with the danger of autointoxication removed.

Addendum

A large number of adults, and some children, have either an absence or a deficiency of the enzyme lactase that is normally present in the intestinal tract. Lactase breaks

Versatile soybeans can be made into milk, as well as tempeh and tofu.

The nutritional value of various kinds of milk compared with orange juice

1 cup (8 ounces):	Orange juice	Whole Milk 3.25% fat	Low-fat Milk 2% fat	Skim Milk	Soybean Milk
GRAMS					
CALORIES	111	150	122	89	87
PROTEIN	1.7	8.1	8.1	8.0	8.9
CARBOHYDRATE	25.8	11.5	11.7	11.9	5.8
FIBER	0.3	–	–	–	–
FAT	0.6	8.1	4.7	0.4	3.9
MINERALS.MG					
SODIUM	3	120	122	128	51
CALCIUM	27	291	298	303	55
PHOSPHORUS	42	228	282	251	126
POTASSIUM	498	370	374	418	310
MAGNESIUM	–	33	34	27	57
IRON	0.5	0.1	0.1	0.1	2.1
VITAMINS.MG					
THIAMINE	.22	.09	.10	.10	.21
NIACIN	1.0	0.2	0.2	0.2	0.5
A(I.U.)	498	307	500	502	105
RIBOFLAVIN	.07	.39	.40	.34	.08
C 124	2	2	2	–	
D –	100	100	100	–	

From Bowes and Church's *Food Values of Portions Commonly Used*, Thirteenth ed., 1980; J.B. Lippincott Company.

Table 1

down the lactose (the sugar in milk) to simple sugars so that they can be absorbed. If the milk sugar remains unchanged as it passes through the digestive tract, it causes gas, bloating, cramps, and diarrhea. If you find that milk or milk products cause these symptoms, they should be eliminated from the diet, and special milk that already has lactase added should be used.

Fat content and calories in milk and dairy products

Percent Fat		Calories per Cup
Whole milk	3.3	150
Low-fat milk (2%)	2.0	120
Low-fat milk (1%)	1.0	100
Nonfat (skim) milk	trace	85
Buttermilk	trace	100
Chocolate milk	3.3	210
Chocolate drink (low fat)	2.0	180
Plain yogurt (low fat)	2.0	145
Flavored yogurt (low fat)	2.0	230

Source: Nutritive Value of Foods. U.S. Department of Agriculture, Home and Garden Bulletin No. 72, Washington D.C. 1977, p.5-7.

Table 2

Plain yogurt is a source of protein, calcium, and other minerals and vitamins.

Milk and allergies

It is probably true that more people are allergic to cow's milk than to any other food. Infants and children seem to be especially susceptible and may develop severe diaper rash or some other type of skin rash, diarrhea, breathing trouble, asthma, or irritability. These symptoms may begin shortly after cow's milk is first used, or they may not show up for several years.

Milk and nutrients

Milk is an excellent source of calcium and also supplies good amounts of phosphorus, riboflavin, vitamin D, and high-grade protein (refer to Table 1). One-and-one-half pints of milk a day provides 855 mg of calcium, which is more than the recommended daily allowance of 800 mg. One cup (8 ounces) of milk supplies 300 mg or about one-third of the daily requirement. It also supplies 20 percent of the protein and 5 percent of the vitamin D requirement. Women who have passed the menopause need more calcium, because of weakening of the bones with the

consequent possibility of fracture. The recommended daily intake of calcium for such women is 1200 to 1500 mg.

Milk and fats

The disadvantage of whole milk is its high content of cholesterol and saturated fats. Low-fat or nonfat milk should be used instead (See Table 2). Since this form of milk does not have the fat-soluble vitamins, it is usually fortified with vitamins A and D. In a cup of whole milk there are over 8 grams of fat, while in the same amount of nonfat milk there is less than half a gram of fat.

Nondairy creamers have about 30 calories per tablespoon and in addition they usually contain coconut oil, which is very high in saturated fats.

While modern methods of milk processing have eliminated most of the serious diseases once spread by contaminated milk, it is true that even today pasteurized cow's milk can be the source of bacteria that cause serious illness.

Salt

Vital mineral for body function

Salt in the diet

Salt should be used sparingly. It is sodium chloride, which is an inorganic mineral and cannot be used by any cell structure in the body. It irritates the stomach and the bloodstream, is indigestible, and hinders the digestion of other foods. It is one of the causes of high blood pressure and should be restricted in the diets of patients with heart disease as well as those with certain types of kidney and liver disease.

Sodium salts are plentiful in fruits and vegetables such as tomatoes, asparagus, celery, spinach, kale, radishes, turnips, carrots, lettuce, strawberries, and many others.

Salt is naturally present in vegetables such as celery.

When no salt is added to food, a person soon learns to enjoy the flavor more. The main taste of people who use any quantity of salt is a salty one. But without salt, more food flavors may be enjoyed. Salt must not be used by patients with dropsy, which is a swelling of the soft tissues due to an abnormal collection of fluid and is commonly seen in those who have heart failure or kidney disease. Swelling of the ankles may be an early sign of heart failure. Salt should also be restricted in persons who have

Foods High in Salt	
Cheese	Frozen dinners
"fast foods"	Bread
Processed meat:	Celery salt
luncheon meat	Garlic salt
corned beef	Onion salt
franks	Salted snacks and nuts
sausage	Sauces:
salami	Worcestershire
cured ham and bacon	ketchup
Canned soups	soy sauce
Canned fish:	Pickles, olives
herring	Frozen entrees
sardines	Sauerkraut
anchovies	Drinking water, especially if water softener is used
Bouillon broth	
Canned vegetables	

Table 1

hyperacidity, Bright's disease, gastric ulcer, obesity, epilepsy, and high blood pressure.

The word salt comes from the Latin word "salus," meaning health. Salt has been used as a preservative for centuries. Roman soldiers at one time received their pay in salt, not in coins, and from this custom the word "salary" originated.

Salt and health

During the past 10 to 15 years, salt has been so widely proclaimed as a health hazard that 40 percent of adults are now trying to cut down on their salt

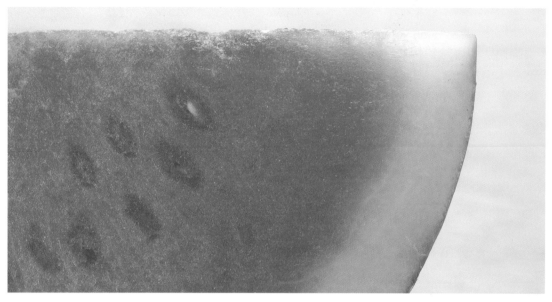

Eating fresh fruit and vegetables rather than canned produce will help you to reduce the amount of salt in your diet.

consumption and another 20 to 30 percent are worried lest they get too much salt in their food.

Sources of sodium

The sodium in our diet comes from three approximately equal sources:

1 Salt that is naturally present in food.
2 Salt that is added to food by commercial processors.
3 Salt that we add to food, either during cooking or at the table.

Table salt is composed of sodium (40 percent) and chloride (60 percent). The sodium is responsible for fluid retention in the tissues of persons with some types of heart, liver, or kidney disease.

But sodium is an indispensable mineral in our bodies. It helps maintain the proper water balance, assists in muscle contraction, aids in the proper functioning of the nervous system, maintains the correct balance of acids in both the blood and urine, and aids in the absorption of nutrients through the cell membranes.

The recommended daily allowance of salt is 3 to 8 grams, or 1100 to 3300 mg of sodium. The average daily intake of salt is 6 to 17 grams, or 2300 to 6900 mg of sodium. One teaspoon of salt has about 2000 mg of sodium.

Spinach is another vegetable with a high sodium content.

Nervous system function depends on sodium, along with other vitamins and minerals found in leafy green vegetables.

Sodium, found in radishes, helps with muscle contraction.

How to reduce your salt intake

Following are some ways to reduce the amount of sodium in your diet.

- Remove the saltshaker from the dinner table. This may be done gradually over two or three weeks.
- Cut down by one-half the amount of salt added to food while cooking.
- Omit or limit salty foods.
- Eat fresh fruit and vegetables when possible. Canned vegetables may have up to 10 times as much sodium as fresh vegetables.

Most common food additives containing sodium

- Table salt (sodium chloride)
- Monosodium glutamate (MSG)
- Baking powder
- Baking soda

Table 2

Sodium content of some selected foods

Food	Portion	Sodium (mg)	Food	Portion	Sodium (mg)	Food	Portion	Sodium (mg)
Coffee, instant:			Fast foods:			Vegetables:		
regular	1 cup	1	cheeseburger	1 each	709	asparagus:		
with flavoring	1 cup	124	chicken dinner	1 portion	2243	frozen	4 spears	4
Cheese, natural:			fish sandwich	1 sandwich	882	canned	4 spears	298
Cheddar	1 ounce	176	hamburger	1 each	461	lima beans, cooked	1 cup	2
Swiss	1 ounce	74	taco	1 each	401	lima beans, canned	1 cup	456
Roquefort	1 ounce	513	pizza, cheese	¼ pie	599	corn, cooked	1 ear	1
cottage cheese	1 ounce	114	Grains:			corn, canned, cream	1 cup	671
Milk, whole or low-fat	1 cup	122	bread:			peas, green, cooked	1 cup	2
Buttermilk	1 cup	257	white	1 slice	114	peas, green, canned	1 cup	493
Fish:			whole wheat	1 slice	132	potatoes:		
herring, smoked	3 ounces	5234	Cereals:			baked or boiled	1 medium	5
halibut	3 ounces	114	Cream of Wheat:			canned	1 cup	753
shrimp, canned	3 ounces	1955	regular	¾ cup	2	au gratin	1 cup	1095
Meat:			quick	¾ cup	126	sauerkraut, canned	1 cup	1554
chipped beef	1 ounce	1219	All-Bran	⅓ cup	160	spinach, cooked	1 cup	49
cured ham	3 ounces	1114	Raisin Bran	½ cup	209	spinach, canned	1 cup	910
frankfurter	1 frank	639	Cheerios	1¼ cup	304	tomatoes, raw	1 tomato	14
Prepared dishes:			Rice Krispies	1 cup	340	tomatoes, canned	1 cup	584
beef and macaroni	1 cup	1185	Corn flakes	1 cup	256	tomato juice	1 cup	878
chili con carne	1 cup	1194	Pancake mix	1 cup	2036	Condiments, Fats, Oils:		
Frozen dinners:			Legumes and nuts:			baking powder	1 tsp	339
beef	1 dinner	998	almonds, salted	1 cup	311	baking soda	1 tsp	821
meat loaf	1 dinner	1304	beans, baked, canned			catsup	1 tbsp	156
chopped sirloin	1 dinner	978	Boston style	1 cup	606	garlic salt	1 tsp	1850
Corned beef hash	1 cup	1520	kidney, canned	1 cup	844	meat tenderizer	1 tsp	1750
Swedish meat balls	8 ounces	1880	pinto, cooked	1 cup	4	olives, green	4 olives	323
Veal parmigiana	7 ounces	1825	cashews, salted	1 cup	1200	onion salt	1 tsp	1620
			peanut butter	1 tbsp	81	dill pickle	1 pickle	928
			Soups:			salt	1 tsp	1938
			beef broth (cube)	1 cup	1152	soy sauce	1 tbsp	1029
			chicken noodle	1 cup	1107	French dressing	1 tbsp	214
			minestrone	1 cup	911	Thousand Island dressing:		
			pea	1 cup	987	regular	1 tbsp	109
			tomato	1 cup	872	low calorie	1 tbsp	153
			vegetable beef	1 cup	957			

Table 3

- Eat unsalted frozen vegetables rather than canned.
- Cut down on the consumption of prepared foods.
- Avoid foods with MSG on the label. Oriental food is high in MSG (monosodium glutamate), which has been reported to cause mental confusion and/or headaches in some people. This has been termed the "Chinese Restaurant Syndrome."

Probably the best-known harmful effect of salt is its propensity to cause high blood pressure, particularly in susceptible individuals.

Some processed foods contain quite large amounts of sodium. If you are concerned about the amount of sodium you are eating, be sure to check the food labels. If you must reduce your salt intake, look for foods with "low sodium," "salt free," or "no added salt" on the label.

Garlic

Ancient foodstuff and remedy

Garlic in the ancient world

For nearly as long as there has been a written record of history, garlic has been mentioned as a food. It probably originated in central Asia, but now it is cultivated in many countries and grows wild in Italy and southern Europe. The garlic bulb is divided into 10 to 20 smaller sections called cloves, and the entire bulb is covered with a rather scaly membrane.

During the time of the Pharaohs, when Egypt was at the peak of its power, garlic was given to the

Thought to have originated in Asia, garlic is now widely cultivated.

laborers and slaves who were building the great pyramids in order to increase their stamina and strength as well as to protect them from disease. In the fifth century AD, the Greek historian Herodotus wrote that on an Egyptian pyramid there are inscriptions in Egyptian characters describing the amount of garlic, onions, and radishes consumed by the workers and slaves who were building the great pyramid of King Khufu (Cheops).

It was not until centuries later that certain substances were isolated from garlic and onions that were found to be effective against such constantly present Egyptian scourges as cholera, typhoid fever, and amebic dysentery. Garlic was also used by the Egyptian soldiers as a way to increase their courage during battle.

Garlic in ancient literature

The Ebers Papyrus, an Egyptian medical papyrus dated sometime around 1500 BC, mentions garlic twenty-two times as a remedy for a variety of diseases. Hippocrates, the father of modern medicine, used garlic as a laxative, a diuretic, for tumors of the uterus, leprosy, epilepsy, chest pains, toothaches, and for wounds incurred during battle. Aristotle also mentions the value of garlic and Aristophanes used garlic as a treatment for impotence.

The Bible clearly states that for 400 years (probably around 1730 to 1330 BC), while the Israelites were slaves in Egypt and no doubt being forced to help build some of the pyramids, garlic, as well as some of the other herbs in the same family, was a part of their diet. Shortly after they had been delivered from slavery by Moses, and were traveling through bleak

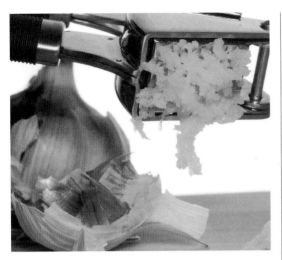

Garlic is often crushed before use.

Chopped garlic is a staple ingredient in savory dishes around the world.

desert country of the Sinai peninsula, they began complaining of their food and wishing for the same things they had been eating while they were slaves: "Oh that we had some of the delicious fish we enjoyed so much in Egypt, and the wonderful cucumbers and melons, leeks, onions, and garlic!" Numbers 11:5, *The Living Bible.*

Garlic is mentioned in the literature of all of the great ancient world kingdoms: Babylon, Medo-Persia, Greece, and Rome. The great Roman naturalist Pliny the Elder recommended garlic for intestinal disorders, dog and snake bites, asthma, tuberculosis, convulsions, tumors, and scorpion stings in his *Historia Naturalis*. Garlic was probably introduced into Japan from Korea along with Buddhism in about 30 BC Dioscorides, the chief medical officer in the Roman army in the first century AD, used garlic to treat intestinal worms.

Garlic as medicine

Down through the centuries garlic has been used as a treatment for all sorts of diseases. Some of the most common of these are: lung problems, including pneumonia, asthma, and bronchitis;

various skin disorders such as leprosy, acne, athlete's foot, dandruff, and ringworm; intestinal illnesses such as gastric ulcer, gastritis, constipation, diarrhea, worms, hemorrhoids, pinworms, cholera, amebic dysentery; arthritis, rheumatism, high blood pressure, tuberculosis, some forms of cancer, diabetes, anemia, heavy metal poisoning, epilepsy, whooping cough, colds, typhus, conjunctivitis, cold sores, hypoglycemia, spinal meningitis, diphtheria, and snakebites.

Garlic has been used to treat disease for thousands of years.

Leeks are a member of the garlic family but have a milder flavor.

Garlic may be eaten raw, but most people can eat only small amounts of raw garlic, and even then it is usually mixed with other foods. In some countries in southern Europe, however, larger amounts of garlic are a common ingredient in the food. Raw garlic, when eaten to excess, is not completely harmless; it may cause anemia as well as various digestive problems. It may also result in burns in the mouth, throat, esophagus, and stomach. Garlic can be taken in tablet form, either with or without parsley. The parsley is added to the tablets in an attempt to neutralize the offensive garlic odor. Odorless capsules are also available at most health food stores.

Chemical properties of garlic

During the 1940s Dr. Arthur Stoll, a chemist working in Switzerland, was able to extract an oil from garlic that he named alliin. He also discovered an enzyme in the garlic, to which he gave the name of aminase. Aminase was found to change the alliin to allicin when the garlic was cut or crushed. It is the allicin that is responsible for the garlic odor as well as for the antibacterial properties used during both World Wars. It is an oxidizer and a strong disinfectant. In fact, even when it is diluted with water 1/80,000 or even as much as 1/120,000, it is still able to kill the germs that cause cholera and typhoid fever.

Garlic contains more allicin than any of its close relatives—onions, leeks, chives, or scallions. The allicin can be destroyed by heating the garlic, but

Use of garlic today

Because of its strong, disagreeable odor, garlic is most often used today only in small amounts, either mixed with other foods or as a seasoning, so even though it does contain vitamins A, C, and B_1 as well as the minerals copper, iron, zinc, tin, calcium, potassium, aluminum, sulphur, selenium, and germanium, the limited amount that is eaten prevents these nutrients from being a significant factor in our diets. The assimilation of vitamin B_1 (thiamine) is reportedly enhanced by the presence of garlic.

Garlic, whose scientific name is *Allium sativum*, belongs to the lily family and is closely related to onions, leeks, scallions, and chives. All of these are known for their pungent, irritating, and unpleasant odor.

Garlic is one of the best plant sources of sulphur. There are about 67 mg of sulphur in every 100 grams of garlic. It is mainly the sulphur-containing compounds in garlic that are responsible for its medicinal effects.

unfortunately heat also destroys the other nutrients that are present. Allicin is also slowly destroyed by aging: it takes nearly two years for all of the allicin to become inactive. The other nutrients survive the aging process.

Medicinal use of garlic

Interest in the possible medicinal uses of garlic has increased markedly within the last decade or so, and during this time numerous experiments have been conducted in animals as well as in humans. The effect of garlic on the cardiovascular system (the heart and blood vessels) has been the subject of much recent investigation. Studies show that animals fed garlic extract have increased physical endurance, decreased blood pressure, and less buildup of fatty deposits in the walls of the blood vessels. There has also been considerable study given to garlic acting as an antibiotic and also as an anticancer agent.

As discussed in Your Body and Its Needs, Fats, the heart muscle is supplied with blood and oxygen by the coronary arteries. If these arteries

Garlic is most often used in small amounts as a seasoning in cooked dishes, mixed with other foods.

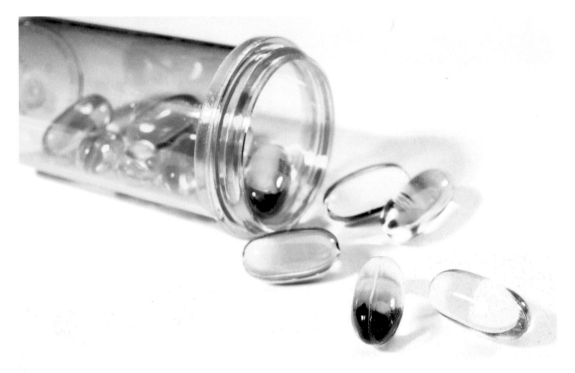

Regular consumption of garlic capsules reduces harmful blood cholesterol levels.

become narrowed by plaques forming on their inner lining, the heart muscle cannot obtain as much oxygen as it needs to function properly, and the well-recognized pain of angina pectoris results. If an artery should become completely blocked, a fatal heart attack may occur. Coronary artery disease is still the number one killer in the United States. Over $60 billion is spent each year in treating this disease.

Blood cholesterol levels

Our blood cholesterol level is an important indicator of the risk we run of having a heart attack. A total cholesterol level below 150 mg is best, and the simplest way for most people to keep their blood cholesterol level down is to reduce the amount of cholesterol and saturated fats in their diet.

Lipoproteins

In order for cholesterol, a fat-like substance normally produced in the liver and essential for several important body functions, to be transported in the blood, it must be connected to a special protein. This union of cholesterol, which itself is a fat (lipid), with a protein is known as a lipoprotein. The total cholesterol in the blood is made up of several of these lipoproteins. The two most important are low-density lipoproteins (LDL) and high-density lipoproteins (HDL).

The LDL is bad. It promotes the formation of cholesterol deposits, called plaques, on the inside of the arteries, causing them to become narrow or sometimes completely blocked. When the total blood cholesterol is elevated, the LDL is almost always increased also.

HDL is good. It opposes the LDL and tends to prevent the formation of cholesterol plaques in the arteries. Since women in general have higher levels of HDL than men, this is probably the reason they have fewer heart attacks.

The importance of both lowering the total blood cholesterol and LDL and raising the HDL is clear. The simplest and least expensive way for most people to do this is to cut down on the total fat in the diet, use more unsaturated and less saturated fat, stop smoking, get regular exercise, and maintain a normal body weight.

Garlic and blood cholesterol

Now what is the connection between garlic and all that we have just been saying? Simply this. Recent studies have shown that garlic prevents or slows down the formation of plaques in the blood vessels. It does this by lowering the total amount of cholesterol in the blood as well as the amount of injurious low-density lipoproteins, while at the same time increasing the amount of protective high-density lipoproteins.

A well-controlled study was recently reported in the *American Journal of Clinical Nutrition* written by A. Bordia, MD. He gave capsules of garlic oil each day for six months to healthy volunteers. The amount given was equivalent to eating 10 average-sized garlic cloves each day. At the end of six months, he found that the total blood cholesterol level had dropped 14 percent, LDL-cholesterol dropped 17 percent, while the beneficial HDL-cholesterol rose by 41 percent. Triglycerides were also significantly decreased.

Garlic and blood pressure

Garlic has been used for centuries in China and Japan to treat high blood pressure. In 1948 Piotrowsky published a paper showing that he was able to lower the blood pressure in nearly one-half of 100 patients that he treated with garlic. The blood pressure decreased 20 mm Hg or more after only one week of treatment. He felt that this beneficial effect was due to dilatation of the blood vessels caused by the garlic.

Along with garlic consumption, regular exercise improves health.

Further health benefits of garlic

Some studies have shown that garlic acts to prevent the blood from clotting so readily. The compound responsible for this action has been named ajoene, and has recently been isolated from garlic by Dr. Eric Block and his co-workers at New York State University. In 1979 Sainani, at the University of Poona, India, studied three groups of people living in the Jain community in India. All of these people were vegetarians and their diets were all essentially the same except for the amount of garlic and onions that were eaten daily. One group ate garlic and onions liberally every day; the second group ate a lesser amount every day; the third group never ate either garlic or onions. It was found that those who ate the most garlic and onions (the first group) had the least tendency for the blood to clot; that is, they had the longest blood clotting time. This study also revealed that the fasting cholesterol blood levels for the three groups was respectively: 159, 172, and 208 mg percent. The total triglycerides in the blood were 52, 75, and 109 mg percent. This clearly demonstrated that those who never ate garlic or onions had the highest blood levels of triglyceride and cholesterol.

Relieving fatigue

An experiment using two hunting dogs was reported in *Runner's World* of December 1979 by D. Gasque. The two dogs were initially found to run equally well behind the trainer's truck. Fresh garlic was then added to the diet of one of the dogs for two weeks, but otherwise there was no difference in the diets. After two weeks, the dogs were again allowed to run behind the truck, and it was found that the dog that had been fed the garlic showed much less fatigue after running for a distance of three miles, and was several hundred yards ahead of the other dog.

Antibiotic properties

Garlic has been regarded by some as having the effect of a broad spectrum antibiotic, the active ingredient being allicin. Garlic was reported to have saved many lives during the great plagues of the Middle Ages that

The odor of garlic is released in sweat.

The antibacterial action of garlic and its success in treating many infections has long been recognized.

swept through Europe killing millions. Even as early as 1858, Louis Pasteur noted the mild antibacterial action of garlic. Near the turn of this century, several reports indicated that garlic was remarkably effective in the treatment of tuberculosis. During both world wars garlic was used successfully as an antiseptic and disinfectant to prevent infection and gangrene in wounds. Dr. Albert Schweitzer, while working as a medical missionary in Africa, used garlic to treat cholera, typhus, and also amebic dysentery with apparent good results. In Russia today garlic is used extensively in treating various infections; in fact, it has earned the name of "Russian penicillin." Garlic juice has been found to be active against many fungi and yeasts as well as bacteria; it inhibits the growth of several bacteria that are resistant to some antibiotics.

Effects on cancer

Garlic has also been studied as a possible cure for cancer. During the 1950s and 1960s, several animal studies were published that gave encouraging results. Germanium and selenium, both present in garlic, have also been investigated as possibly having a beneficial effect on cancer.

While the majority of studies have given encouraging results, a few problems have arisen. When raw garlic was fed to rats in high doses it was found to cause anemia, weight loss, and failure to grow properly. The unacceptable odor of garlic, that affects not only the breath but also the perspiration, is another problem. Moreover, an occasional person will be found who is allergic to garlic and will develop a contact dermatitis, with redness and itching of the skin.

Healthful Diets

For healthful living and elimination of toxins

The fundamental principal of true healing consists of the return to natural habits of living. Proper diet is of much more value than medicine in the production and maintenance of good health. There is today a greater menace to civilization than that of war. This menace is malnutrition.

We eat too much and most of what we eat is poison to our system. Half of what we eat keeps us alive, and the other half keeps the physicians alive. As well as eating too much, we do not masticate our food thoroughly. Since many of our diseases can be traced to improper diet, the cure for these ailments is a correct, well-balanced diet.

For maximum nutrition, eat foods raw whenever possible.

A true diet is not based on calories but on the organic and inorganic elements that promote and sustain life. Many of our most common and serious diseases are caused by wrong habits of eating and drinking, including the use of tobacco, alcohol, and drugs. This has been proven by numerous scientific experiments in recent years. When food is absorbed by the body, it will nourish, repair, and furnish life force and heat to the body, but if in its preparation and refining the life-giving elements are taken away, it cannot furnish life force, but instead it will clog the normal functions of the body and result in many disorders.

Many diseases are nature's effort to free our system of poisons that result from wrong habits of eating and drinking. When we assist nature in expelling impurities and in reestablishing right conditions in the system, we can overcome disease.

The whole nation needs more vitamins, better cooks, more care exercised in the preparation of our food, and smaller hospitals.

The human race has been growing more and more self-indulgent until health is being sacrificed on the altar of appetite. God gave our first parents food that He designed for the human race to eat. Only after the world was destroyed by a flood did He give permission to eat flesh foods, since all vegetation was dead, but then only the clean animals, as given in the Bible in Leviticus, Chapter 11. Animal foods are not, however, the most healthful foods for humans. Recent scientific research and experiments have proven this beyond a doubt. The diet given to Adam and Eve in the Garden of Eden did not include flesh meats.

Foods to consume

Fruits

all berries	apricots	apples	pears
grapefruit	cherries	lemons	plums
pineapple	raisins	grapes	figs
quinces	bananas	prunes	dates
peaches	oranges	melons	limes

Vegetables

asparagus	onions
beets	okra
beet tops	parsley
celery	greens of all kinds
cabbage (uncooked)	watercress
cauliflower	parsnip
carrots	pumpkin

cucumbers	rutabagas
turnips	sweet potatoes
tomatoes	squash
dandelions	Swiss chard
Irish potatoes (unpeeled)	all sprouts
kale	spinach
lettuce	beans

Legumes

soybeans	garbanzos (chickpeas)
green beans	peanuts
dried beans of any kind	wax beans
split peas	navy beans
lentils	string beans
lima beans	peas

Table 1

We should learn how to avoid and overcome sickness by correct eating and living.

Normal diet for the average person

First, observe the following rules for eating.

Diet rules

- Do not eat fruits and vegetables together.
- Do not eat between meals.
- Do not drink any liquid with meals.
- Allow five hours between meals.

Second, more care must be exercised in the cooking of food every day so as not to destroy during preparation the vitamins, minerals, and other life-giving properties.

Third, 75 to 85 percent alkaline food should be used in the everyday diet. If you have any ailments, your diet should be at least 90 percent alkaline base-forming foods. Eating acid foods brings on disease, while alkaline foods overcome disease and help to prevent it.

Do not use cane sugar on fruits. Do not eat bananas unless they have dark spots on the skins and the ends are not green. Dried fruits are good if they are not sulphured. Do not mix more than two kinds of fruit at a meal. It is best to eat fruits raw. Applesauce is very good if the whole apple is cooked—skin, core (unless wormy), and seeds—then strained through a colander or sieve. Raisins added to applesauce make very delicious dish.

Legumes are very high in protein and therefore are useful as meat substitutes. As an example, peanut butter contains four grams of protein per tablespoon. The proteins contained in legumes are an adequate substitute for meat proteins if they are combined with the proteins in wheat or corn products.

Freshly prepared juices contain the most vitamins and minerals.

Raw diet

I believe in eating everything in its raw and natural state as far as possible, of the foods that can be digested. I just read an article by a man who thinks we should never cook anything, but eat it raw as people did in the beginning of time. But this fact is generally overlooked: foods are not as they were in the beginning.

In the beginning, fruits, grains, and nuts grew all the year around, and there was no need to can, cook, and bake as there is today. The wheat, rye, barley, oats, beans, and nuts were never hard and dry as they are now. There were fresh fruits and grains the year around, and they were eaten in their milky or grape sugar state, in which they needed scarcely any digestion. When our green corn is in the grape sugar state, it can be easily digested and requires very little cooking. After it matures and gets dry, it has turned into a starchy

state, and will take a longer time to digest. Therefore, we need to grind and bake it. If properly baked, it turns the starch back into grape sugar, to a great extent.

Starch comes only from plant foods but there is an abundance of it in our food supply. Some foods rich in starch are nuts, grains, peas, corn, lentils, dried beans, sunflower seeds, potatoes, parsnips, and winter squash.

Much impurity is produced in the system by too much protein. Now we know how to prepare our food, and also what foods to eat to balance the amount of protein with other foods. Too much protein overtaxes the system. The corn, wheat, peas, and beans in their milky state, before they are full-grown, contain three or four percent protein, but are high in minerals and life-giving properties. When they mature, the wheat has from eight to

Approximate time required for digestion (in hours)

Rice, boiled	1	Parsnips, boiled	2½
Barley, boiled	2	Green corn and beans, boiled	3¾
Carrot, boiled	3¼		
Beets, boiled	3½	Milk, boiled	2
Egg, soft-boiled	3	Milk, raw	2½
Egg, hard-boiled	3½	Turnips, boiled	3½
Egg, fried	3½	Potatoes, Irish, baked	2½
Egg, raw	2	Potatoes, Irish, boziled	3½
Butter	3½	Cabbage, raw	2½
Bread, whole wheat	3½	Cabbage, boiled	4½
Bread, corn	3¼	Apples, hard and sour, raw	3
Vegetable, hash, warmed	2½	Apples, sweet and mellow, raw	2

fourteen percent protein; the dried corn a little less; while the beans have from twenty to thirty percent more. All beans, lentils, and corn may be picked and canned in the milky state. Being thus very low in protein, all can eat freely of them. Peas, beans, lentils, and grains can be sprouted, which turns the protein into peptogen to a great extent, and starches and sugars into dextrose and grape sugar. They are then very easy to digest. Moreover, the sprouts have a very good flavor, and are high in life-giving properties. Sprouting increases the amount of protein and also the water-soluble vitamins, B complex and C. Leafy vegetables, such as spinach, lettuce, celery, and cabbage, are good when eaten in their natural state.

Clean, freshly prepared raw vegetable juices are excellent to supply the body with natural minerals, salt, and vitamins. Of course, it is necessary that they be properly macerated so that the life elements are released into the liquid.

Sprouted legumes are easier to digest and contain an increased amount of protein.

Fruit diet

All fruits contain acids, which are necessary for the proper elimination of various toxins, poisonous acids, and other impurities. These natural acids are highly alkaline after they have been reduced in the body.

The value of a fruit diet cannot be overestimated, especially in sickness, ill health, or whenever the body is filled with poisons. Germs cannot grow and live in fruit juices. The germs that cause typhoid fever and cholera cannot resist the action of fruit juices such as lemon, orange, pineapple, strawberry, apple, and grapefruit. A fruit diet will disinfect the stomach and alimentary canal. Fresh fruits are more effective for this purpose than stewed or canned fruits.

Malic, citric, and tartaric acids are powerful germicides found in fruits. Malic acid is found in pineapples, apples, quinces, pears, apricots, plums, peaches, cherries, currants, gooseberries, strawberries, raspberries, blackberries, elderberries, grapes, and tomatoes. Citric acid is found in strawberries, red raspberries, cherries, red currants, cranberries, lemons, limes, grapefruit, and oranges. Tartaric acid is obtained from grapes and pineapples. Tartaric acid is important in treating all diseases that have hyperacidity, such as lung diseases, sore throat, indigestion, peptic ulcer, etcetera.

Oxalic acid is found in plums, tomatoes, rhubarb, sorrel, yellow dock, and spinach. It is especially good for both constipation and an inactive liver. But a word of caution should be given about eating foods high in oxalates. About 10 percent of Americans will, at some time during their lives, develop a kidney stone, and most kidney stones are at least partly composed of oxalates. Therefore, if you have trouble with kidney stones you should not eat foods that have a high content of oxalates.

Lactic acid is found in buttermilk, clabber milk and soybean buttermilk. It is good for the treatment of fermentation and putrefaction, and in treating hardening of the arteries it is especially good.

Fruit grows slowly and receives the benefits of sunlight and air.

It is best to use fruits uncooked. Never sweeten them with cane sugar. A fruit diet is an excellent cure for chronic constipation, and is also good for reducing. Fruit gives the body strength and energy. Fruits are solvents and should always be used abundantly while on an eliminating diet.

Fruit is an ideal food. It grows more slowly than other foods, and therefore it receives the beneficial effects of the sunlight and air for a longer time.

Dates, raisins, figs, and many other dried fruits have become staple foods in many countries. Dates and raisins are high in natural sugar, so they are very easily assimilated. Dried figs, especially Black Mission figs, are rich in the bone-building elements, calcium and phosphorus, as well as iron.

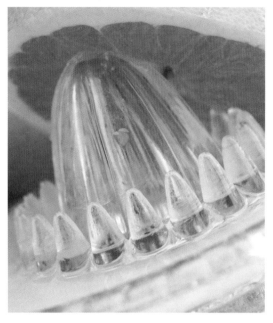

Drink fresh orange juice immediately after squeezing.

Orange cleansing diet

Drink from 5 to 8 glasses of orange juice daily. Drink the juice immediately after the oranges have been squeezed or the container opened. Keep orange juice tightly covered even when in the refrigerator. Do not let it stand exposed to the air as it rapidly loses its vitamin C content.

Take a high enema every night while you are on this diet. Herbal enemas are preferable, especially if there is colon or intestinal trouble: it is excellent to use slippery elm, because it is very cleansing, nourishing, and healing to all the mucous membrane surfaces in the body.

After taking the orange juice from 5 to 10 days, eat a very plain, simple, and nourishing diet. This will improve anyone's health. If the person who wishes to take a cleansing diet is undernourished and weak, and feels that a little something else is

necessary, eat apples, masticating them thoroughly; a few nuts might also be eaten.

If you are troubled with skin diseases of any kind, boils, carbuncles, etcetera a most helpful treatment is to eat 8 or 10 oranges a day, and drink 3 or 4 glasses of sanicle tea each day. Take the tea after the orange juice has left the stomach, which usually takes an hour or so. Take a high herbal enema with white oak bark every evening for 8 or 10 days. This will bring results beyond all expectation.

Some will find that the orange juice itself acts as a strong cathartic so that the bowels may move several times a day. If you find this to be true, the enemas may be omitted after the first or second day.

Carrots are a suitable vegetable to eat while on an eliminating diet.

The eliminating diet

All the good food that may be eaten cannot do the body any good until you have first cleansed the body by eliminating excess acid and mucus. The intestines retain these poisons, and they are one of the main causes of disease and premature aging. By eating an abundance of alkaline or base-forming foods, one can rid himself of these poisons and acids. To correct these unnatural and unhealthful conditions and make it possible for the food that is eaten to be assimilated and absorbed by the system, the body must be flushed and cleansed. Eating these foods will bring about a natural rejuvenation by constantly supplying the bloodstream with its original elements. These elements are found in natural foods, which should be either eaten raw or cooked as little as possible so as not to destroy the minerals or life-giving properties. You will be feeding the entire body,

not starving it. Leviticus 17:11, "The LIFE is in the blood" and in the same chapter, fourteenth verse, "For the life of all flesh is in the blood." Health and happiness depend upon the bloodstream containing all of the necessary elements; when one is missing, disease in some form often results. To make the bloodstream pure and healthy, eat food in its natural state as far as possible, drink freely of pure water, bathe frequently, exercise in the pure air and sunshine, and use nonpoisonous herbs that were given for the "service of man." Psalms 104:14.

In most of the civilized world we are able to do this almost any time of the year, as we have citrus fruits and fresh vegetables available the year around.

We repair our homes, buy new parts and have our automobiles repaired, and give regular care to other machinery that we may be using. Just so, we must take care of our bodies by supplying them with natural elements and minerals to build and repair the parts that are constantly being worn out.

If pure and alkaline, the bloodstream, which provides nutrition to every cell in the body, will dissolve all poisons and carry them away. No disease can exist with a pure bloodstream.

Fruit

Use all kinds of fruit liberally. All fruits must be ripe before being picked or else they will not have the eliminating qualities.

Eat at least 2 grapefruit a day, 6 oranges, and 3 lemons. Do not use cane sugar with your fruit or lemonade as it destroys the benefit of the fruit.

Fresh pineapple, ripe peaches, cherries, plums, pears, apples, ripe strawberries, blueberries, and raspberries are excellent.

If fruits do not seem to agree with you, take one-fourth teaspoon of golden seal in one-half glass of water twenty minutes before you eat.

Persons wishing to eliminate who have an ulcerated stomach and cannot take fruits should drink two quarts of potassium broth a day. This is also excellent for invalids.

Vegetables

The best vegetables to use are spinach, celery, carrots, parsley, tomatoes, asparagus, mild green onions, red or green, cabbage (best raw), lettuce, cucumbers, radishes, okra, eggplant, etcetera. Eat a large raw vegetable salad each day. Have one meal of properly cooked vegetables each day.

Cook all vegetables in as little water as possible, and if salt is necessary, use only a small amount for seasoning.

Fresh blueberries are packed with antioxidants that cleanse the bloodstream.

General rules while on the eliminating diet

All the above foods, when taken in abundance, will cleanse the bloodstream. Therefore, the greater the quantity taken of these foods, the sooner the body will be cleansed.

The eliminating diet is not a fast. It is a feeding process. It feeds the body through the blood with the necessary life-giving minerals that everybody needs. The eating of fresh fruits and vegetables in large amounts prevents shrinkage of the stomach and intestines, and also prevents lines and wrinkles from forming on the face and body.

An Epsom salts bath stimulates the skin and opens the pores.

Drink water copiously between meals. Take moderate exercise in the open air. Eat nothing but fruits and vegetables.

When taking the eliminating diet, do not use any of the following: milk, cane sugar or cane sugar products, gravies, butter, free fat of any kind, macaroni, spaghetti, tapioca, corn starch, meat, tea, coffee, chocolate, ice cream, pastries of any kind, white flour products, any kind of liquor or tobacco, bread, oils of any kind, canned fruits or vegetables, potatoes, cakes, eggs, or any food that is not mentioned in the eliminating diet.

It is highly important that the bowels move freely. If they do not completely evacuate at least once a day, it is wise to cleanse them once or twice a week with an herbal enema.

We have 5 organs of elimination—skin, lungs, bowel, kidneys, and liver. The bowels will be greatly improved by these foods and the help of nonpoisonous herbs. The lungs eliminate poisons freely when we practice deep breathing and exercise. The skin cannot eliminate poisons when it is dry and inactive. There are millions of pores that breathe and eliminate poisons. Therefore, a daily bath should be taken by everyone and, during the eliminating, it is excellent to take an Epsom salts bath every other day to stimulate the skin and open the pores.

Use 3 pounds of Epsom salts to a tub full of water. Drink plenty of water or broth while in the tub. Massage the body while in the tub. Salt glows are also highly beneficial. Rub the body thoroughly all over with half common and half Epsom salt. This increases the activity of the skin and stimulates the circulation. Finish with a cool shower or sponge-off, rubbing vigorously with a Turkish towel.

Many people do not understand why they cannot eat other good wholesome natural foods while on the eliminating diet. This is because they would upset the reaction of these cleansing foods. Do not take any starchy foods, sugars, or proteins as these things congest and clog the system.

When the cells of the body are clear, they function normally and harmoniously. Therefore, the whole body is rejuvenated and the vitality is restored.

Before beginning to eliminate, cleanse the system with an herbal laxative. This will rid the body of much waste matter and mucus and prevent such a great stirring up.

Immediately after taking the eliminating diet, eat sparingly of easily digested foods, such as baked potatoes, green lima beans, tender peas, corn, tomatoes, carrots, etcetera.

An abundance of oxygen assists elimination greatly. So above all things breathe deeply. Use grape juice, orange juice, grapefruit juice, and sweet apple juice liberally. Oxygen hastens elimination and burns up poisons.

How long should one stay on an eliminating diet?

This depends entirely upon the individual. If you have been sick or eating unnatural foods for years, or almost a lifetime, you may have to follow the eliminating diet many times. Eliminate a week or longer if you are stout or overweight, and repeat if necessary. One pound a day may be lost by faithfully eating just the elimination foods and that

which is lost is mostly waste and poisons. If one has taken patent medicines, drugs, serums, etcetera, it will take longer to eliminate these poisons from the system. When all pains and discomfort in the body are gone, the poisons will have been eliminated. Until they are, you will have to go on the eliminating diet again. Everyone could safely eliminate seven days in every month. Very little healthy tissue will be lost. The most that is lost is unhealthy tissues and waste, and the sooner you rid your body of these, the better it will be for your health.

Golden seal is a mild laxative and internal body cleanser.

Obesity

Dealing with the effects of poor eating habits

Calories are not a sufficient foundation to determine the nutritive value of food. Foods that have a high caloric value are often deficient in nutrient elements and organic salts. In order to determine the true nutritive value of food it is important to study their composition in regard to the amount and type of vital elements they contain. For perfect health we must have perfect digestion, assimilation, and elimination. The ignorance of the average person regarding the laws of his being is appalling.

Health problems linked to obesity

Overeating or too frequent eating produces a feverish state in the system and overtaxes the digestive organs. The blood becomes impure, and diseases of various kinds occur. It also produces

Desirable weights for men and women of age 25 and over

Weight in pounds (in indoor clothing)

Height (in shoes)[a]	Small frame	Medium frame	Large frame
Men			
5'2"	112-120	118-129	126-141
3"	115-123	121-133	129-144
4"	118-126	124-136	132-148
5"	121-129	127-139	135-152
6"	124-133	130-143	138-156
7"	128-137	134-147	142-161
8"	132-141	138-152	147-166
9"	136-145	142-156	151-170
10"	140-150	146-160	155-174
11"	144-154	150-165	159-179
6'0"	148-158	154-170	164-184
1"	152-162	158-175	168-189
2"	156-167	162-180	173-194
3"	160-171	167-185	178-199
4"	164-175	172-190	182-204

Weight in pounds (in indoor clothing)

Height (in shoes)[a]	Small frame	Medium frame	Large frame
Women			
4'10"	92-98	96-107	104-119
11"	94-101	98-110	106-122
5'0"	96-104	101-113	109-125
1"	99-107	104-116	112-128
2"	102-110	107-119	115-131
3"	105-113	110-122	118-134
4"	108-116	113-126	121-138
5"	111-119	116-130	125-142
6"	114-123	120-135	129-146
7"	118-127	124-139	133-150
8"	122-131	128-143	137-154
9"	126-135	132-147	141-158
10"	130-140	136-151	145-163
11"	134-144	140-155	149-168
6'0"	138-148	144-159	153-173

Reprinted with permission of the Metropolitan Life Insurance Company.

Note: Data are based on weights associated with lowest mortality. To obtain weight for adults younger than 25, subtract 1 pound for each year under 25.

[a] 1-in. heels for men; 2-in. heels for women.

Table 1

A person who has a sedentary job uses fewer calories than a manual worker.

encourages excessive eating. After having eaten enough, a person adds this extra rich food, which becomes a burden and poison to the system.

When the intestines are already full of food, any additional food that is eaten is forced to remain in the stomach overtime and sour. When this food putrefies, its poisons are absorbed into the blood and consequently the whole system is affected. Overeating makes the work of the heart, stomach, liver, kidneys, and bowels much harder.

There is probably no other country in the world that has as many obese people as the United States. If obesity is defined as being more than 20 percent over the ideal weight (Table 1), it has been estimated that 80 million Americans fall into this category. And it is not only adults that are affected. More and more children and adolescents are overweight, largely due to their poor diet that is high in refined, high caloric foods and also snacking between meals and during the many hours spent daily watching television.

excessive acid and causes the mucous membrane lining of the stomach to become congested. Hyperacidity is a common result. An excessive intake of food is much more common than a deficiency. Overweight people are much more likely to have a serious illness than those who maintain a normal weight. Cancer of the breast and womb, kidney disease, diabetes, gallstones, osteoarthritis, arteriosclerosis, high blood pressure, and apoplexy (strokes) are some of the consequences of overeating. Obese persons frequently have high levels of cholesterol and triglycerides in their blood and are much more likely to die suddenly of a heart attack.

It must always be remembered that what is enough food for a hard-working man would be a great excess for a person of sedentary habits of living.

The modern order in which food is served at meals is very destructive. The meal is arranged so that the most highly tempting dishes are presented last, such as pastries, ice cream, etcetera. This

Those who eat a healthy breakfast tend not to overeat later in the day.

Learn to recognize high calorie foods so you can avoid them or have as occasional treats.

How to lose weight

The secret to losing weight is simple. Use more calories than you take in. For almost everyone this is easier said than done. Less than 10 percent of those who go on special diets or other types of reducing programs are able to keep the weight off. So they try a different diet, lose weight again, but then go back to their old way of eating and soon gain all the lost weight back. Dr. Mayer of Tufts University has aptly termed this "the rhythm method of girth control."

In order to lose weight you must first of all decide that you really want to and then you have to attack the problem sensibly, safely, and slowly. If you were trying to overcome a drinking problem, you wouldn't stop in at the neighborhood bar on the way home from work, or if you were trying to stop smoking you wouldn't purposely place yourself in a position where others all around you were smoking. The same principle applies when you are trying to lose weight. When you go shopping, don't linger in front of the candy counter or saunter slowly by the bakery, admiring all the beautifully decorated pies, cakes, and other desserts. Why make it harder on yourself than necessary? Learn what foods are fattening and avoid them. If there is a nutritional label on the food you are about to purchase, read it and see how many calories you will be getting in an average serving. It is amazing how quickly eating only a few extra calories a day will put on the extra pounds. Eating an excess of only 100

How calorie intake can be doubled

Food	Calories	Added Item	Calories	Total Calories
Bread, whole wheat, 1 slice	56	Butter and Jam	110	166
Milk, skim, I cup	90	Milk, whole, 1 cup	150	
Salad, lettuce and tomato	40	Mayonnaise, 1 tbs	100	140
Peas, 1 cup	95	Butter, 1 tsp	60	145
Potato, baked, 1 avg. size	95	Butter, 1 tbs	108	203
Entree	150	Gravy	100	250
Baked apple	90	Apple pie, homemade	410	
Total Calories	**616**		**1038**	**1654**

Table 2

calories a day will cause a weight gain of about 10 pounds in a year. If you don't know your daily calorie requirement, you can figure it out roughly by multiplying your weight by 15 if you are a moderately active adult.

Remember that eating 3,500 calories more than you use up in daily living puts on one pound of fat. So in order to lose one pound a week you must decrease your caloric intake by 500 calories per day. Table 2 shows how the calories in a simple nutritious meal can be more than doubled by adding or using high calorie items.

If you have a dessert, choose healthier options such as baked fruits.

Exercise and weight loss

Proper exercise is almost a must to include in any reducing program. It doesn't even have to be vigorous exercise like jogging, aerobics, or swimming. Just taking a brisk 20-to-30 minute walk three times a week will be very helpful and will increase the rate at

Gardening is an effective way of burning calories.

Minutes needed to use 100 calories during certain sports activities

Activity	Weight of person	
	155 lb	130 lb
Skiing	8	9
Swimming at 2 mph	10	11
Running	11	13
Football	11	13
Tennis	14	17
Horseback riding	16	19
Gardening	17	21
Skating	19	23
Walking, rapid	19	23
Bicycling	24	29
Walking, moderate, 3 mph	28	33
Golf	33	40

Table 3

which the excess calories are burned off. Table 3 gives a list of common exercises and activities and shows how many minutes it takes to use up 100 calories. Table 4 gives the number of calories that are used during an hour of various kinds of vigorous exercise.

Tips for losing weight

Here are some positive suggestions to help you get down to and then maintain your weight within the ideal range.

- Don't be in a hurry to lose weight. You should lose between one-half and two pounds a week, never more.
- Don't eat or snack between meals.

- Eat a good nutritious breakfast and lunch, but go easy on supper. Do not eat before going to bed.
- Learn to recognize the foods that are high in calories, and avoid them.
- Skip desserts; eat fresh fruit instead.
- Don't take seconds; leave the table while you are still somewhat hungry.
- Use lots of fruits, vegetables, and whole grains. These will give you a feeling of fullness while keeping the calories down.
- Cut down on fatty foods such as fatty meats, meat products, mayonnaise, salad dressing, nuts, etcetera.

Jumping rope is a fun way to keep fit and use up a lot of calories.

Exercise and calorie expenditure

Activity (for one hour)	Calories
Bicycling 6 mph	240
Bicycling 12 mph	410
Cross-country skiing	700
Jogging 5 mph	740
Jogging 7 mph	920
Jumping rope	750
Running in place	650
Running 10 mph	1280
Swimming 25 yards per minute	275
Swimming 50 yards per minute	500
Tennis-singles	400
Walking 2 mph	240
Walking 3 mph	320
Walking 4 mph	440

From *FDA Consumer*, July-August, 1985, page 27.

Table 4

- Purchase and learn how to use a calorie counter. Lower your caloric intake to a point where you are losing about one pound a week, never more than two pounds. Don't forget: *you lose weight by eating fewer calories than you use.*
- Establish a regular exercise program that fits your needs, and stick to it.

Fasting and Healthful Eating

For physical and spiritual well-being

There is much said throughout the entire Bible about fasting. We will consider some of its uses and benefits. God instituted fasting for both spiritual and physical blessings. The priests in Christ's day fasted twice a week. Throughout the history of the Old Testament the people fasted and prayed in order to gain victories. Fasting has two useful purposes—the upbuilding of the body and the spiritual upbuilding of the soul. Christ fasted 40 days to get the victory over appetite on man's behalf. On this point of appetite our first parents fell, and thousands have gone to an untimely grave because of indulgence.

I have made many experiments with fasting. I fasted for one day a number of times just to get the victory over appetite and to gain spiritual strength. I have also fasted a number of times

When fasting, make sure you drink plenty of water.

for 3 days. Once I fasted for 21 days, and worked from early until late and never rested during the day. Another time I fasted for 23 days, and worked every day. I could have fasted 40 days, but was working too hard.

There are persons who advocate long fasts for health (and otherwise), but I WARN EVERYONE AGAINST LONG FASTS, as they do not benefit physically, and are not a spiritual requirement.

Benefits of short fasts

Short fasts for a day or two are very beneficial, both spiritually and physically. Make sure you drink plenty of water and take the deep-breathing exercises as outlined earlier in this book. To abstain from rich food, and to eat but very little plain food, even for days or weeks, would be very beneficial. This would give the system a chance to purify itself of poisonous substances. *But the weak, the lean, and the undernourished must be very careful about fasting.*

At one time I was with others eating dinner at an outing and we noticed a man who was not eating. I went to him and asked, "Friend, have you anything to eat? We have plenty and some to spare." This man replied, "I am fasting. I do not care for anything to eat." I then asked him his reason for fasting. He said, "I used to have rheumatism so bad that I was unable to do anything. All the doctors and their medicine didn't help me. One day a man came to me and said if I would fast two days a week my rheumatism would leave me." I asked him who the man was who told him this. He replied that he did not know, that he had never seen the man

Deep breathing exercises will help to improve your physical and spiritual well-being.

before, and had never seen him since. He said, "I followed his instruction, and it was but a short time until my rheumatism was gone, and I have never had it since. This was a number of years ago."

In Bible times when one fasted an entire day, it was counted that he had gained a victory. I know of different times when people fasted one day, and then in the evening after sundown they ate a lot of food. This should not be considered as fasting for one day. Fasting means to eat nothing all day until the next day. A serious mistake is often made when too much food is taken after the fast, and much injury to the system is the result. A great deal of the effect of the fast is thus lost.

Fasting and health problems

There are several medical problems that may arise with fasting, and for this reason, even though fasting may be beneficial, if it is carried on for longer than a day or two you need to keep on your guard for the following possible complications.

- Kidney stones
- Low blood pressure
- Irregular heart beat
- Gouty arthritis
- Headaches or light-headedness
- Abdominal pain or nausea
- Decreased urine output
- Severe cramps

If any of these or other complications develop, the fast should be stopped immediately.

Aside from spiritual and health reasons, fasting is also used to treat obesity and certain convulsive disorders. It has also been used with varying degrees of success as a means of political protest. Gandhi in India, well known for his passive resistance, fasted

All the nutrients a cow and calf require are present in grass.

as a political protest many times and for as long as three weeks, on at least three occasions. In quite recent times ten men from the Irish Republican Army died in prison, following fasts ranging from 45 to 61 days. The longest fast of which we have any record was that of an obese 27-year-old man. While under constant medical supervision, he fasted for 382 days and lost a total of 276 pounds.

Our food today

I am thoroughly convinced that a great many people eat too much. Americans are the most overweight group of people in the world, but this does not necessarily mean that they are properly nourished. In fact, many eat food that does not give them proper nourishment. It is also true that many people are undernourished because they eat devitaminized (refined) food improperly prepared, and improper mixtures of food that ferment and make poor blood from what they do eat.

But if we eat food as God made it, containing all of its natural vitamins and minerals, we will not get nervous, irritable, unreasonable, and out of sorts. When the minerals, vitamins, and other nutrients that would keep the body healthy are removed from the food during its preparation, we become malnourished and subject to all kinds of diseases, of which there are as many as there are different concoctions made for us to eat. When we feel so tired all the time, it is because those nutrients that give us pep and make us strong have been removed from our food.

I have seen many herds of horses, cattle, sheep, and other animals, and they are all very much alike

A field of wheat ready for harvest.

raised the calf, in this pasture. She was never out of the pasture and had nothing to eat but the grass that grew in that pasture. The calf had nothing but the milk she got from her mother until she was large enough to eat the grass too. This calf was beautifully developed, had a well-proportioned body, nice hair, good solid bones, good sound teeth, good hoofs, and good eyes. Now there was not anything in the milk that was not in the grass, and this milk produced this calf. That shows very plainly that all of the vitamins, minerals, protein, and carbohydrates were in the grass.

Now it is just the same with all of the food that God has given us. Of course it is true that different kinds of fruits, grains, and vegetables have somewhat different properties, and I would not recommend that anyone should choose a particular food and live on it to the exclusion of all others. As large a variety of food as possible should be eaten. This is very important.

But if the natural life-giving properties, which are in the foods as God made them, were not destroyed in their preparation, we wouldn't have to worry about calories, or alkaline and acid-forming foods. If a wide selection of food from the four basic food groups is eaten every day, the body will be kept in perfect health and there will be no need to wonder whether or not we are getting the proper amount of protein, carbohydrate, fat, vitamins, and minerals. I was born and raised on a farm in the northern part of Wisconsin, and we raised practically everything we ate, and we were a large family. We were never sick and we all lived to an old age.

because they eat the food the way God made it for them. Just stop and think! There is not anything in any of the meats that is not in the grains, hay, and grass that the animals eat. Why eat it secondhand? Let's eat it in its pure original state. What do you say?

A diet of acid-forming foods and combinations causes waste matter in the system, which in turn causes wrinkles and makes us look old.

There is so much written about foods today that it becomes confusing. They write about calories, acid-forming foods, alkaline foods, vitamins, minerals, etcetera; and one writer who claims to be an authority says this, while another one says that. I have heard people say many times that they did not know what to eat any more. In the accompanying picture (left), we see a cow with her calf. This cow

Food Preparation

Useful Hints to Preserve Vitamins

How to retain nutrient content

How nutrients are lost

Many important nutrients are lost to a greater or lesser degree when food is cooked by ordinary methods. In particular, the water-soluble vitamins—B-complex and C—may be largely lost by careless cooking and storage. Vitamin C is the most unstable of all the vitamins and if, by observing the following rules for cooking, this vitamin can be largely retained, other important nutrients, including iron, will also be preserved in significant amounts. Fortunately, some of our food sources that are highest in vitamin C, the citrus fruits, are best eaten raw. Fruits and vegetables together supply well over 90 percent of our vitamin C.

Tips for retaining nutrients

Follow the practical suggestions listed below in order to retain the most nutrients while cooking your food, and remember the four nutrient robbers are air, water, heat, and light.

- Use as little water as possible during cooking.
- Have the water boiling for about 1 minute before adding the food.
- Let the water simmer rather than boil vigorously.
- Save the leftover water to use as vegetable stock for gravy or soup.
- Cut the vegetables in large, uniform pieces just before cooking. Leave the peeling or skin on when possible. The smaller the pieces being cooked, the larger the area exposed to

Cut vegetables into large, uniform pieces just before cooking and use the shortest cooking time possible.

Timetable for cooking

Apples, sour	baked, medium hot oven, 30 minutes		Peas	boiled 10 to 12 minutes
Apples, sweet	baked, medium hot oven, 45 minutes		Potatoes	boiled 15 to 30 minutes
Asparagus, whole	boiled 10 to 15 minutes		Potatoes	baked in hot oven, 45 to 60 minutes
Beans, dried	boiled until tender, about 2 to 3 hours		Rice, brown	boiled 40 to 50 minutes
Beets, whole	boiled until tender, 20 to 30 minutes		Rolled oats	direct boiling, 15 minutes double boiler, 1 hour
Broccoli	boiled 10 to 15 minutes		Salsify (oyster plant)	boiled 2 hours
Carrots, whole	boiled until tender, 15 to 20 minutes		Squash	boiled, whole, 10 to 15 minutes boiled pieces, 8 to 12 minutes
Carrots, sliced	boiled until tender, 10 to 15 minutes			
Cauliflower, pieces	boiled until tender, 8 to 10 minutes		String beans, whole	boiled until tender, about 10 minutes
Corn on the cob	boiled 6 to 10 minutes		Sweet potatoes	baked, hot oven, 45 to 60 minutes boiled 20 to 35 minutes
Eggplant	baked in hot oven, 30 minutes steamed, 15 to 20 minutes			
			Tomatoes, whole	boiled 10 to 15 minutes
Onions, small	boiled 10 to 15 minutes		Turnips, sliced	boiled until tender, 20 to 30 minutes
Onions, large	boiled 20 to 30 minutes		Turnips, sliced	boiled 15 to 20 minutes
Parsnips, whole	boiled 20 to 30 minutes			

Table 1

water, and therefore the greater the vitamin loss will be.

- Use the shortest cooking time possible. Serve vegetables tender and crisp, not soggy and mushy.
- Serve food immediately after preparation. Do not keep it hot for a long time before serving. Plan your meals so that the reheating of food is done as seldom as possible. Cover and refrigerate leftover foods right away.
- Keep cooking vessels tightly covered.
- Cooking by steaming or pressure cooker will preserve about 30 percent more of the vitamins than boiling.

- Do not add soda to cooking water, because this destroys vitamin C and some B-complex vitamins.
- Food that is high in vitamin C should not be cooked in copper or iron vessels.
- Store fresh fruits and vegetables in a refrigerator and prepare them immediately before they are to be used. Do not let them stand in water or remain exposed to air any longer than is necessary.
- Place frozen food directly into boiling water after removing from the freezer. Do not permit the food to thaw first.
- Keep orange juice covered and in the refrigerator. Drink fresh orange juice immediately after squeezing. Do not leave it exposed to the air.

Ways to cook vegetables

The best way to cook vegetables is to bake them. Boiling is good if very little water is used and none of the liquid is thrown away. Waterless cooking, casserole baking, and low pressure steam cooking are also good.

Boiling

When boiling vegetables, put them in just enough boiling water to cook them and don't overcook them. If there is any water left, save it to add to your soups or broths. The vegetables must boil or simmer continuously after placing them in the water; otherwise they will become water-soaked.

Seasoning, peeling, and serving

Add sea salt sparingly just before the vegetables are entirely done; if salt is added as they are beginning to cook, it has a tendency to toughen them. Cook vegetables only until they are tender; prolonged cooking destroys the life-giving properties. Do not add fat to the vegetables while they are cooking; add your seasoning just before they are done, and serve them at once.

Vegetables such as radishes can be used without peeling.

Never peel or remove the eyes of Irish potatoes before cooking; the life of the potato is in the eyes and the peel. Do not peel any vegetable that can be used without peeling. Carrots, parsnips, salsify (vegetable oysters or oyster plant), rutabagas, and others may be scraped lightly, so as not to lose the minerals that are found just under their skins.

Green vegetables are very desirable during the winter months; if you think them expensive remember that they are far cheaper than the cost of an illness, and when properly prepared they are real medicine.

Canned or frozen vegetables, even if you get a good brand, are not as good as properly prepared fresh vegetables. But they are better than fresh vegetables that are poorly prepared.

To obtain protein with your vegetables, serve one of the many meat analogs on the market, or any nuts you like best. Nuts require thorough mastication,

Scrape carrots lightly to retain the minerals found just under the skin.

Cook vegetables in as little water as possible and if there is any water left, save it to add to soups.

however, and they should be chewed to a creamy consistency in order to get the most good out of them. The meat substitutes that contain nuts are better for most people, because the nuts used have been ground.

Vegetables can be seasoned with soy mayonnaise that has been made without the lemon if desired. Either dilute the mayonnaise with cold water to the consistency of cream, or use it as is. Either rich soybean milk or one of the nut milks is good when added to hot vegetables; heat the vegetables for only a few minutes after the milk has been added, and serve at once. Good soybean milk can now be purchased; thus, you can always have it on hand.

All the nonstarchy vegetables, such as carrots, cabbage, cucumbers, radishes, and parsley, should be eaten raw if they agree with you.

Kloss's Favorite Health Recipes
Vegetable Recipes

Mashed potatoes

- *Select the dry, mealy variety, such as the Idaho potato.*
- *Wash them thoroughly and boil or steam them until they are thoroughly done. Steaming is better than boiling.*
- *When done, peel the outer thin skin off, being careful not to remove the eyes.*
- *Mash, add rich soybean milk, salt to taste, and bake in a greased casserole dish for 20 minutes in a hot oven.*

Boiled cabbage

- *Select a head of cabbage that has many green outside leaves in good condition. Slice into eighths, put in cooking pan, and cover with sliced onions. Pour 1 to 2 cups of boiling water over it and cook for about 20 minutes, or until tender. Salt sparingly when about half done.*

Carrots and peas

- *Equal parts of sliced or cubed carrots and peas can be cooked together until tender; season with rich soybean milk or soybean butter if desired. Salt to taste.*

String beans

- *Wash, string, and break the beans about one inch long, or slice them lengthwise. Cover*

Chopped herbs can be added to simple favorites like mashed potatoes.

the bottom of a pan with a little vegetable fat and put the beans in the pan. Salt, and cover the pan with a tight lid, cooking over moderate heat until the beans are a bright green, stirring them often so they will not stick. Then barely cover the beans with boiling water, and cook until tender.

Mixed greens

- Use as many kinds of greens as you wish, having them all as near the same tenderness as possible. Wash and chop. Rub the cooking kettle with a little garlic, add enough fat to just cover the bottom of the kettle well, put the greens in, cover tightly and cook over medium heat for about 10 minutes. Salt and serve at once.

Eggplant

½ cup chopped onions	1 or 2 cloves of garlic
½ cup green peppers	2½ cups of tomatoes,
3 tbs. vegetable fat	chopped
3 cups raw eggplant,	salt
unpeeled, diced into	
½-inch cubes	

- Put onions and peppers in hot fat and brown them lightly. Add eggplant and garlic and cook a few minutes. (Eggplant can be peeled very thinly if you prefer.) Then add tomatoes and salt to taste. Put in greased baking dish and bake for about 30 minutes in a 350°F oven.

Beets

- Always use young beets when obtainable. Cut the tops up fine and cook in hot water for about 5 minutes. Then dice the beets about ⅛-inch square, add them to the tops, and cook until tender; salt, and just before serving add a little soybean butter if you wish.

Okra

- Select even-sized, tender pods of okra. Cook until tender, in just enough water to keep from burning. Salt and season with soybean butter (optional) just before serving.

Spinach

- Wash thoroughly. Put in a tightly covered kettle and cook until tender; from 5 to 10 minutes. Salt when partly done. Add a little lemon juice if desired for extra flavor.

Cook spinach for a short time only.

Use any kind of dried bean to make beans with tomato sauce.

Beans with tomato sauce

- *Use any kind of dried beans. Soak them overnight in cold water, and the next morning drain them, cover with cold water and tomato sauce, or other seasoning if you prefer, and cook in a crock pot for about 4 hours. Those who cannot eat beans prepared in the ordinary way may be able to eat them when they are cooked in this fashion.*

- *After soaking the beans overnight, they may also be put in cans. Fill the cans about three-quarters full of beans, and then fill to the top with water, salting the water before pouring it in the can; or use half tomato sauce and half water. Seal and cook in a steam pressure cooker, using 10 pounds of pressure for about 1½ hours. Some beans require a little less cooking and some a little more. Test them for yourself. Old beans require longer cooking than new ones, but all beans should be thoroughly soft and tender. When prepared properly, they will not produce gas and will digest more easily.*

- *Another way to prepare beans is to boil them until almost dry, then put them in a baking dish, add some soybean milk, put in the oven, and bake thoroughly. This method adds to the flavor and digestibility of the beans, and makes them more alkaline.*
- *The Great Northern bean is very fine and cooks easily. The lima bean is alkaline and therefore one can eat it more freely than the navy bean and some of the others.*
- *Soybeans are, no doubt, the most nutritious of all beans, but the flavor is not as pleasant. This can be overcome by using various seasonings, such as tomato sauce, a little onion, and celery.*

To sprout soybeans, lentils, or grains

- *Cover well one pint, or any amount you desire, of soybeans (or others) with water and let stand overnight. Pour off the water but keep the beans moist. Rewash two or three times daily, keeping them moist, and in a dark place, for approximately three days until well-sprouted. Allow to stand until the sprouts are about ½ inch long. Lentils are prepared in the same manner, but they do not take as long to sprout as soybeans. Soybeans may be allowed to sprout until they are an inch long, and then only the sprouts are eaten. The sprouts need only about 10 minutes cooking.*

- *The sprouting of any bean or pea turns the protein into peptogen to a great extent, and the starch into dextrose or maltose. The sprouts are very high in vitamins, more so than spinach, lettuce, or celery.*
- *Cook sprouted beans or peas the same way you cook any fresh beans or peas; but be careful not to overcook. Salt to taste. A little tomato and onion added make a very palatable and wholesome dish.*

Soybean sprouts and rice

- *Boil the sprouted soybeans until tender. Boil brown rice separately. Mix approximately equal parts, add tomato sauce and some cubes of nut roast or loaf (recipes given later in this chapter). Mix these all together and place in the oven at 350°F for 30 to 60 minutes.*
- *If the flavor of the soybeans is too strong, they may first be parboiled in strong salt water for a few minutes.*

Soybean sprouts have a high protein content.

Soybeans

A knowledge of the value of the soybean here in America is one of the greatest things that was ever launched in the food line in the history of the nation, and at this time of great poverty, want, and disease, it is the most important thing that could be given to the people.

Anyone with a piece of ground may raise his own soybeans. They will not only greatly improve the soil, making fertile soil out of worn-out soil, but at the same time they will supply the family with most delicious and nourishing food. Soybeans should be planted at different intervals throughout the summer in order to have shelled soybeans all summer. The green soybeans can be shelled just like any other bean or pea. Some varieties do not shell easily, but these can be easily removed from the shell by first boiling for just a few minutes.

Soybean milk can be made from soybeans at home for less than two cents a quart. The Yellow Mammoth, Dixie, Illinois, and Tokyo soybeans are among the best varieties for making soybean milk. There are other varieties that are better for green shelled beans. W. J. Morse, senior agronomist of the U.S. Agriculture Experimental Station, Washington, D.C., can give most valuable information along this line, as he has made, and is still making, extensive experiments with soybeans, and is thoroughly acquainted with that subject.

For stomach ulcers, duodenal ulcers, cancer, and diabetes, as well as liver, kidney, and bladder troubles, soybean milk in not only a good food, but a real medicine. It is easily digested, it does not curd, is highly alkaline, and is rich in mineral matter.

Green soybeans can be shelled just like peas.

The soybean is one of the greatest and most complete foods that we have. In the Orient, it has been used for thousands of years, and in this country it has been used for some time for stock feed, and to improve the soil. But only recently has much effort been made to use it for human consumption. At the present time, there are many people in various sections of the United States who are experimenting with it to some extent with considerable success.

The objection to the soybean is that it does not have a flavor as pleasant as some of the other beans. The flavor can be improved, however, by preparing the beans for human consumption in a different way.

Using soybeans

I have experimented with soybeans for fifteen years and have produced a fine, acceptable soybean milk as well as many other soybean products.

I use soybeans in more than fifty dishes. I can make soybean bread, buns, pie, pones, roast,

Analysis of human, cow's, goat's, soybean, and nut milks

Type of milk	Water	Ash	Protein	Fat	Carbo-hydrates
Human	89.95%	0.25%	1.30%	2.50%	6.00%
Cow's	87.30	0.80	3.20	3.50	5.20
Goat's	87.00	0.50	4.00	4.50	4.00
Soybean	87.03	0.52	2.40	3.15	6.90
Nut	87.00	2.03	5.60	5.50	7.23

Table 1

cottage cheese, and soybean cheese (which is very similar to both Philadelphia cream cheese and American yellow cheese); also soybean coffee and ice cream, without any cane sugar in any product. My soybean milk is simply delicious, very palatable, and both children and adults like it.

Soybean milk, properly made, is a wonderful food for the sick. Soybean milk does not form hard curds in the stomach and putrefy as cow's or goat's milk can do, and it can be used in the same ways they are used. Beans and peas cook quicker when they are boiled in soybean milk than when they are boiled in water. Soybean milk can sour and clabber like cow's milk, and after souring, can be beaten up into most delicious buttermilk. The beauty of it is that it is highly alkaline, and is well adapted for the human system, for both adults and children.

Many pay a big price for goat's milk, while soybean milk is infinitely better for human consumption. It does not have the contamination of the animal in it, nor the tendency to disease and putrefaction.

Table 1 is an analysis of human, cow's, goat's, soybean, and nut milks as given by the United States Department of Agriculture, Bureau of Chemistry and Soils, Washington, D.C.

To the soybean milk used for the above analysis, I had added a little emulsified soybean oil and a little malt.

Soybeans are also used for industrial purposes in the manufacture of artificial petroleum, automobile steering wheel rims, cable insulators, candles, casein, celluloid, core oil, crude and refined oil, emulsifier, electric distributor parts, illuminant (for lamps), hard and soft soaps, horn buttons, glue, hard curd soap, cooking oil, glycerine, enamels, foundry sand-cores, linoleum, lard, lubricant, laundry oilcloth, paints, photographic films, paper, plastic material, potassium soap, printer's ink, rubber substitute, silk-scouring soap, seawater soap, shampoo mixture, silver soap, soy vinegar, varnish, textile dressing, waterproof cement, etcetera.

Soybeans are easy to grow and are extremely versatile.

Legumes and grains can be combined to make complete proteins.

The following quotation is from an address delivered by Dr. J. A. LeClerc before the annual meeting of the American Soybean Association, Sept 15, 1936.

The nutritional value of the soybean

The soybean is going to revolutionize the food of humanity more than the potato did two hundred years ago, when it was a curiosity—and today is a staple food. It differs from the potato in the respect that it has been used for thousands of years as one of the principal foods of the Chinese. The Chinese nation exists today because of the use of the soybean as a food. China has survived five thousand years, its people have endured not only one, but hundreds of severe economic depressions, floods, earthquakes, famines, and wars.

Their recovery from these calamities is due largely to the use of the soybean, as it is a food which perfectly takes the place of disease-producing meat, milk, and eggs. It (the soybean) contains all the life-sustaining properties of meat, milk, and eggs, and is far more economical and easier to produce than any of these.

If Americans were suddenly deprived of meat, milk, and eggs and no more thought was given to planning our diet than most of us do, the result would be a condition of malnutrition due to a shortage of protein in our food.

The Chinese under similar circumstances have gone on living normal lives, simply by eating soybeans in some form. The Buddhist priests in the Orient are forbidden meat by their religion; in place of it they eat tofu, a soybean curd, and other soybean foods. The Chinese coolies, whose strength and endurance are traditional for carrying heavy burdens, pulling rickshaws, etcetera, live chiefly on soybeans and rice. Chinese babies are dependent on the soybean for food, dairy products being rare in the Orient. Those babies that must be fed artificially are given milk made from soybeans. It is a scientific fact that physical development on a soybean diet is perfectly normal. History proves the value of soybeans as a food.

Food chemists have conclusively proven that soybeans cannot only be substituted for more expensive foods but are more wholesome than those articles of diet. Today soybeans are one of the most economical sources of nourishment.

Not only are soybeans suitable for all kinds of baked products but soya flour or soybeans can also be used in breakfast foods, diabetic and infant foods, in pancake and self-rising flours, macaroni, doughnuts, pretzels, soy sauce, pate de foie gras, potted meats, meat loaf, and sandwich spreads, mayonnaise, soups, confectionery, beverages, coffee substitutes, beer, milk, cheese, ice cream, dog food, besides numerous industrial products. It is understood, of course, that food products containing soya flour should be properly labeled.

Soya flour is considerably richer in protein than are the flours made from such other legumes as the navy bean, pea, lentil, lima bean, etcetera, and about four times as rich in this constituent as are the cereal flours. Soya flour protein is of especially good quality. Soya flour contains less than two percent starch, whereas starch is the main constituent in other cereal flour, containing as it does about thirty times as much.

Soya flour is especially rich in the vitamins and in minerals. The amount of calcium is twenty times greater than that in potatoes, twelve times that found in wheat flour, five times that in eggs, about two times the amount present in liquid milk, and one-fourth as much as in dried milk. Milk has always been regarded as the calcium food par excellence.

One pound of soya flour is equivalent to two pounds of meat in protein content. To the extent that people might consume one-half pound of soya bread per day instead of ordinary bread, the extra amount of protein in the soya bread is sufficient to replace a quantity of protein in over one-fourth of the daily intake of meat on the average. Meat protein costs five times that of soya protein.

Proteins are muscle-builders and are absolutely indispensable. There is a high quality protein content in soybeans, which makes them such a successful substitute for meat, milk, and eggs. They are the only natural food in the vegetable kingdom that contains a higher protein value than milk or eggs.

The soybean has life-giving properties that meat and other proteins do not have.

The soybean is king of the beans. It is a fine alkaline food, and there are many varieties of the soybean. For cooking purposes get the "easy cook" variety, as it cooks much quicker than other varieties. It is best to cook soybeans under a low steam pressure, five pounds of pressure for 40 to 60 minutes for most varieties. They should be cooked until tender, not mushy. Always soak the beans overnight before cooking. It is best to cook all beans under a low steam pressure.

Tofu is a low-calorie, high protein, cholesterol-free food.

Soybean Recipes

Soy patties

2 cups soybean pulp 1 onion, chopped fine

2 cups natural brown 1 tbs. soy sauce

  rice (cooked) ¼ tsp. salt

2 tbs. vegetable fat flavor with garlic, sage or

                whole wheat bread crumbs

- *Mix the first seven ingredients thoroughly together, and shape into patties. Roll the patties in whole wheat bread crumbs. Bake in a greased pan until brown, or warm in a frying pan, but do not fry.*

Soybean loaf

2 cups soybeans, cooked 1⅓ cups whole wheat

  and ground zwieback crumbs,

2 cups pinto bean pulp toasted

1 cup tomato juice 1 onion, chopped fine

1 cup finely 2 tbs. soy sauce

  chopped nuts spices to flavor

salt to taste

- *Mix ingredients thoroughly together. Add sage, celery seed, thyme, or other flavorings you like. Put in a greased baking dish and bake for 1 hour in a moderate oven.*

Use sage to flavor soybean loaf.

Onions are a basic ingredient in many savory dishes.

Soybean cottage cheese loaf

½ cup celery 3 cups soybean cottage cheese

parsley (see Cheese section, following)

1 cup onion 1 cup whole wheat bread crumbs

½ cup green pepper (toasted)

6 tbs. lemon juice ¼ cup peanut oil

6 tbs. soy sauce 1 tbs. chopped garlic

¾ cup raw peanut butter 1 heaping tsp. sage

salt to taste pinch cayenne pepper

- *Chop the celery, parsley, onion, and green pepper fine. Mix in the lemon juice, soy sauce, peanut butter, and cottage cheese. Then add the other ingredients and mix thoroughly. Put in a greased baking dish and bake in a moderate oven.*

Soybean milk no. 1

- *Take 1 pound soybeans, cover with water, and soak them overnight. In the morning wash them thoroughly, cover with fresh water, and bring to a boil. If the water is changed again a couple of times and brought to a boil each time, it helps to remove the soybean taste after the milk is made. Then drain and grind the beans. Put the beans in a fine-meshed sugar sack or cheesecloth and tie the top securely. Put the sack of ground soybeans in a large dish or pail. Pour 2 quarts of water over them; warm water is preferable as the milk has fat in it. Knead the sack of ground beans well, washing and squeezing the milk out. Pour off the milk into a large pan or pail. Pour 2 more quarts of water over the beans, and knead and squeeze out well again. Combine the second 2 quarts of milk with the first 2 quarts in a large flat-bottomed pan, and boil for 20 minutes or more, stirring constantly with a pancake turner from the bottom of the pan as it boils, so that it will not stick to the bottom of the pan. You may add a little malt honey, honey, or malt sugar, but do not make it too sweet. Add salt to taste. Do not cook in aluminum.*

Soybean milk no. 2

- *Take 1 pound soy meal (do not have it ground too fine) and 3 quarts of cold water. Mix and boil for 25 minutes. Strain, sweeten, and salt to taste. It is best to use a flat-bottomed pan, and stir with a pancake turner, as it burns very easily. If you desire it richer, add some soybean cream, the recipe for which is given later in this section.*
- *These soybean milks may be used in the same way as cow's milk. When using for cooking, do not sweeten. You may add the sweetening to the milk as it is used: it keeps fresh longer if the sweetening is not added. This milk is highly alkaline. It must be handled in the same way as cow's milk. When cooled, keep in an ice box or cool place, as it will sour in about the same length of time as cow's milk.*
- *This soybean milk makes a more nourishing and healthful chocolate milk than dairy milk.*

How to curd soybean milk

- *After making the soybean milk, while it is still boiling hot, add enough citric acid so it will curd at once. Use 3 or 4 tablespoonfuls of citric acid to the quart of boiling milk. Stir briskly and let set. The curds form within a few seconds, and it doesn't take long until the milk is curded. Skim the curd off the clear water and place in a double cheesecloth, squeezing out all the water, making the cheese as dry as possible.*
- *If a smooth cheese is desired, use less citric acid. If a granular cheese is liked, use more citric acid.*

Soybean jelly

4 cups soybean milk (unsweetened)
2 rounded tbs. agar-agar (flaky)
4 tbs. malt sugar

- *Soak the agar-agar in the soybean milk for 1 hour. Put in a saucepan, bring to a boil, and simmer slowly until the agar-agar is entirely dissolved. Add the sweetening and cool. Fresh fruit or fruit juice may be added for flavoring, if desired. Put on ice.*

Soybean butter

½ pint water
2 tbs. soybean flour
1 pint oil

- *Mix the water and flour together, put in a heavy iron frying pan, and boil for 5 minutes, or until thickened. Strain into a mixing bowl. Pour in 1 pint of soybean oil, very slowly, as in making mayonnaise, beating constantly. (You may use any good vegetable oil, but preferably not palm or coconut oil.) Use a blender for easier mixing.*

Soybean cream

1 pint rich soybean milk
½ pint soybean oil (or any vegetable oil)

- *Place the milk in a mixing bowl, and pour in the oil in a very small stream, beating constantly, until it is the desired thickness; if you desire a thick cream use more oil; if a thin cream, use less.*
- *If you do not have any soybean milk, use a heaping tablespoonful of soybean flour, and ½ pint of water. Mix and place in a frying pan, stirring with a pancake turner, and let it boil until thickened, for 5 minutes or a little more. Then strain, and proceed as above, beating in the oil until you have the desired thickness.*

Firm tofu (soybean curd) is made from soybean milk.

the malt sugar, and butter or mayonnaise. Put on stove and let boil for 5 minutes. Strain through a fine sieve or cheesecloth. Add vanilla or any crushed fruit or fruit juice you desire. Put in a freezer and freeze the same way as any other ice cream. Made in this way, ice cream can be melted and fed to invalids and infants.

"Egg yolk"

- You may use the following "egg yolk" in any recipe that calls for the yolk of an egg; it looks very much like egg yolk, tastes like it, and has very much the same properties, but no cholesterol.
- Take 1 heaping tablespoonful soybean flour, mix with ½ cup of water, put in a frying pan and boil until it thickens, stirring constantly so that it does not stick. Strain into a mixing bowl, and beat in soybean oil until it becomes thick enough to be cut with a knife. Use this wherever a yolk of egg is desired. Season with a pinch of salt, and use dandelion butter coloring for a little added color.

Vanilla adds flavor to soybean ice cream.

Soybean ice cream

1 tbs. agar-agar

2 quarts rich soybean milk

2 lbs. malt sugar

½ pint soybean butter or soybean mayonnaise

1 tsp. vanilla to taste, or crushed fruit or fruit juice as desired to taste

- Soak the agar-agar in cold water until it swells. Drain and put in soybean milk, add

Soy pancakes

1 cup cornmeal

1 cup soybean mash

1 cup soybean milk

½ cup malt sugar

salt to taste

½ cup soybean butter

- *To the corn meal and soybean mash add the soybean milk and beat up as ordinary pancake batter. Add the malt sugar, salt, and beat in the soybean butter.*

- *If the batter is used when very cold, the pancakes can be made nicely without yeast or baking powder. If the pancakes are for breakfast, it is well to soak the cornmeal in the soybean milk the night before.*

- *Some like these pancakes made with yeast. For raised pancakes, take one cake of Fleischmann's yeast, dissolve it in the soybean milk, and proceed as above, letting the batter rise for about an hour before baking.*

Soy pancakes can be made without yeast or baking powder.

Cheeses, Nuts, and Vegetable Protein Dishes

Soybean cottage cheese

- *This is made in the same way as ordinary cottage cheese. Use unsweetened soybean milk. Allow the milk to sour or clabber, then heat to body temperature until it separates from the whey. Drain in a very fine sieve or through cheesecloth. When it has drained dry, add a little rich soybean milk to soften and flavor, as you would add cream to ordinary cottage cheese. The addition of a little Kloss's Mayonnaise also improves the flavor and makes a richer product. Salt to taste. Some add a little honey; this makes it a tasty spread for children, and is a splendid nerve builder.*

Soybean cheese

5 lbs. raw peanut butter

1 or 2 quarts tomato purée

5 quarts soybean milk

- To 5 pounds of raw peanut butter add 1 quart of tomato purée, or if you prefer a strong tomato flavor, use 2 quarts. Stir in gradually 5 quarts of soybean milk, and put in a warm place until it develops lactic acid, or until it gets about as sour as cottage cheese. Then it is ready to use and can be placed in the refrigerator in a covered container. If you

Soybeans can be transformed into a number of dairy substitutes, including milk and cheese.

wish you may put it in cans (either No. 2 or No. 3), place in a large pan and cover with boiling water. Let this cook for 4 or 5 hours. If you have a steam pressure cooker, cook under 5 pounds of pressure for 2 or 3 hours. The cheese is then ready for serving.

Soybean cream cheese

- Use unsweetened soybean milk. Let stand until it thickens (not sour). Then put on the stove and boil a minute or two until the water separates from the whey. Put in a cheesecloth and wring dry. Run through a mill or blender until it is a smooth paste. Add a little rich soybean milk to soften and make a creamy consistency. Salt to taste. Kloss's Mayonnaise may also be added for richness.

Nut cheese no. 1

1½ pints water or soybean milk

1 lb. raw peanut butter

½ lb. soybean butter

salt to taste

- Pour the water into the peanut butter very slowly, stirring to a paste, gradually adding water until the entire amount has been used. If soybean milk is used instead of water, a better product is obtained. Let stand until it sours to suit the taste, thus developing lactic acid like the lactic acid found in buttermilk. Beat in the soybean butter and salt to taste.

It is now ready to use. Keep it covered in the refrigerator. You may also put it in cans and prepare as for Soybean Cheese, preceding.

Nut cheese no. 2

1 lb. raw peanut butter

4 tbs. ground oatmeal flour

1½ pints water

salt to taste

- Prepare in the same manner as Nut Cheese No. 1.
- Some of the Nut Cheeses which I make are much like the yellow American cheese, while others are similar to cream cheese. They are very agreeable to the taste, are high in food value and emulsified nut oils, are much easier to digest, and contain none of the harmful bacteria of ordinary cheeses found on the market. These nut cheeses may be put up in cans to keep them pure and sanitary. They are prepared in a way that develops lactic acid such as is found in yogurt, buttermilk, and cottage cheese.
- Those who cannot eat ordinary cheese made with rennet can eat freely of nut cheese, and there is no exposure to disease, as is the case with other cheeses.
- Nut cheese is more economical, and may be used in any way that the cheeses on the market are used. More food value is obtained for the money.

Malted nuts

1 cup raw peanut meal or raw peanut butter (peanut meal is preferable)
½ cup malt honey
few grains of salt

- *Mix all ingredients well. Place in a slow oven until thoroughly dried out, but do not brown. Then run through a mill, but do not grind it too fine because it must remain in a powder form, and not be as a butter. If iron pans are to be used, lay heavy brown paper in the bottom so that the nut mixture will not come in contact with the iron. If the oven is too hot, the nuts will turn too brown. Another way is to dry the nuts in the sun and then put in the oven for a while, or just long enough to cook them.*

Nut milk

1 cup raw peanut butter
½ cup milk sweetening (malt sugar or honey)
1 cup boiling water
few grains of salt

- *Mix the peanut butter and the milk sweetening thoroughly together. Use a heaping teaspoonful of this mixture to a cup of boiling water. Thoroughly mix, adding salt.*
- *This may be used as any other milk.*

Uses for kokofat

- *Kokofat is a trade name for the pure fat extracted from the coconut, one of the richest fats on the market. One-fourth less Kokofat than any other fat is needed in cooking. For instance, if a recipe calls for 1 pound of butter or Crisco in cooking or baking, you need only ¾ pound of Kokofat to get the same results.*
- *You can melt it, add some dandelion butter coloring, salt to taste, cool, and use in place of cow's butter. It can be used for baking and cooking in any way that you would use butter, makes very nice pie crust, is sweet, has no foreign taste, and keeps a long time without getting rancid.*

Coconut oil and nut butter

1 lb. coconut oil
½ lb. peanut oil
butter coloring
salt to taste

- *A fine butter is made by mixing these ingredients with an egg beater or an electric*

ADDENDUM

Coconut and palm oil are now known to be high in saturated fatty acids, and should be used sparingly if at all.

Shelled peanuts still in their skins.

Peanut butter

1 lb. blanched, raw peanuts

- *Run the peanuts through a peanut butter mill. This is a very excellent and wholesome butter. Peanut butter made this way can be diluted with water and used like cream, or spread on bread.*

Mock almond butter

- *Take 1 pound blanched peanuts, cover with water, and boil until they just begin to get tender, but not mushy. Drain off the water and dry the peanuts thoroughly. This can be done in the sun, or in a very slow oven if they are stirred frequently, but the nuts must not be browned at all. Grind them fine. This makes an excellent butter, which can be used in many ways. To eat with vegetables or fruit, add water until it is of the consistency of milk or cream.*
- *This same butter may be reduced with water, and lightly salted to taste, making a palatable and nourishing butter that is easy to digest.*

The entire peanut plant is removed during harvesting.

beater, beating until they are thoroughly blended. It is a wholesome butter with a delicious flavor.

To blanch peanuts

- *Buy shelled nuts and steam them for 2 to 5 minutes. Rub the nuts between the hands, or place them on a table and lightly press with a rolling pin to loosen the skins sufficiently to enable one to blow them away. Place on a cookie sheet in the oven at 350°F until they are a very light golden brown.*

Original meat or vegetable protein

- *Take 5 pounds strong gluten flour, which is ordinarily called bread flour. The gluten flour to use is not like ordinary white flour. It has more food value and more vitamins. Add 2 quarts of water, and make into a fairly stiff dough, about the consistency of bread dough. Let stand for 1 hour after mixing. Then put in a large pan and cover with water. Wash out the starch by working it with both hands. When the water becomes white with starch, pour it off, and put on fresh water. Repeat this until the water is clear; then all the starch will be washed out.*

- *If it is desired to have it very tender, cover this gluten with water and let stand a day or two under water. If the weather is cool it should stand about two days, but in warm weather, a day will be sufficient time. Do not let it stand too long, however, for the gluten will dissolve.*

- *Then cut the gluten mass in small pieces, dropping, as it is cut, into a pan of boiling water, containing enough water so that the gluten will float. Stir on the bottom of the pan with a pancake turner to prevent burning. Cook for half an hour.*

- *Remove from the water what is desired for immediate use and add a little soy sauce. This gives it a meat flavor.*

- *Always keep the gluten covered with water, both before it is cooked and afterwards.*

- *It can be warmed in a frying pan with a little Mazola or corn oil, seasoned with finely cut onions, if desired. Too much frying makes it tough, however.*

- *This vegetable protein can be used in stews, pot pies, vegetable roasts, or any place where lean beefsteak is used. It is excellent in vegetable soup.*

Vegetable roast

8 oz. strong cereal coffee

1 lb. washed gluten

5 oz. raw peanut meal

salt to taste

- *Mix all ingredients in a blender and thoroughly blend. Put it in cans, seal, and cook in a steam pressure cooker for about 4 hours under 5 pounds of pressure; or if in an open kettle, cook for 6 hours. This can also be put in a stone crock, placing the crock in a dish of water, and baked for 4 hours in a moderate oven. The placing of the crock in the dish of water is to prevent the meat from burning.*

- *This vegetable roast will be found to be an excellent product when cut in cubes, to combine with any kind of a vegetable stew that the housewife may wish to prepare.*

Vegetarian roast no. 1

2 tbs. ground onions

2 cups raw peanut butter

½ cup boiled kidney beans

3 cups water

ground celery seed to suit taste

- *Mix the ingredients, put in cans, seal, and cook for 4 hours under 5 pounds of pressure. This can also be placed in a crock and baked in the oven, as described in the directions for Vegetable Roast.*
- *Vegetarian Roast No. 1 can be used diced in casseroles, stews, and soups. It is also good sliced and browned for sandwiches.*

Vegetarian roast can be sliced for sandwiches.

Vegetarian roast no. 2

1 lb. raw peanut butter

1½ pints water

salt to taste

- *Add the water to the peanut butter a little at a time, stirring continuously to make a paste free from lumps. Add salt to taste. Cook from 1 to 4 hours. Can be boiled in a double boiler or cooked in the oven by placing the dish containing the roast in a dish of water to prevent it from burning.*
- *This roast should be of such a consistency that when it is cold it can be sliced and eaten. This is good made up into sandwiches, also diced in casseroles, stews, and soups.*
- *For Tomato Vegetarian Roast, prepare it just like the Vegetarian Roast No. 2, except use half water and half tomato juice; or all tomato juice if you like.*

Peanut butter is used in vegetarian roast.

Gluten patties

2 cups ground gluten

1 onion, finely chopped

2 cups crumbed zwieback, or cooked brown rice

½ cup soy sauce

½ tsp. salt

- *Flavor with garlic, Vegex, or sage. Mix thoroughly, make into patties, and brown in oven or frying pan.*

Vegetable salmon

1 lb. raw peanut butter

1 medium-sized carrot, ground very fine

1 No. 2 can of tomatoes, put through a fine sieve

1 pint water

- *Mix ingredients thoroughly and salt to taste. It is then ready to be put in cans, if desired, and cooked under 5 pounds of steam pressure for 4 hours. If cooked in an ordinary kettle, well covered with water, it will require 1½ to 2 hours longer boiling. This mixture can also be baked in the oven. First boil it a few minutes in an open saucepan, stirring constantly until it thickens, and then bake in a slow oven for 1 hour. It is then ready to serve. This is a very wholesome and palatable dish.*

How to cook brown rice

- *One cup brown rice will make 3 cups cooked rice. Bring 2½ cups water to a boil. Add ¾ tsp. sea salt. Stir in 1 cup of brown rice. Bring to a boil again. Cover tightly. Turn heat as low as possible. Steam for 50 minutes. Remove cover and leave over heat for a few minutes.*

Nut loaf

2 tbs. onions

2 tbs. celery

2 tbs. soy sauce

2 cups brown rice, cooked

1 cup nuts, chopped

½ cup whole wheat bread crumbs, toasted

soy milk to moisten

salt to taste

- *Chop onions and celery fine. Then mix all ingredients together thoroughly. Add more soy milk if too dry. Put loaf in a greased pan and bake in a moderate oven for ¾ hour.*

Gluten roast

2 cups sprouted lentils

2 cups washed gluten

- *Mix lentils and gluten together and run through an Enterprise grinder two or three times. Season with a little tomato, Vegex, or sage. Salt to taste. Cook for 4 hours in sealed tins under 5 pounds* of pressure. If cooked in an open vessel or double boiler, 6 hours cooking is required.

- To cook in the oven, make the material into a loaf, put in a greased pan and just barely cover the loaf with water. Place this pan in another larger pan containing water and bake for 1 hour in a moderate oven at 350°F. When done, pour the liquid off the loaf and use this for a gravy. It may be thickened with cornmeal and seasoned with Vegex or any vegetable extract.

A selection of sprouting legumes.

Soups

Soups can be made from any combination of vegetables one likes, such as celery, carrots, potatoes, parsley, onions, and okra. Other good vegetables for soup are dried beans such as navy, lima, Great Northern beans, or green split peas, soaked overnight in water and cooked very slowly until thoroughly done, then put through a fine sieve or colander to remove any of the outside covering of the bean that may not have cooked up soft. If the sifted pulp is too thick, thin out with soy or nut milk, flavor with onion, garlic, or parsley, which should be cut very fine, added to the sifted pulp, and heated about ten minutes before serving. Soy sauce, Savorex, or Vegex is good for flavoring. Use salt sparingly. Never use black or white pepper.

A good soy soup is made just as you make any other bean soup. Soybeans can be purchased in cans, which makes it easier for the average home to use them more freely. They are a wonderful food.

All nut milks may be used in place of soybean milk. Flavor with a little soy sauce if desired, to taste.

Much is said about vegetable juices, and they are good, but not everyone can digest raw vegetable juices. Make your own vegetable juices by using any vegetable or vegetables you wish. The dark leafy vegetables are very good. Cut the leaves fine, put them in cold water, bring to a boil, and boil gently for a few

Many different vegetables and beans can be made into soup.

minutes. Then pour the leaves into a fine-mesh bag and squeeze it to extract the juice. Then you have a real vegetable juice; use hot or cold. Flavor with soy sauce, onion juice, or any vegetable flavoring you like.

Vegetable soup no. 1

- *In a large soup kettle put about 1 cup each of the following vegetables: carrots, cabbage, celery, potatoes (do not peel the potatoes, but scrub with a wire brush, so the eyes will remain in the potatoes, as they are the life-giving part); and also ½ cup onions. Be sure to use the green leaves of the celery and the green leaves of the cabbage. The green leaves of the cauliflower are even better although they are generally thrown away. Add 1 gallon of water. After the soup has come to a boil, add 1 cup of brown rice, and simmer slowly from one to two hours, or more. Salt to taste.*

- *When the soup is done, you may, if desired, add 1 quart soybean milk, more or less to suit the taste.*
- *If the soup is to be fed to invalids, to small children, or to those who have ulcers or cancer of the stomach, let it simmer at least 2½ or 3 hours slowly. Then mash the vegetables with a wire potato masher and boil them a few minutes longer. Then strain the soup through a fine wire strainer, and add the soybean milk. Tomato juice may be added instead of the soybean milk if you like. This is a most wonderful alkaline dish and highly nourishing.*
- *When the soup gets cold, it is a very nourishing drink and very high in vitamins and life-giving properties, far superior to sauerkraut juice or tomato juice.*
- *One can add different kinds of green vegetables to suit one's own taste, and may also use more of one kind and less of others if preferred.*

Vegetable soup no. 2

2 large carrots, scraped

4 turnips

4 onions

parsley (use generously)

green leaves of cabbage, chopped

medium bunch of celery, using stalks and leaves

1 cup lima beans, fresh or frozen

1 cup green peas, fresh or frozen, or you may use a cup of puree made from the dried split peas and lima beans

soy sauce to taste

- *Cut the vegetables in small pieces, and do not boil hard. Let them simmer until cooked soft. Add a little salt and soy sauce when finished, if desired.*

Potato and onion soup

6 medium-sized unpeeled potatoes, sliced fine

3 good-sized onions, cut fine

5 tbs. parsley, chopped

2 quarts water

- Let simmer for 1 hour. Then add one heaping table-spoonful each of soybean flour and oatmeal flour, mixed thoroughly with a little cold water, and then added to the soup. Let boil for five minutes, salt sparingly, and serve.

Potato and onion soup.

Fruit soup

My parents used a great deal of fruit soup when I was a child.

2 cups raisins

2 cups prunes

4 quarts cold water

1 cup grape juice (unsweetened)

2 lemons

malt sugar or honey to sweeten to taste

- *Soak the raisins and prunes overnight. Then add them to the water and let them simmer until done. Add the grape juice and lemons,*

Theere are many versions of tomato soup, all good for health.

sliced very thin, and the sweetening to taste. This can be served hot or cold as you desire. This soup can be thickened with cornstarch or agar agar.

- Do not serve this soup with a vegetable meal; use whole wheat toast, whole wheat zwieback, whole wheat crackers, or any of the whole grain products, soybean gems, and nut products, or nuts; used in this way it makes a fine luncheon or fruit meal.

Cream of tomato soup

6 cups very rich soybean milk

6 cups tomato juice

6 rounded tbs. soybean flour

(make into a thin paste with cold water)

- You may also use a milk made from any nuts in place of soybean milk. Milk made from raw peanut butter is excellent, and so is almond milk.
- Heat the soybean milk. Then heat the tomato juice, add the soybean flour paste, stirring constantly. Do not let it boil, just simmer. After 5 minutes stir the thickened tomato juice into the hot milk, let heat a few minutes, add a pinch of salt and serve.
- Oatmeal water, made by soaking four parts of water to one part of oatmeal overnight and then strained, is an excellent addition to any soup stock. It increases the vitamins and makes the soup creamy.

Tomato soup no. 1

3 cups tomato juice

3 cups cold water

3 heaping tbs. soybean flour

- Mix the tomato juice and water, and bring to a boil. Make a thin paste of the soybean flour mixed with cold water, stir this into the hot tomato juice, and let simmer for 5 minutes. A heaping tablespoonful of soybean butter may be added to this. Let the soup get real hot, add a pinch of salt and serve.

Tomato soup no. 2

1 tbs. 3-minute oats

1 quart water

1 quart tomatoes

1 tbs. Kokofat

salt to taste

- Cook the 3-minute oats in boiling water for 10 minutes. Mash the tomatoes and put them through a flour sieve. Add the tomatoes to the water and then add the Kokofat. Boil for 5 minutes. Salt sparingly.

Cream of corn soup

1 pint fresh or canned corn

3 pints rich soybean milk

salt to taste

- Heat the milk. Put the corn through a sieve, and add to the hot milk. Salt to taste and serve.

Cream of celery soup

1 cup diced celery

1 pint soybean milk

½ pint water

½ tsp. salt

2 tbs. soybean butter

- *Cook the celery in the milk and water and when nearly done, add salt. Simmer until celery is soft. Add soybean butter just before serving.*

Cream of lentil soup

3 cups cooked lentils

1 pint rich soybean milk

1 quart water

salt

1 small, fresh onion, chopped fine or ¼ cup dried onion

vegetable extract such as Savorex or Vegex

parsley

2 tbs. soybean butter

- *Put the lentils through a sieve, add the soybean milk, and 1 quart of water; salt to taste. Season with onion, and a little vegetable extract. Just before serving, add finely cut parsley, and 2 tablespoonfuls soybean butter.*

Lentil soup

2 cups cooked lentils

¼ cup chopped, cooked carrots

¼ cup chopped green onions

1 cup tomato juice

2 cups lentil juice (the water that the lentils are cooked in)

½ cup finely cut parsley

- *Mix all the ingredients, heat to boiling point, add 1 tablespoonful soybean butter, salt to taste, and serve.*

Lentil soup is a nutritious recipe.

Potatoes add starch to soups.

Vegetable oyster (salsify) soup

3 cups vegetable oysters (cut in small rings)

2 cups water

2 cups rich soy milk

1 tbs. soybean butter

- *Cook the vegetable oyster rings in the water until tender. Add the soybean milk and butter. Salt to taste and serve.*

Cream of spinach soup

1 cup spinach pulp

2 cups rich soy milk

1 cup mashed potatoes

(as given earlier in this chapter)

2 cups potato water

1 tbs. soybean butter

- *Mix the spinach pulp and soybean milk, add the mashed potatoes and potato water, salt to taste, bring to a boil, add 1 tablespoonful soybean butter and serve.*

Potato soup

3 cups mashed potatoes

2 tbs. chopped onions

1 pint rich soybean milk

1 quart parsley or watercress for seasoning

- *Make the mashed potatoes by following the recipe given earlier in this chapter. Mix all the ingredients together, bring to a boil, add 1 tablespoonful soybean butter, and serve.*

Split pea soup

- *Cook until tender either green or yellow split peas. Rub the cooked peas through a sieve. To the pea puree add rich soybean milk until it reaches the desired consistency. Some gluten meat, diced small, will add greatly to this soup. Season with onions, garlic, parsley, or soybean sauce. Vegetable extract may also be used. Simmer for 5 minutes and serve hot.*

Gravies

Oatmeal gravy

1 quart boiling water

4 oz. oatmeal flour or 3-minute oats

1 tbs. oil

seasonings such as bay leaf, onion, or desired flavoring

Vegex or vegetable extract (to taste)

salt

- *Into 1 quart of boiling water stir gradually the 4 ounces of oatmeal flour, or 3-minute oats. Boil until thickened. If 3-minute oats are used, a little longer boiling is necessary than when oatmeal flour is used. Add about 1 tablespoonful corn oil, or any other good oil. The gravy may be seasoned with a little onion, bay leaf, or other seasoning as desired. Also add 1 teaspoon Vegex or vegetable extract, which will give it a meaty flavor.*
- *This makes a very wholesome and well-flavored gravy.*

Soybean gravy

- *Into 1 quart boiling soybean milk, add oatmeal flour or 3-minute oats (about 4 ounces) to make the desired consistency, or thickness. Oatmeal flour works quickest.*
- *Let simmer until thickened, stirring constantly with a pancake turner so it will not burn on the bottom. Add a little soy sauce or vegetable extract to lend a meaty flavor.*
- *This may be made with water instead of milk, and enriched with a little Kloss's butter, and a little fine cut onion to add to the flavor.*

Add a little chopped onion to soybean gravy to enhance the flavor.

Salads and Salad Dressings

Salads are refreshing and life-giving if made of any combination of vegetables that are fresh and crisp.

Do not combine fruits and vegetables in the same salad, as it is not a healthful combination. Have your vegetable salads with your vegetable meals, or make a good nourishing vegetable salad and eat with nuts or some good meat substitute for luncheon. Another time have a fruit salad with nuts or some good meat substitute for luncheon or with a fruit meal.

Do not use mayonnaise that has vinegar, mustard, black or white pepper, or cane sugar in it. If you wish to use mayonnaise, make your own. (See the recipe for soy oil mayonnaise later in this section.)

or slices of green pepper around the mixed vegetables and garnish with whole sprigs of parsley. Finely chopped or ground-up nuts sprinkled over this make a very nourishing salad or you can use the nuts whole. Ground-up nuts are the best, however, as very few people will chew the whole nuts enough to thoroughly emulsify them; thus they do not get the good of the nuts. Soy mayonnaise is very nice with this salad, and so are a few olives arranged around or over it.

Vegetable salad no. 1

1 cup finely diced or grated carrots
1 cup finely diced celery
1 cup cabbage, chopped fine
1 green pepper, cut in thin rings or
    fine slices
1 cup finely cut parsley
finely chopped nuts
olives

- *Mix the carrots, celery, and cabbage together and put as large a serving as you wish of these on lettuce leaves, arranging the rings*

Use any combination of crisp, fresh vegetables to make a salad.

Use radishes to make a vegetable salad.

Vegetable salad no. 2

green onions (spring)

green peppers

cucumbers

celery

parsley

radishes

watercress

- *Use equal parts of these vegetables. Chop or dice the green onions, celery, and green peppers; mince the parsley and watercress; mix and place a serving on lettuce leaves. If the cucumbers are nice, with a thin fresh skin, do not peel, but wash well. Cut in thin round slices or lengthwise and arrange with radishes around and over the other vegetables.*

Potato salad

potatoes

ripe olives

onions

parsley

celery

cucumbers

nuts

cayenne pepper

soy oil mayonnaise

radishes

- *Prepare the potatoes by boiling with the skins on, and drying them on the hot stove burner when done so they are dry and mealy. Cool the potatoes and skin them.*
- *Have the onions, celery, and ripe olives chopped quite fine, mince the parsley, and mix with your diced cucumbers and potatoes. Leave the skin on the cucumber if it is a nice thin skin. Salt moderately, add finely ground-up nuts or halves of walnuts, and a pinch of cayenne. Mix with soy oil mayonnaise, and garnish with radishes and parsley.*

Potatoes should be cooked in their skins.

Fruit Salads

In making fruit salads be careful of your combinations. Citrus fruits do not combine well with other fruits, such as dates and figs. Avocados may be used with citrus fruits. Combine these as you wish, using figs and dates as a garnish. When using avocados, sprinkle some lemon juice over them. Any kind of nuts may be used with a fruit salad. Finely ground nuts sprinkled over the salad make it more nourishing.

Good combinations for fruit salads

- Ripe bananas, fresh or dried coconut, shredded or ground, cherries, and pineapple
- Apples, raisins, and walnuts
- Bananas, apples, and pineapple
- Ripe strawberries and ripe bananas
- Red raspberries and bananas
- Black raspberries and bananas
- Ripe pears, strawberries, and bananas
- Fresh peaches, cantaloupe, and Thompson seedless grapes

Fresh coconut is a good combination with fresh fruit.

All berries and fruits must be vine-ripened and tree-ripened to be really valuable for food. Be sure that bananas are fully ripened; they must not show any green on the ends and must be sprinkled with brown spots.

Salads look nice served on lettuce leaves. Soy oil mayonnaise diluted to the consistency of cream is delicious with fruit salads.

Make sure fruits are fully ripened before eating.

Fruit salad

½ cup wheat flakes

½ cup diced or chopped raw apples

½ cup chopped raisins

- *It is best to soak the raisins overnight before using. More or less of any ingredient may be used to suit the convenience and taste. Mix ingredients together and serve. This makes a salad that anyone can live on.*

Soy oil mayonnaise can be made to any consistency you wish.

Soy oil mayonnaise

1 heaping tbs. finely ground flour

½ pint cold water

½ pint soy oil

1 tbs. lemon juice (more or less to taste)

pinch of salt

paprika and cayenne

vegetable butter coloring

- *Mix the soy flour into the cold water; boil for five minutes. Cook in a smooth flat-bottomed dish, using a pancake turner for stirring to keep free from the bottom of the dish, as it burns very quickly. Strain through a fine sieve into a medium-sized mixing bowl.*

While beating rapidly and continuously, or using a blender, pour in the soy oil in a very fine stream. If the oil is poured in fast, the mayonnaise will separate after standing awhile. (If this should happen, pour the oil off, and beat again.) It will be very simple after you have made it a few times. Then add the salt, paprika, cayenne, and vegetable butter coloring and beat just enough to mix well. It needs only a small pinch of cayenne to make it taste snappy. Using more or less soy oil, you may make it any consistency you wish. Peanut oil may be used in place of soy oil, but I prefer the soy oil and soy flour.

- *A clove of garlic cut and rubbed on the bowl in which the mayonnaise is made greatly adds to the flavor.*

Kloss's mayonnaise

½ cup water

¼ cup soy milk powder

¼ tsp. sea salt

¼ tsp. paprika

¼ tsp. seasoning of your choice

½ cup oil

lemon juice

- *Blend the first five ingredients in a blender. Add ½ cup oil slowly while blending at high speed. Remove from blender. Add 3 tablespoons lemon juice or according to taste.*

Lemon adds a zesty taste to homemade mayonnaise.

- *This mayonnaise can be used anywhere that dairy cream is used. It makes a very fine dressing for coleslaw or any kind of greens.*
- *A little cayenne pepper may be added if a snappy mayonnaise is desired. To add the cayenne pepper, sprinkle it a little at a time directly into the mayonnaise, beating until it is thoroughly mixed.*
- *Red pepper or cayenne is a wonderful medicine, and does not injure the product. Cayenne pepper should not be classed with black and white pepper, or mustard and vinegar, which are found in the mayonnaise on the market and are highly injurious to the digestive tract and stomach.*

"Nut mayonnaise"

- *Dilute ½ cup raw peanut butter or mock almond butter (see recipe given earlier in this chapter) with 1 cup of water. Then beat in 1 cup of oil, either corn or olive oil. Add about 1 tablespoonful lemon juice. Salt to taste.*
- *This can also be boiled for 2 or 3 minutes, and then beaten thoroughly.*

Milk sweetening

1 cup malt honey

1 cup corn or olive oil

- *Pour the corn or olive oil into the malt honey, beating constantly. Pour slowly. In this way the fat is emulsified and easily digested.*

Breakfast Foods

French toast

- *Slice soybean or other bread about one-half inch thick and let dry in a moderately warm oven. When thoroughly dry, increase the heat in the oven enough to turn the bread a golden brown. This browning turns the starch into dextrose or grape sugar, making it practically like the juice in ripe fruit.*

- *Now immerse the toast in soybean milk, being careful not to leave it too long. Lift out with a pancake turner, and spread a thin coating of Kloss's Mayonnaise on each slice. Have your frying pan hot with a little oil in it, place the toast in with the side down that has the mayonnaise on it. Now, spread the top side with mayonnaise, leaving until the under side is browned, then turn it over until the top side is browned.*

- *Serve with diluted malt honey, honey, or maple syrup. French toast can be served with any meal, but is especially nice for breakfast. French toast, with a cup of hot soybean milk, is nice for a light supper.*

- *This toast makes a wholesome and easily digested dish, containing all the necessary food elements.*

Zwieback is a wholesome, easily digested food that can be served with any meal.

Zwieback

- *Bread baked in the ordinary way is never entirely dextrinized, so that the starch turns into grape sugar. But zwieback, or twice-baked bread, is very wholesome and easy to digest.*

- *To make zwieback, slice the bread about ¾ inch thick, and let it dry in a slow oven until it is entirely dry. Increase the temperature of the oven and brown the bread to a golden brown. It must be carefully watched, as it burns easily.*

Breakfast wheat

1 cup natural whole grain wheat

3 cups water

salt to taste

- *Place all ingredients in a double boiler and cook until the kernels burst. Raisins, pitted dates, or chopped figs may be stirred into the wheat just before serving. These give a natural sweetness and are far better for the system than cane sugar.*

- *This can also be cooked in a steam pressure cooker until the kernels are done, for about 1 hour, or in a crock in the oven; set the crock in a pan of water to keep the wheat from burning and cook about 4 hours; or cook in an electric crock pot overnight.*

Malt honey

- *Take 1 pound of wheat or cornmeal. Add 8 quarts of water. Let it come to a boil and boil it until it thickens so that the starch is cooked. Cool to between 140° and 170°F. Then add 2 ounces of barley malt, either in powder or syrup form. Stir. Let stand until the starch is changed into dextrose or malt honey. When the water is clear, pour or siphon it off, being careful not to get any mash from the bottom, otherwise the malt honey will not be clear. Now boil it down to the consistency of syrup.*

Malt honey can be diluted before use.

Old-fashioned granola

- *Take whole wheat flour and enough water to make a stiff dough. Roll it out about a quarter or half an inch thick. Put in oven and bake until it is partly dextrinized, nearly a golden brown. Take a hammer and break it up and grind through a Quaker City Mill made by the A. W. Straub Company of Philadelphia. After grinding, put in a baking pan and reheat to slightly dextrinize it.*

Boiled rice

1 cup natural brown rice

3 cups water

salt to taste

- *Put 1 cup of rice and 1 teaspoon of salt into a pan, pour on 3 cups of boiling water, cover tightly and simmer on low heat without stirring for 45 minutes, when the rice will be thoroughly cooked but not mushy.*

Baked rice

½ to ¾ cup natural brown rice

2 cups soybean milk

½ tsp. salt

- *Wash and drain the rice. Pour the hot milk into a baking dish and add the rice. Cover and bake in a slow oven for 2 to 3 hours without stirring, or until the milk is thickened and creamy with rice. If the milk boils out under the cover, the oven is too hot.*

Natural brown rice is wholesome and versatile.

- *This makes a very delicious dish, and does not require any additions. If a dressing is desired, however, milk sweetening, the recipe for which was given earlier in this chapter, may be diluted with a little water or soybean milk and poured over the rice. Fig marmalade may also be used with rice: see the recipe for Fig Marmalade Pie.*
- *An excellent rice pudding can be made by adding ½ cup malt honey and 1 cup of raisins just before placing the rice in the oven to bake.*

Dixie kernel

1 cup cornmeal

1 cup oatmeal

1 cup whole wheat flour

1 cup finely ground bran

1 tsp. salt

- *Mix all ingredients and add enough water to make a stiff dough. Roll out to about ½ inch thickness. Bake in a moderate oven until slightly browned. When a day old, grind up while still a little moist.*
- *Add 1 cup of water to a cup of malt honey, mixing thoroughly. Sprinkle this over the ground cereal product. Do not let the mixture get too moist. Now spread out to partly dry, and then place in an oven to dextrinize, making a slight golden brown.*

Graham crackers can be ground to make breakfast food.

Old-fashioned dixie kernel

- *Take various kinds of broken crackers, such as bran, whole wheat, oatmeal, graham and white, and grind them together.*
- *Take equal parts each of malt honey and water, stirring well together, and sprinkle over the ground crackers, mixing them up thoroughly to slightly moisten them. Place in the oven, stirring frequently to prevent burning, and slightly dextrinize to a golden brown.*
- *This makes a very delightful breakfast food.*

Cooking Under Steam Pressure

The best way to preserve nutrients when cooking

We hear much about cooking with steam pressure. Some condemn it and some recommend it. In this chapter I will give some of my practical experiences, which I believe prove its value. I have had much experience with steam pressure cooking for many years, and had the honor of securing the first patent on a home steam pressure cooker ever granted in the United States. This cooker is now used over practically the entire civilized world.

Some time ago I read a long argument against steam pressure cooking. The doctor who made this argument is well-known in the United States; therefore, I shall not mention his name. His experiment proves that he is not a competent judge of steam pressure cooking. He spoke of having cooked wheat, corn, oats, barley, rye, buckwheat, and sunflower seed for two hours under thirty pounds of steam pressure. These cooked grains were fed to such animals as rats, guinea pigs, etcetera. These small animals became sick and paralyzed in a few weeks. From these facts the doctor concluded that steam pressure cooking is detrimental to food.

I have operated canning factories large and small, and have visited many other large canning factories, but have never yet heard of anyone cooking food under thirty pounds of steam pressure for two hours, nor even for one hour under any such pressure. People used to cook navy beans and corn under ten to fifteen pounds of pressure for one hour. Most steam pressure cooking is done at about five pounds of steam pressure, which is ideal. In California a law was passed forbidding certain foods to be cooked using more than five pounds of steam pressure.

There is no kind of cooking, either in a kettle or in a baking oven, that preserves the life-giving properties better than closing the foods tightly in a steam pressure cooker and cooking them until thoroughly done. I have had the privilege at different times of feeding groups of people where everything was cooked under steam pressure. We use the steam pressure cooker in our home with most gratifying results.

Potatoes are very delicious cooked in this way. Medium-sized potatoes will cook in twenty minutes

Comparative amount of heat developed for each pound of pressure in the pressure cooker

Steam Pressure (Lbs. per square inch as shown on steam gauge)	Degrees of Heat Fahrenheit (Boiling point of water is 212°F)
1	216
2	219
3	222
4	225
5	227
6	230
7	233
8	235
9	237
10	240
11	242
12	244
13	246
14	248
15	250

Table 1

Spinach retains its vitamins and minerals when cooked under steam pressure.

in a steam pressure cooker under five pounds of pressure. When you take them out, they are dry and mealy and have an excellent flavor, providing of course that they had a good flavor to start with.

Spinach is wonderful when cooked under steam pressure. It retains all of its life-giving qualities when cooked under a low pressure, say five pounds for 2 to 5 minutes, depending somewhat on the condition of the spinach. A canning recipe book comes with every steam pressure cooker, giving all the details on how to cook each food and how to use the steam pressure cooker.

The following table shows the comparative amount of heat developed for each pound of pressure in the pressure cooker.

The steam pressure cooker is one of the finest cooking utensils that has ever been invented. You can cook everything without putting water on it.

You can also put several different foods in the cooker, cook them all at the same time, and each food will retain its natural flavor. Another advantage is that breakfast food or any other food can be cooked in a steam pressure cooker without having to stir it. It does not have to be watched, for it will never burn.

There is no way to cook foods that will preserve the life-giving properties, vitamins, and flavor more perfectly than under steam pressure. At the same time, it is a great fuel saver. After the food starts to cook, only a little heat is required to keep up the temperature. It also requires less attention than any other way of cooking, because, as previously mentioned, food will not burn or stick to the cooker. After you have set the pressure where you want it, you can go away and let it cook as long as necessary.

Baking and Breads
Tips and techniques

General principles

Food must be prepared properly to be easily digested and thoroughly assimilated. Our physical well-being depends on this. Considering cooking's importance to health, we do not give it the attention it deserves. A thorough knowledge of healthful cooking is just as essential to health as is eating good food.

Successful cooking and baking depend largely upon using the best quality of food. But even the best food is often damaged during preparation. When food is not prepared in a wholesome, appetizing manner, it is more difficult for it to make good pure blood that is necessary to build up wasted tissues. For health's sake, food must be prepared in a simple manner and be free from grease.

Flour, salt, yeast, and water are mixed together to make fermented bread.

Ninety percent of all human ills originate in the stomach, and are caused from overeating wrong combinations of food, or unwholesome, unnatural foods. Remember, properly cooked food is always much easier for the body to digest.

All food should be prepared in one of the following ways: boiled, steamed, simmered, stewed, braised, roasted, broiled, or baked. Do not eat fried foods; they are indigestible and harmful to the system.

Making bread

Breads are divided into two classes: fermented and unfermented. Fermented bread is made light by a ferment, yeast usually being employed. Unfermented bread is made light by the introduction of air into the dough or batter. This method will be discussed later.

Yeast or fermented bread

Fermented bread is generally made by mixing flour, water, salt, and yeast into a dough. A small amount of malt extract, malt honey, or honey may be added, if desired, as it increases the food value and hastens fermentation. This is the straight dough method. The dough is kneaded until it is elastic to the touch and does not stick to the board, the object being to incorporate air and to distribute the yeast uniformly. The dough is then covered and allowed to rise until it has doubled its bulk, and does not respond to the touch when tapped sharply, but gradually and stubbornly begins to sink.

At this stage, the dough is "ripe," and ready to be worked down (kneaded). It will require from

The dough is kneaded until it is elastic to the touch.

2 to 3½ hours to rise, depending on the grade and consistency of the flour used, the temperature of the room in which it is set, and the amount of yeast used. This process is best accomplished at a temperature ranging from 80° to 90°F.

After rising, the bread is again worked down well, turned over in the bowl, and left to rise until about three-quarters its original bulk.

Then it is turned out on a board, kneaded together enough to work out the air, and cut up in loaf-size pieces. It takes 1 pound plus 3 or 4 ounces of the dough to make a one-pound loaf.

Knead the dough until the air has been worked out and leave it on the board a few minutes so it will rise just a little. You will find that this improves the texture of the bread.

Then form into loaves and knead just enough to work out the air. Do not knead too much.

With a little experience you will become a master at bread making.

Instructions for baking bread are given in the section titled "The Oven," following.

Sponge bread

Bread is also made by setting a "sponge" at the beginning. That is, by making a batter of the water, the yeast, and part of the flour, and letting it rise until it is light. Then the remaining ingredients are added and the mixture worked into a dough. Bun and cracker dough is usually set with the sponge method, because it produces a very fine and light texture. Ordinary white and whole wheat breads are often made by the same process.

A sponge is light enough when it appears frothy and full of bubbles. The time required will vary with the quantity and quality of yeast used, as well as with the temperature of the room in which it is set to rise.

Yeast

The most convenient yeast is dry yeast, which is always reliable and can be obtained in most grocery stores.

In Bible times families used to keep a little of their dough in an earthen vessel from one baking time to another. This sour dough was used for yeast in bread making. My mother used this.

Sometimes in the early days we would go to a brewery and for two pennies we would get nearly a two-quart pail full of yeast. This yeast was just the same as the Fleischmann's yeast today, only it was in liquid form.

Bread raising

A proper place for bread to rise when you make your own bread is of great importance in order to have good bread and to have it good every time. I have at different times used an ordinary, clean, wooden dry goods box, put some shelves in it, and made a door through which I could put my big bread pan. Then I made a place below the lower shelf where I could set a lighted lamp with a little dish of water above it to keep the box at an even temperature. You can also put in a large dish of hot water, or heat some soapstones or bricks wrapped in a piece of paper or cloth to heat the box to an even temperature. There must be considerable space between these soapstones and the first shelf upon which your bread is set. In such a compartment the sponge can be raised as well as the bread after it is put in pans.

I have also found a common oats sprouter, made of galvanized iron, very convenient. They are easily obtained and sold everywhere, by Sears, Montgomery Ward, and others. An oats sprouter

Whole wheat bread should not rise as high as white bread.

has a hot water tank over a lamp, which can be regulated to get an even temperature to raise bread. This is a very valuable device to have in any household and will pay for itself in a short time. You can also use this useful device to make malt, as well as to sprout different grains and legumes for table use. Of course, anyone handy with a saw and hammer can make a wooden box, as described in the preceding paragraphs, to serve the same purpose.

Sometimes, bread is left standing around on the table subject to drafts and it gets too cold while it is trying to rise. Furthermore, I never advise that bread be set to rise all night, unless the proper yeast cannot be obtained, in which case a slow and long process of rising is made necessary because of the yeast.

Put enough yeast in the bread to cause it to rise in 2 or 3 hours. The first time the bread should rise high enough just before it falls so that when it is touched it will go down. Should it happen that it rises so much that it falls, it is necessary that it be kneaded and allowed to rise again before it is put in the pans. After it is in the pans, it should rise half its size before it is put in the oven. If the bread rises too much while in the pan it will be coarse and full of holes. Should it accidentally rise too high, knead it over and let it rise again.

Whole wheat flour bread must not be permitted to rise as light in the pans as white flour bread. Care in this respect will preserve in the bread that sweet, nutty, wheat flavor that is so characteristic of bread made from the entire grain, but which will be lacking if the loaves rise too light in the pans.

Good bread is easy to make at home—white and brown breads are usually made using the same method.

Make it a business to have good bread, and do not give up until you do. Be determined, and say as many others have said, "I can make anything that anyone else can."

Some years ago I held a food demonstration in one of the Southern states. A Southern woman who attended one of these demonstrations had never made a loaf of bread in her life. All she had ever learned to make was soda and baking powder biscuits. She learned to make some very fine bread in only a single lesson. I furnished the flour, so I knew it was whole wheat flour. The first batch she made did not turn out very well, for the sole reason that the oven was not hot enough. The second batch was very fine. After one learns how it is very easy to make good bread.

If you will only be determined to have good bread, with a little experimenting you will succeed. I know a twelve-year-old girl who bakes delicious bread.

The oven

Daughter's Note: *This section refers to the old wood-burning range in common use at the time this book was written, and not to a modern gas or electric range.*

It is very important that one has a good oven in order to make good bread. I have many times found ovens in which the side of the bread nearest the fire box would burn, or sometimes it would burn on top, or on the bottom. This can be remedied to some extent in most ovens. If the bread does not bake evenly on the top, side, and bottom, there is something wrong with the oven.

If the bread burns too quickly on the side where the fire is, you can take the grate out of the firebox, spread a layer of fire clay next to the oven, or put asbestos paper behind the grate. If the bread burns

Traditional wood-fired bread cooked in a brick oven.

on the bottom, you can lay a piece of asbestos or a piece of tin on the bottom of the oven. Often if a piece of wire fencing with small mesh is placed on the bottom of the oven, a little bit of air space being left between the bread pan and the bottom of the oven prevents the bread from burning on the bottom. If the bread does not bake enough on the bottom, it is evident that too much soot and ashes are in the oven and the stove needs cleaning out

For whole wheat bread, the oven should be heated to 450°F, then gradually reduced to 350°F to 300°F. It is well to have an oven thermometer, which you can find for sale in any department store for around $1.50 to $2.50. If you have no thermometer, the oven should be hot enough so the bread will begin to brown in fifteen minutes.

Be sure your oven is hot enough. If it is not, your bread will not be good. After the bread is thoroughly heated, reduce the oven temperature. If the same temperature were kept, it would burn the bread on the outside. Therefore, as mentioned in the preceding paragraph, the temperature should be gradually reduced from 450°F to about 350°F and then at last to about 300°F. Bake your bread thoroughly, allowing an hour to one and one-quarter or one and one-half hours in the oven.

Old-fashioned clay oven

Before the iron stove came into existence, people baked bread in various ways. Sometimes they baked on the hearth of a fireplace, sometimes between two hot stones, and sometimes they baked it in hot ashes, and toasted ears of corn upon the coals. In some countries they made

Bread cooked in a wood-burning stove has a delicious crust.

ovens of clay and straw, similar to the way the Egyptians made brick.

My parents had one of these clay ovens. It was made like this: we built a platform about 2½ feet high of 2-inch thick lumber. The platform we had was about 5 feet wide and 6 or 7 feet long. These boards were heavily covered with clay mixed with cut straw, then one layer of brick was laid over them so it left a very smooth and nice surface on top. Then an arch from wooden slats was built over that. The arch was about 2 feet in height in the center. The back was closed except for a short chimney, and this was covered with a small piece of tin to hold the heat after the fire was taken out of the oven. The arch was covered with two or three layers of clay mixed with cut straw. A door was left in front, through which the oven was fired, and also for putting in and taking out the bread. After the oven was all finished, a slow fire would be started in it, which would dry out the clay. After the clay was partly dried, the fire would be increased, and it would burn this clay into brick in much the same way as bricks are made.

When we wanted to get the oven ready for bread making, we built a fire inside. When the bread was ready to go, all the coals and fire were raked out and the oven cleaned off. Many times the bread was put right on the brick, but we usually put it in pans. In this oven we baked lovely bread with a beautiful crust. We generally arranged the fire so we could leave the bread in the oven from an hour to an hour and a half.

It would be a great blessing if every home had an oven of this kind and people made their own bread today.

The finest bread may be made in this kind of an oven, because it bakes just right. The oven should be hot enough so that in 15 minutes the bread will begin to brown. Then allow the heat to gradually diminish, as it naturally would in the clay oven, as the fire was all taken out. Such ovens can also be made so there is a little fireplace on the front part that opens into the oven, with a chimney on the opposite side. Then you can fire while you are baking.

Use of steam in the oven

It is much easier to get a good crust on bread without burning it if there is steam in the oven. This may be accomplished by placing a small pan of water in the oven. Some of the big bakeries that have chain ovens bake bread in 900°F heat in 20 to 25 minutes, using considerable steam in the oven to keep the bread from burning.

Toasted homemade bread.

Zwieback

No bread is entirely dextrinized, or turned into grape sugar; therefore zwieback or twice-baked bread, in which this process is completed, is very wholesome and very easy to digest. A good way to make zwieback is to slice the bread about one-half inch thick, and let it dry out in the sun, or in a slow oven, until it is entirely dry.

I have kept zwieback an entire year in fine shape in a common barrel lined with heavy brown paper. During this time there was a long period of wet weather, and it seemed as if the zwieback had gathered a little moisture, but there was not a trace of mold; I put it outdoors on paper in the sun and let it dry out thoroughly again, and after it had

been heated in the oven, it was just as good as when it was freshly made. I did this for experimental purposes.

Zwieback should be made an important part of our diet, and if rightly handled, will save a great deal of time and expense. I have at times, when I was not in a position to bake my own bread, had some bakery make twenty-five, fifty, and even up to four hundred loaves of good whole wheat bread, using my own recipe, for myself and neighbors to make into zwieback. As mentioned earlier, the bread can be sliced evenly and dried out in an oven or out-of-doors in the sun until it is perfectly dry. Then heat the oven and brown it slightly on both sides. Use for breakfast or lunch time. To make an excellent lunch, serve it with fruits, or fruit juices, soybean milk or malted nut cream. Use it any way you like, but make it a practice to have a large supply of zwieback on hand.

Combinations of grains and legumes in breads

In Bible times they used to combine different grains and legumes and make them into bread. "Take thou also unto thee wheat, and barley, and beans, and lentils, and millet and fitches, and put them in one vessel, and make thee bread thereof." (Ezekiel 4:9)

A number of seeds have been used in bread since Abraham's time and are still used by the Germans and others, such as caraway, gimmel, anise, rue, fennel, and dill. All of these have medicinal properties. They are all good for indigestion, and

Aromatic caraway seeds are often added to rye bread.

prevent fermentation. For gas and colic, rue was quite frequently used, even by the priests in Christ's time. It has a wonderfully quiet, soothing effect upon tired and weary brains.

People would do well today if they would use more of these things instead of the abundant luxuries that destroy both soul and body.

Bread baking in Bible times

In early Bible times when ovens were rare, sometimes a number of women would bake their bread in one oven, as in Leviticus 26:26, where ten women baked bread in one oven. From ancient times until recent years, bread, legumes, and fruit seemed the main diet. In ancient times, bread, raisins, and figs were used a great deal. Abigail brought two hundred loaves of bread, one hundred clusters of raisins, and two hundred cakes of figs with some other things to David. (1 Samuel 25:18)

All kinds of seeds can be used when making bread.

Bread Recipes

Many good bread recipes can be found in almost any cookbook. Leave out the harmful ingredients and use only those that are wholesome.

Where these recipes advise grease or oils of any kind, use a little raw peanut butter, which is very rich in oil; and for the sweetening use malt sugar or Karo syrup, which enriches the bread, gives it a very excellent flavor, and keeps it moist.

The bread is done when it shrinks away from the sides of the pan. Remove at once from the pan and cool on a wire rack, away from drafts.

Whole wheat bread

(3 loaves)

1 cake compressed yeast

3 cups warm water

2 tbs. Karo syrup

1 tbs. salt

7 cups whole wheat flour

- *In a large mixing bowl, crumble the yeast into the warm water. Stir in the Karo syrup, and salt. Add the flour and mix all the ingredients to a medium soft dough. Turn out on a slightly floured board, and knead until elastic to the touch, about 20 to 30 minutes. Then return the dough to the bowl, cover, and let stand in a warm room. The dough should rise until, when tapped sharply, it begins to sink. This takes about 2 hours. Work the dough down well, turn*

Whole wheat bread is wholesome and tasty.

over in the bowl, and let rise again to half again its size; then shape into loaves and put into pans for baking.

- *Let rise until half again its original bulk, then bake in a preheated 400°F oven for at least 1 hour or longer. These coarse breads must be watched closer during the rising than* those made from white flour, as they get light in much less time.

- When taking bread from the oven, sponge it off with a cloth that has been dampened in cold water or oil. Soybean or nut milk, however, may be used in place of water to improve the bread. Set the loaf on a wire rack to cool off quickly, and the crust will be brittle and tender.

Rye bread

(2 loaves)

1 cake compressed yeast

3 cups lukewarm water

1 tbs. caraway seed (optional)

5 cups rye flour

1 cup sifted white flour

1 tbs. salt

- The white flour should be flour strong in gluten. It should be the same as that used when making washed gluten for nut foods.
- Dissolve the yeast in 1 cup of lukewarm water. Add the caraway seed, if used, and 2½ cups rye flour, or enough to make a sponge. Beat well. Cover and set aside in a warm place, free from drafts, to rise for about 2 hours.
- When the sponge is light, add the white flour, the rest of the rye flour or enough to make a soft dough, and the salt. Turn out on a board and knead for at least 10 minutes. Place in bowl, cover, and let rise until it doubles in bulk. This takes about 2 hours.

- Turn out on a board and shape into two long loaves. Place in shallow pans, cover, and let rise again until light—about 1 hour. Turn on the oven to 375°F. With a sharp knife lightly cut three strokes diagonally across the top of each loaf, and place in the oven. Bake at 375°F, a slower oven than when making white bread, for 30 to 35 minutes.

Note By adding ½ cup of sour dough, left from a previous baking, an acid flavor is obtained that is considered by many a great improvement for rye bread. This should be added to the sponge. My mother made nearly all her bread from sour dough, saved from previous baking, both rye and whole wheat. As nearly as I can remember now, she would save about a pint of dough from her baking and keep that until the next baking. It would be sour enough to start the yeast germs. Then she would work the bread the same as directed.

Rye bread can be worked much the same as whole wheat bread. Rye flour does not contain as much gluten as wheat, and therefore it does not rise as light as whole wheat flour without the addition of wheat flour strong in gluten. I have made a splendid loaf of rye bread with 3½ cups of rye flour and ½ cup of strong white gluten flour. You may also use 3 cups of whole rye flour and 1 cup of whole wheat flour, strong in gluten, to make a splendid rye loaf.

Whole wheat raisin bread

(2 loaves)

1 cake compressed yeast

1 cup lukewarm water

6 cups whole wheat flour

¾ cup malt honey, malt sugar, or Karo syrup

1 cup raisins, well-floured

1 tsp. salt

1 cup raw peanut butter

4 tbs. oil

Raisins are a popular addition to bread.

All kinds of dried fruits and nuts can be added to the bread mix.

- *Dissolve the yeast in 1 cup lukewarm water. Add 2 cups flour, and the malt honey, and beat until smooth. Cover and set aside to rise in a warm place, free from drafts, until light, which will take about 1½ hours.*
- *When well risen, add the floured raisins, the rest of the flour or enough to make a moderately soft dough, and the remainder of the ingredients. The raw peanut butter should be dissolved in a cup of lukewarm water. If the dough is too soft, add a little more flour, and the next time use less water.*
- *Knead lightly. Place in a well-greased bowl, cover, and let rise again until double in bulk about 1½ hours. Shape into loaves, fill well-greased pans half full, cover, and let rise until light about 1 hour.*
- *Bake at 400°F for 10 minutes and then at 375°F for 40 to 50 minutes longer.*

Steamed graham bread

(2 loaves)

1 cake compressed yeast, dissolved in a little warm water

3 cups nut milk

1 tsp. salt

1 cup malt honey or Karo syrup

2 cups cornmeal

3½ cups of graham flour

- *Mix the yeast, nut milk, salt, and malt honey together; then mix the cornmeal and flour, and stir into the liquid. Put into two well-greased basins or empty cans and steam under 5 pounds of steam pressure for 2½ or 3 hours. Then the bread can be put in a moderate oven and browned a little for 15 minutes, if desired.*

Health gems or crackers

These gems (an old-time name for muffins) are good for those suffering with Bright's disease, diabetes, liver, or kidney troubles and may be made as follows.

- *Put 2 cups of whole wheat flour in a pan on the stove, over a medium heat. Stir it frequently with a wooden paddle until it is very slightly golden brown or what we call dextrinized. Remove from the heat.*

- *To the whole wheat flour add 1 cup of soybean flour and 1 cup of boiled spinach or ½ cup of powdered spinach. Then add some peanut milk, made from raw peanut butter. (To make peanut milk, mix raw peanut butter into a cream with water to the consistency of thin cream or cow's milk.) The batter should be just thick enough so it will drip from a spoon. Salt to taste. Place batter in paper baking cups in a muffin pan or you may grease the pan instead. Bake at 425°F. for 20 minutes or until nicely browned.*

- *If you wish to make a cracker, more flour will need to be added. Roll it out to any thickness you want, and cut it to any size you desire. This makes a most wonderful product, either as a cracker or a gem. Mashed, cooked carrots may be used in place of spinach, and also 2 or more tablespoonfuls of malt honey or Karo syrup may be added. Bake in the oven at 350°F for 15 minutes or until lightly browned.*

Honey can be used when making sweet breads and muffins.

Soybean bread no. 1

(2 loaves)

2 lbs. whole wheat flour

1 lb. soybean mash or ½ lb. soybean flour

1 cake compressed yeast

1 pint lukewarm water

½ cup malt sugar or Karo syrup

salt to taste

- *Mix 2 pounds fine whole wheat flour and 1 pound soybean mash, after the milk is taken out; or in place of the mash, ½ pound soybean flour may be used.*

- *Dissolve one cake of compressed yeast in a little lukewarm water; add 1 pint of water, ½ cup of malt sugar or Karo syrup, and salt to taste. Mix this with the flour and mash to make a fairly stiff dough, about the consistency of regular bread dough. If the dough is not stiff enough, a little more flour may be added.*

- *Let it rise, to about double its size in a warm place. Then knead the dough down and fold it over toward the inner side. Turn it over and let it rise again to about half*

Soybean flour, used for making soybean bread.

Whole wheat soybean bread.

again its size. Then knead it and shape into two loaves, put in pans, letting it rise to about double its size. Bake at 400°F for 10 minutes, then at 375°F for 45 minutes longer. It should begin to brown about 15 minutes after placing in the oven. Bake the bread thoroughly; this gives it a good flavor and makes it easy to digest

Soybean bread no. 2

(3 loaves)

3 lbs whole wheat flour, finely ground

1 lb. soybean meal (out of which the milk has been washed)

1 cake compressed yeast

1 pint lukewarm water

1 cup malt sugar or Karo syrup

salt

- Mix this together following the method given in the recipe for Soybean Bread No. 1; work

the dough as described above, and bake thoroughly.

- About 2 or 3 tablespoonfuls of malt honey added to the water will add very much to the flavor and value of the bread, giving it a deep nutty flavor. Or to make the bread even better, use malt extract, which is high in diastase and aids in the digestion of starch.
- When this bread is made into zwieback, thoroughly dried out until it is a light golden brown, diabetics can eat it because the starch has been changed into grape sugar. Zwieback is excellent for everyone.

Soybean buns

4 cups whole wheat flour

1 cup soybean meal (mash) or ½ cup soybean flour

½ cup soybean butter

2 packages of dry yeast

1 cup water or soybean milk

- To the whole wheat flour and the soybean meal or flour, add the half cup of soybean butter. Dissolve the yeast in the water or soybean milk and add to the flour mixture. After the dough has risen (in 2 or 3 hours) mix it down, turn over, and let rise to half again its size. Now shape into the size of buns that you like and let them rise to about half again their size. Bake for 20 to 30 minutes, according to the size of the buns, at 350°F.

Unleavened Bread

Unfermented or unleavened bread is made light by the introduction of air into the dough or batter. This is done by beating the batter breads and kneading the dough breads.

When making unleavened gems or muffins, have your water, nut milk, and other ingredients as cold as possible and salted to taste. Have your gem pans greased and sizzling hot, and have your batter just stiff enough so that it will drip from the spoon. Place the gems in a preheated oven and bake for 20 minutes at 400°F. This will make a very palatable bread.

Cornmeal gems

1 cup soybean milk

2 tbs. oil

1 tsp. salt

1 cup cornmeal

1 cup whole wheat flour

- *Place the milk, oil, and salt in a bowl. Now beat the cornmeal and flour into this mixture. The ingredients should be cold as described above, and your gem pans greased and sizzling hot. Bake in a preheated oven at 400°F for 20 minutes.*

Oatmeal or soybean gems

1½ cups milk	1 cup cornmeal
3 tbs. oil	1 cup whole wheat flour
1 tsp. salt	1 cup oatmeal or soybean meal

- *Follow mixing and baking directions for making cornmeal gems.*

Potato or carrot gems

1 cup milk	2 cups whole wheat flour
3 tbs. oil	1 cup mashed Irish potatoes,
salt to taste	sweet potatoes, or carrots

- *Follow mixing and baking directions for making cornmeal gems.*
- *In the three foregoing recipes, soybean butter may be used instead of oil.*

Soybean gems

½ lb. soybean mash (out of which soybean milk has been washed)

½ lb. dextrinized cornmeal

½ cup soybean milk or water

- *To dextrinize cornmeal, put the meal in a large baking pan in the oven. Do not have the oven too hot as the meal should not be burned. Stir frequently with a pancake turner or a wooden paddle until it turns a golden brown. This turns the starch into dextrose and makes it palatable and easy to digest.*
- *Mix the mash and the dextrinized cornmeal with the soybean milk. Salt to taste. Pour them in hot, greased cast-iron gem pans and bake for 20 minutes in a hot oven at 400°F.*
- *This makes a very wholesome gem, one that diabetics can eat.*
- *This mixture, made thin enough with more milk added, may be spooned out on a greased cookie sheet as drop cookies, and baked in a 375°F oven for 10 minutes.*

Pones

¹⁄₃ lb. cornmeal

¹⁄₃ lb. whole wheat flour

¹⁄₃ lb. oatmeal flour

1¹⁄₂ cups soybean milk or water

2 tbs. malt honey or Karo syrup

- *Mix together all the ingredients. Have batter cold and greased gem pans and oven hot (400°F). Bake for 30 minutes.*

Beaten biscuit

2 cups whole wheat flour

²⁄₃ cup soybean milk

¹⁄₂ cup soybean butter

2 tbs. Karo syrup

salt

- *Put your flour into a bowl, add the milk, then the soybean butter, Karo syrup, and salt. Mix into a stiff dough as you would in making ordinary bread. Beat with a rolling pin or any heavy stick. This beating is done to make the biscuit tender and mellow.*
- *Make into sticks or roll about one-half inch thick and cut in sizes to suit your taste. This can be rolled still thinner and made into a cracker if you like. Prick with a fork to keep it from blistering. Bake at 325°F for 30 minutes to light brown.*

Whole wheat crisps

- *Mix 5 ounces of raw peanut butter, with ¹⁄₂ pint of water, making a milk. Stir 1 pound of whole wheat flour into the raw peanut butter milk, and salt to taste. Make the dough stiff enough so mat it can be rolled thin. Cut into squares and bake at 375°F for 10 to 15 minutes. This makes a lovely cracker.*
- *It can be improved by adding to the milk about 2 big tablespoonfuls of malt honey or Karo syrup. This is a complete food and very palatable.*
- *These crisps may also be made from raised dough. Make the dough as for sponge bread. Take a scant 1¹⁄₂ pints of water, ¹⁄₂ pound of malt honey or Karo syrup, and about 4 ounces of raw peanut butter. Make the peanut butter into a milk, and set the sponge as for bread, as outlined previously. Use for this amount about 1 cake of compressed yeast. When it has risen as for bread, knead it and work it into thin rolls. Prick them with a fork so they will not blister, cut into strips and bake in a 350°F oven until brown. This makes a very delicious cracker.*
- *These recipes may be divided or multiplied, according to the size of the batch you make.*

Pies

Raised pie crust

1 yeast cake

warm water, to dilute yeast

½ cup cooking or salad oil

malt sugar, small amount

1 cup whole wheat flour

1 cup soybean flour or soybean mash

- *Dissolve the yeast cake in the warm water and add the oil and malt sugar. Now add the whole wheat flour and soybean flour. Mix in the same way as bread dough and let rise for an hour or more in a warm place. When it has risen, knead down and let rise again for 10 or 15 minutes before rolling out Then roll out thin and put in pie tins, allowing it to rise about 15 minutes. Bake for 10 minutes at 450°F.*

Soybean pumpkin pie

2 cups hot soybean milk

2 tbs. fine zwieback crumbs

⅓ cup malt sugar, malt honey, or regular honey

a few grains of salt

1 cup drained, mashed pumpkin

½ tsp., or less, of almond flavoring

prepared pie crust

- *The crust for this kind of pie should have a built-up edge.*
- *Heat the milk. While the milk is heating, mix the zwieback crumbs, sugar, and salt and stir them into the mashed pumpkin. Mix*

thoroughly and add the hot milk. Add seasoning. Pour into a crust and bake in a moderate oven (350°F) until set, about 35 minutes.

- *Instead of almond flavoring, ½ teaspoon each of nutmeg and cinnamon may be used.*

Fig marmalade pie

1 cup figs

1 cup pitted dates

1 cup raisins

3 cups soybean milk

prepared pie crust

- *Mix the figs, dates, and raisins and run together through a food chopper. The holes in the plate of the mill should be quite fine so as to puree the fruit, so that it is easier to digest. Reduce the thickness of the fruit with soybean milk to the right consistency. Pour this filling into a raised pie crust, directions for which are given in the foregoing recipes, and bake for 15 or 20 minutes in a moderate oven (350°F). No top crust is needed for this pie.*
- *To thicken the filling, about 2 teaspoons of agar-agar may be soaked in the cold milk for a short time; then boil this mixture before adding to the fruit.*
- *Vanilla may be added for seasoning, which gives the pie a very different flavor.*
- *If the crust is allowed to rise to the thickness of the filling, it makes a healthful pie, one*

that would make an excellent school lunch for children. It is something they will like and which will nourish as well as satisfy them.

• *This pie filling may be prepared without the raisins. It may also be made with pitted dates alone, which makes a very sweet pie.*

Soybean pumpkin pie is delicious, and simple to make.

Preparing Wholesome Desserts and Beverages

Desserts

Fruit pies may be considered healthful when the crust is made of whole wheat flour and well baked. A whole wheat crust has a rich nutty flavor and requires a little less shortening than when made of white flour. But rich starchy pie fillings and custards are among the most objectionable of all desserts.

Unleavened pie crust

1 cup whole wheat flour

1 cup soybean flour

1 tsp. salt

½ cup cooking or salad oil

3 tbs. ice water

- *Mix flours and salt in a mixing bowl. Add oil and mix well with a large fork. Sprinkle ice water over the mixture and mix well. Press the mixture into a smooth ball with the hands. Divide the ball into halves and flatten both parts slightly. Roll each half between wax paper. Makes one 2-crust pie shell.*

Brown betty

1½ cups seedless raisins

½ tsp. salt

1 quart chopped apples

1 tbs. lemon juice

1 scant cup brown sugar

½ cup water

1 cup whole wheat zwieback crumbs

- *Spread half the raisins over the bottom of a greased pudding dish, cover raisins with half the chopped apples, sprinkle over the apples half the sugar and half the crumbs, sprinkle over this the remainder of the raisins and chopped apples. Sprinkle on the rest of the sugar and crumbs, add salt and lemon juice to ½ cup water and pour this over the top of the pudding. Cover the pudding and set in a pan of water, cover, and bake for an hour. Remove from the pan of water and bake without the cover long enough to brown the top slightly. Serve with vanilla sauce.*

Vanilla sauce

- *To the desired amount of soy bean cream you may add malt sugar and vanilla to taste. This makes a delicious sauce, to be used in the place of starchy sauces and whipping cream.*

Vegetable gelatin

- *To prepare agar-agar for dessert, soak 1 tablespoon of agar-agar in 1 pint of warm water for 30 minutes, drain and then simmer for 20 minutes in another pint of warm water; cook until dissolved. The quantity of liquid will be reduced by boiling. Strain the liquid and add a pint of any desired fresh fruit or fruit juice. Bananas, peaches, or any*

Vanilla sauce can be used instead of whipping cream.

other fresh fruit may be sliced in the bottom of each mold to give variety. Before serving, decorate with crushed or chopped nuts. For dressing, use either the vanilla sauce or soybean cream.

Orange jelly

¾ cup orange juice

1 cup malt sugar

1 tsp. grated orange rind

¾ cup water

3 tbs. lemon juice

1 tbs. vegetable gelatin (see Vegetable Gelatin)

salt

- Mix the orange juice, rind, lemon juice, pinch of salt, and sugar, add the water; when boiled gelatin is ready, add the other ingredients. Mold until firm. Serve with soybean cream.

Orange jelly is a simple and nourishing dessert.

Baked apples make a delicious, healthy dessert.

Strawberry jelly

1 tbs. agar-agar

1¾ cups crushed strawberries

2 tbs. lemon juice

1 cup boiling water for agar-agar

few grains salt

1 cup malt sugar

- *Prepare as for orange jelly; when cool decorate with strawberry halves, and serve with crushed nuts or soybean cream.*

Baked apples

- *Wash the apples and remove the cores without cutting completely through the apple. Then fill the cavities with raisins or dates, and bake until done (about 45 minutes) at 350°F in a flat baking dish with a little water in the bottom. With the raisins, chopped nuts may also be used, which add to the flavor. Serve with a nut cream.*

Stuffed dates

- *Remove the pits with a sharp knife, cutting lengthwise, and replace with pecan meats or other nuts if preferred. If you wish to remove the skins, scald them, draining well. As a rule they should always be scalded to remove dirt.*

Rice pudding

1 cup soy cream

1 cup cooked brown rice

pinch of salt

1 cup drained, crushed pineapple

- *Mix together, chill, and serve. Other fruits may be used in place of pineapple.*

Cream tapioca

½ cup tapioca (minute)

2½ cups soybean milk

⅓ cup malt sugar

1 tsp vanilla

pinch of salt

½ cup soy cream

- *Soak the tapioca in soybean milk for 15 minutes. Add the sugar and salt, and bring to a boil, stirring constantly. Place in a double boiler, and cook until tapioca is transparent. Add vanilla, chill, and serve with soy cream.*

Rice pudding is a simple, sustaining dessert.

Broths and Beverages

Soybean coffee

- *Place the quantity of soybeans you desire in a flat baking pan and heat in a hot oven, stirring frequently to prevent burning.*
- *Watch them closely and thoroughly stir them as they will get much darker inside than on the outside while roasting. The outside hull seems to brown less rapidly than the inner portion, so you will find it necessary to take a few out occasionally, and break them open with a hammer to see just how they are roasting. To get a good-flavored coffee, it is necessary to have an even roast. If some of the beans are not roasted quite enough, and some of them a little too much, it spoils the flavor of the coffee.*
- *After roasting, grind the beans in a mill, to a coarse grind. Brew the coffee in a pot the same as you would regular coffee.*

Soybean milk is a healthy alternative to cows' milk.

- *Get some coffee and compare the color so you will know how brown to make it. Half bran and half soybeans may also be used for a good coffee.*

Soybean milk

- *The recipe for soybean milk is given earlier in the section.*

Cereal coffee no. 1

- *Cereal coffee is a product that is used very much nowadays, and can be made very easily at home.*
- *Place the quantity of rye grain you desire in a large flat baking pan and roast in a hot oven. Stir the grain with a wooden paddle until it becomes as brown as coffee. Grind rather coarse in any small hand mill. It is now ready for use.*
- *When roasting the whole grain, take a little out with a spoon when it gets nearly done, lay it on a solid board and break it up with a hammer in order to determine the brownness.*
- *It is helpful to have handy a little regular coffee in a glass container so its degree of brownness can be easily compared with that of the homemade coffee.*

Cereal coffee no. 2

- *Wheat bran is used in this recipe. Mix equal parts water and malt honey. Moisten the bran, a pound or whatever quantity you desire, with the water and malt honey mixture, let it get quite dry, or altogether dry before roasting. You may use Karo syrup in place of malt honey.*

- *It may be placed in the sun or where it is airy to dry, so it does not sour before it gets dry.*

- *When dry place in a flat baking pan, in a hot oven, stirring frequently, until it is as brown as coffee.*

- *Half bran and half rye may also be used. The rye must be ground before mixing it with the bran. This makes a fine-flavored coffee.*

- *The bran for this coffee may be purchased from a feed store. It is much cheaper than bran put in packages and sold at the grocery stores. The ordinary bran run in large mills is just as clean as the flour from which the bran is taken, not touched by human hands. It runs out of the spout into a bag, and is perfectly clean and safe to use.*

ADDENDUM

There are many good ready-made cereal coffees available on the market today.

Bran water

- *To 2 cups of bran add 1 quart of water, and let it stand overnight. In the morning strain through a fine sieve or cheesecloth.*

- *This bran water liquid can be used in any kind of soup stock, stew, or any breads in place of ordinary water.*

Bran broth

- *Cook 1½ cups of the bran water (see preceding recipe) for about 5 minutes. Add ½ cup of soybean milk. More or less of the bran water and soybean milk may be taken, depending, of course, upon the amount required to suit the need, but this is a good proportion to use. Season with vegetable extract or Vegex and parsley.*

Homemade coffee can be made from cereals or soybeans.

Oatmeal water

- To 1 quart of water, add 1 cup of oatmeal, and soak it overnight. In the morning, strain through a fine sieve or cheesecloth.
- This is to be used in soup stocks, stew, or breads in place of water. It increases the vitamins and makes soups creamy.

Soybean broth

- Place 2 cups of wheat bran in 1 quart of unsweetened soybean milk. In another pan, soak 1 cup of oatmeal in 1 quart of soybean milk. Place these two containers in the refrigerator overnight. In the morning, stir each one several times and strain.
- Pour 1 pint of boiling unsweetened soy milk on 4 heaping tablespoonfuls chickweed; let stand for half an hour and strain.
- Mix the wheat bran, oatmeal, and chickweed liquids together, adding 1 quart unsweetened soy milk. Add diced celery and onions for flavoring, to taste. Simmer for 30 minutes, adding 3 tablespoonfuls Kloss's Mayonnaise. A few minutes before it is finished, add 1 cup of very finely cut parsley. This broth contains all the nutrients the body requires.

Herb broth

2 cups wheat bran

1 cup oatmeal

4 tbs. chickweed water

- Soak 2 cups wheat bran in 1 quart of water, and also 1 cup oatmeal in 1 quart of water overnight. Stir up each mixture several times; then strain.
- Pour 1 pint of boiling water on the chickweed, let steep for half an hour; strain.
- Mix together the wheat bran, the oatmeal, and 4 tablespoonfuls of the chickweed water, and add 1 quart soybean milk. Parsley, finely cut, may be added for flavoring, or season with celery or onions as preferred. Let simmer for a few minutes and serve. A little Kloss's Mayonnaise may also be added.
- This broth contains all the nutrients the body requires.

Soybean buttermilk

- Buttermilk is an excellent article of diet for everyday use, but is especially beneficial in malnutrition, tuberculosis, toxic conditions, and intestinal infections. Soybean buttermilk has the advantage of producing an alkaline effect in the body and is more nourishing than ordinary buttermilk or yogurt buttermilk used under various names. It is rich in minerals and very palatable.
- Use unsweetened soybean milk. Let stand until sour if desired, or until just clabbered and not sour. Beat up with an egg beater, and add salt to taste.

Potassium broth

2 cupfuls bran

2 large onions

1 cup oatmeal

2 stalks celery

4 quarts water

½ bunch minced parsley

4 potatoes, medium sized

2 vegetable oysters (salsify)

2 large carrots

- *Mix the first three ingredients and soak overnight. Beat up with an eggbeater and strain through a fine sieve.*
- *Wash thoroughly 4 medium-sized potatoes and slice thin, also 2 large carrots, 2 medium-sized onions (optional), 2 large stalks celery with the green leaves cut fine, ½ bunch of parsley cut up and 2 good-sized vegetable oysters. Cook in the bran/oatmeal water. Let simmer in a covered kettle until vegetables are done. Mash up vegetables and strain again through a fine sieve.*

Herb Drinks or Teas

Coffee, tea, chocolate, and cocoa are harmful to the system, but all of the teas named in the following list are very fine to drink and take the place of harmful drinks. The herb teas are rich in medicinal and chemical properties. Some are very healing to the stomach and a good tonic. Others prevent fermentation and gas in the stomach and bowels, and also prevent griping. Some are very excellent to overcome nausea and vomiting, and all of them have a splendid beneficial effect on the system. There are some that are nice to take in the evening before retiring to induce sleep. All of them are soothing and quieting to the system.

peppermint	fennel
hyssop	spearmint
strawberry leaves	rue
alfalfa	hop blossoms
chickweed	dandelion
sassafras	catnip
green celery leaves	yellow dock
wintergreen	mint
meadowsweet	camomile
sarsaparilla root	juniper berries
birch bark (small twigs)	chicory
red raspberry leaves	sage
calamus root	wild cherry bark
red clover blossoms	(small twigs)

Herb tea

- *Use 1 heaping teaspoon of the herbs granulated, or if powdered use ½ teaspoon, to 1 cup of boiling water. Place the herbs in a pan, and pour the boiling water over them, allowing it to steep one half hour. Cover.*
- *These teas are less expensive than coffee, tea, etcetera, and they are healthful, beneficial, and not harmful.*

General Tables

Children's dose equivalent to adult dose of 1 tsp. (60 drops)

Child's age	Dose
18 or over	1 tsp.
15 to 18 years	¾ tsp. or 45 drops
9 to 12 years	½ tsp. or 30 drops
4 to 6 years	¼ tsp. or 15 drops
2 to 3 years	10 drops
1 to 1½ years	7 drops
0 to 3 months	2 drops

Weights

Number of grams*	Approximate equivalent
1000 (1 kg)	2.2 lb
454	1.0 lb
100	3.5 oz
28	1.0 oz
16	1.0 tbs.
4	1.0 tsp.

*One paper clip weighs about 1 gram.

Spinach leaves.

Useful household measures (approx.)

Measure	Fluid ounces	Tablespoonful	Fluid drams	cc (ml)
1 Glassful (cup)	8	16	60	240
1 Teacupful	4	8	30	120
1 Wineglassful	2	4	15	60
1 Tablespoonful (tbs.)	½	1	4	15
1 Dessertspoonful			2	8
1 Teaspoonful (tsp.)			1	4 (60 drops)

Table of equivalent fluid measures

Gallon	Quart	Pint	Glass or cup	Ounce	Tablespoonful	Teaspoonful (dram)	cc (ml)
1	4	8	16	128	256	1024	4000
	1	2	4	32	64	256	1000
	½	1	2	16	32	128	500
	¼	½	1	8	16	64	240
				1	2	8	30
				½	1	4	15
						1	4

Grapes on the vine.

Glossary

Amino acid Substance necessary to form proteins. Essential amino acids are those which must be obtained through food because the body cannot manufacture them itself.

Anemia Condition that occurs when there is a reduction of hemoglobin, the oxygen-carrying pigment, in the blood. The most common form is iron-deficiency anemia, caused by lack of iron in the diet, which leads to fatigue, pallor, breathlessness, and poor resistance to infection.

Antibiotic Substance that destroys or prevents the growth of bacteria.

Antioxidant Substance that neutralizes free radicals, thus preventing cell degeneration and decay.

Antiseptic Agent that prevents infection and/or putrefaction in the body.

Antiscorbutic Substance that prevents scurvy, the oldest recognized vitamin deficiency disease.

Autointoxication Ancient theory based on the belief that intestinal waste products can poison the body and cause disease.

Bacteria Microscopic single-cell organisms that may cause disease.

Cholesterol Fat-like substance present in the blood. High levels can damage the artery walls.

Bile Thick fluid made by the liver that helps the body digest fats.

Colon Major part of the large intestine, ending at the rectum.

Detoxification Process by which the body is purged of toxins, through fasting, for example.

DNA (Deoxyribonucleic acid) A chemical that makes up genetic material.

Edema Swelling cause by fluid retention beneath the skin's surface.

Enzyme Protein made in the body that acts as a catalyst to accelerate a biological reaction.

Essential fatty acid One of a group of unsaturated fatty acids that are essential for health and must be obtained from the diet.

Fatty acid Fundamental constituent of fats and oils.

Free radicals Natural byproducts of metabolism, but these particles are potentially dangerous because they can damage cell structure and cause a range of problems, from high levels of cholesterol to a weakened immune system.

Gluten A protein found in wheat and other cereals.

Glycogen The form in which carbohydrates are stored in the liver and muscles.

Hemoglobin Substance in the red blood cells (responsible for their color) that transports oxygen round the body.

Hemorrhage Loss of blood.

Hormone Chemical messengers that regulate body functions.

Immune system Body organs responsible for immunity, the ability of the body to resist infection due to the presence of white blood cells and antibodies (blood proteins that destroy foreign invaders such as bacteria and viruses).

Legume Edible seeds of plants that provide a good source of protein, vitamins, and fiber.

Linoleic acid An essential fatty acid that cannot be made in the body and has to come from food.

Lipoprotein A combined fat/protein important for the transport of fats in the bloodstream.

Metabolism Collective term for chemical processes

Green leafy vegetables such as kale are packed with micronutrients.

that take place in the body, and the means by which food is converted into energy. The metabolic rate describes the energy required to keep the body functioning when at rest.

Micronutrients Substances such as vitamins and minerals that are needed only in small amounts yet are essential for good health.

Nitrosamines Carcinogenic chemical compounds found in foods such as cured meats.

Osmotic pressure The passage of a solvent from a less concentrated to a more concentrated solution through a semipermeable membrane (osmosis) plays an important role in controlling the distribution of water in the cells. The more concentrated the solution, the greater its osmotic pressure (i.e., the pressure by which water is drawn into it).

Osteoporosis Loss of bony tissue resulting in bones that are brittle and liable to fracture. It is caused by a lack of calcium in the diet.

Provitamin Substance that is not itself a vitamin but can be converted into a vitamin in the body, for example, carotene to vitamin A.

Rickets Childhood deficiency disease caused by a lack of vitamin D. The bones become soft and malformed, most evidently in the legs, which become bowed.

RNA (Ribonucleic acid) Genetic material needed for protein synthesis to occur.

Saturated fat Highly concentrated fat, usually derived from animals, containing fatty acids and cholesterol.

Stimulant Substance that increases activity or efficiency of a body system or organ.

Thyroid gland Large gland in the neck concerned with controlling the metabolic rate.

Toxins Poisons and waste products made by the body.

Trace element One of a group of minerals the body needs in minute amounts that can only be obtained from food.

Trans fats Saturated fats made when oils have hydrogen atoms added to them to harden them for use in processed foods.

Viruses Smallest known types of infective agents, capable of replication but only within living cells.

Vitamin Complex organic substance essential for growth, reproduction, good health, and regulation of metabolic processes.

Whitlow Inflamed swelling of the skin surrounding the nails, usually caused by bacterial infection.

Zymotic disease Old-fashioned name for a contagious disease such as measles or cholera that was thought to develop in the body following infection in a process similar to the fermentation and growth of yeast.

Index

Acknowledgments

PICTURE CREDITS

The publisher would like to thank the following for their permission to reproduce the images in this book. Every effort has been made to acknowledge the images, however we apologize if there are any unintentional omissions.

Alamy/Jon Arnold Images Ltd: 153; Bon Appetit: 36BL, 220; Foodfolio: 149, 215; Tim Hill: 199TR; Kim Karpeles: 237; Geoffrey Kidd: 201; John Ferro Sims: 182; Sue Wilson: 191.

Corbis/TH-Foto/zefa: 157; Envision: 218 C; Fleurent/photocuisine: 179; J.Riou/photocuisine: 240; Studio Eye: 184; Viel/ photocuisine: 176, 211.